Recovered, Alive

Amelia Chiarenza

All statements contained herein are the
opinion and experience of the author.

First Edition
Printed in the United States of America

Published by Amelia Chiarenza, November 2025
Sioux Falls, South Dakota

Cover Art by Alisa Burpee

Library of Congress Control Number: 2025921677

ISBN #: 979-8-9932439-5-5

Let today be the day where you take nothing for granted. For life is fleeting, fragile and precious and can change on a whim. Say all the things you really want to say to your loved ones today, say the things you would regret should they pass on and your words remain unspoken. Rejoice, for you and they are alive today – and should you or them pass on to unknown shores, rejoice even more for you have a wonderful love story to tell.

-Jackson Kiddard

Contents

Author's Note

Dear Reader,

My drive to write this book was born shortly after my mother died and continued through the death of my dear friend and then my father. I began *Recovered, Alive* in snippets, which grew into waves, then evolved into full-fledged composition. I wrote in the throes of my shock, sadness and despair and began even before I recognized my emotions and the impact of cavernous grief. The words in this book served as a guiding light, carrying me forward and playing a significant role in my recovery. I was not aware of their role at the time; I was drenched in a force propelling me to write. Only now can I recognize the weaving of them together served such a purpose for my soul.

I was as resolute to put this book out into the world for others, as I was resolute in caring for my loved ones who died. Every decision I have made about this book has been purposeful with the intention of honoring their lives and my own metamorphosis from their dying.

When I was laid off from my demanding corporate job in early 2024, I immediately chose to listen to my intuition, tap into my creative spirit, and attend to my own human transformation. I directed my full attention toward finishing this manuscript and learning how to navigate the world of publishing a book.

As a work of nonfiction, nearly all names remain unchanged. It was my desire to journal and share what was true to my own experience, including the people who were a part of it.

Because of the nature of this personal story, I wanted every detail to reflect the deep meaning of my journey with personal touch. I call them "my bespoke choices." The colors you see in this book are the colors associated with the birth dates and death dates of my mother, my best friend, and my father. The cover art was created by a talented artist, writer, psychologist and friend. It is a rendition of a tree planted at my childhood home the year I was born. It is a silver maple, a rapid-growing gift of nature and symbol of strength, resilience and adaptability. The first print of this book comes from a small and mighty, family-owned and women-run business from Minnesota —the state where my parents were born and grew up. The fulfillment company for *Recovered, Alive* is a local distributor in my hometown —of course it should be shipped from the land of my roots.

❖

May you find a story of your own in mine.

Recovered, Alive

Introduction

This is a curation of thoughts during a period of loss. It is a story of grief and mourning. As such, it is also a story of discovery, learning, strength and life.

I heard my partner's colleague once say, "you know, *this* (she was talking about the death of her mother) isn't something that you can write about because everyone's experience is different." She was right, everyone's experience *is* different and everyone's grief *is* different. At the same time (and where I would challenge her is that), there are inherent commonalities and a simpatico we experience as humankind, including the very essence of grief, the very essence of mourning. It is deeply personal. And it is deeply human.

Before this story, I thought I understood heartbreak, heartache. I did not. I thought I could recognize grief and that I knew what it was. I could not and I did not. I am still learning and growing. And, I have a story to tell: a story of my grief underscored by a love story. It is my mourning.

When my mother died, the world turned upside down. My world turned upside down. She received a sudden diagnosis and then rapidly transitioned to death. I stared her death in the face and then cared for my father, who was sick. He had been ill for quite some time. At the outset of navigating this new reality, my dearest friend, my go-to friend, died of an unexpected diagnosis. And then, my father died.

I recognize now that these three individuals were core to my being. And all three died in rapid succession. While I did not necessarily expect to see it coming, I think (even now), *I did not see this coming*. How could I? How would I? In no way did I expect it to happen as the 1-2-3 punch of a life-changing punching bag.

My life is different now. I am different, changed. I understand heartbreak, heartache. I recognize grief and intimately feel it, mourning and intimately know it. And still I am learning and growing.

This book is a tribute to each of these beautiful individuals, their lives; their being in this world, and my love for them. It, too, is an ode to the life I knew before losing them, to the deep sorrow for having lost them, and to moving with the strong force of remembrance and love.

Stories connect us. To people. And, to experiences. I believe that shared experiences can serve as a form of discovery. It is through sharing stories that we ignite connection and can feel less alone. I am compelled to write about my thoughts, emotions and the happenings from this period of loss both for myself and for others. It has been an immediate, deep craving whilst forging through, up, over, and under emotional pain.

We don't talk about loss like this in our culture and society. At least, not that I have experienced. Or maybe I wasn't looking in the right places? Death, loss and grief will happen. They are things to know and embrace as a part of living. If we could incorporate, recognize, and face them before they completely upend our lives—get familiar with them as we do with other aspects of life—then maybe (just maybe) there would be an opportunity to ease the toughest moments. And, I know, the toughest moments are those that shift us, teach us, and color the pages of our journey to new strength.

I recognize that this loss is a dagger in my soul. I have suffered accelerated and profound loss in my early forties, at a point in my life when most others my age still have a living parent, parents, and living best friends.

I learned from *The Grief Recovery Handbook* by John W. James and Russell Friedman that people will experience a significant loss every nine to thirteen years. I cannot imagine that timeframe. It is not the timeline of my experience. My losses were significant, they arrived all too fast, early, and in rapid succession. There is an uninvited wisdom I have gained because of that.

I also know that there are so many others who have endured

and are experiencing deep loss.

Maybe you have recently lost someone close to you. Maybe it was a long time ago. Maybe you have not yet lost someone dear to you. Maybe you are curious about life-changing events because you know life is short, but you have not yet *felt* that it is short. Maybe you are interested in learning more about loss because while you have not directly experienced the pain surrounding death, you have endured other life-altering events that are exceptionally painful and have served as losses. Maybe you have just had a health scare, maybe you have just been diagnosed with a life-threatening disease, maybe you are watching your loved one struggle. No matter what, I share my journey with you.

This is my mourning, journaled in three acts.

❖

We take in stories through our own experiences. Perhaps my story can provide insight, and at the same time, offer comfort to another, to you.

That is my hope.

Act I: Hijacked

Loss

For Mom.

For Sharon.

For Dad.

Scenes

Life Hijacked

Life hijacked. That is the term that came to mind for me months ago while out walking my dog. It had been sixteen months and counting since my entire world—my life— had become completely hijacked.

Most people during 2020 and 2021 would reference the global pandemic with the shifts in work to telecommuting; the distancing from friends and strangers alike; the fear of contracting the virus; the limbo of "what is next?" as the loss and distance from a former life. So many people have written about COVID-19 and its personal impact, from rebooting careers, voicing frustrations, and sharing experiences remotely via blogs, books, and podcasts.

This is not that story.

While the pandemic plays a role in my story as part of the scenery, so-to-speak, it is not the focus, the main theme, nor the main character. The pandemic for me "pales in comparison" to what 2020 and 2021 were for me. The significance of these two years for me did not reside in the changes due to COVID; rather, it resided in the loss of a parent, a dear friend, and another parent.

In March 2020, I lost my mother to acute myeloid leukemia. In August 2020, I lost my very dear friend, Sharon, to pancreatic cancer. In July 2021, I lost my father to pulmonary fibrosis.

As a result of these losses, I felt completely disconnected from my life and from reality. It was not because of the global pandemic, but because of the very real loss that hit so close to home and in such a relatively short time. It was a hijacking by way of shock and grief. The pandemic was simply icing on a dark cake that has no flavor and too much flavor all at once.

There I was, walking my dog along a sidewalk in a park near my childhood home, feeling the strong, hot wind of the midwestern plains brushing past my face and seeing the hair on my dog slicked back by its airy force. *Where am I?* I wondered. *How did this all happen? I don't know this life, this new way of being at all.* The life previously known to me had been hijacked—taken by force, taken without choice, and leaving a permanent wake for me to navigate.

I know I am not alone. While I have felt acutely and systematically alone at so many points along this journey, I know that there are many others who have experienced, are experiencing, and will experience excruciating loss.

Even then (and now), I pinch myself to know that I *am* living this reality, a hard reality - as though I am living the life of someone else, disconnected and entirely distanced from my own living, from my own life. Yet it is mine.

Life hijacked. My life, hijacked.

…as though I am
living the life of
someone else, disconnected
and entirely distanced
from my own living;
my own life.
Yet it is mine.

Dear Mom

On a Friday afternoon, my dad said, "You better get here. I don't think your mom is going to make the weekend."

My partner, Angela, was flying back home to Virginia from a business trip in Texas. She booked me the last seat available on the next morning's flight from Washington D.C. to Sarasota, Florida. Meanwhile, I called my sister, who lives in Tampa, and we made a plan that she would pick me up at the airport the next morning once I arrived. Angela would join later that day once she could meet the dog sitter at our home and catch a flight to Sarasota.

I packed a backpack, adding one outfit in all black.

On the flight, I wrote my mom a Mother's Day card. It was nearly two months too early, but I felt a distinct impulse to put to paper what I wanted to say to my mother. I knew it was a holiday she so enjoyed, and I also knew that Mother's Day 2020 was not likely to be celebrated as it was in years past.

The following is the card I wrote, and the last thing I read to my mother.

> Dear Mom,
> I want to let you know that I have a great life. I found the love of my life, Angela, who supports and loves me to the fullest. And I have the joy of raising a fantastic pup, Charlie. My love of dogs and the unconditional love they offer runs deep, including their "always so happy to greet you" quality, as you would describe. You and I share that. My home with Angela is an oasis and we have found joy making it so. I still make the bed every morning, without fail. You taught me that. Thank you. I have a wonderful time forging new friendships and nurturing older ones. Angela and I love to "make things pretty" as you would say and to host dinners with friends and neighbors. We find great joy in community. I got this from you. Thank you. I have built a wonderful career, with work that keeps me challenged, inspired, and continuing to learn. I know

how to work hard and the value of a strong work ethic. You taught me that. Thank you. I have developed a strong skill in speaking in public, something for which I am praised at work. The value of that skill I learned from you. Thank you. I know how to write a proper thank you note, the importance of timing and understand why it is important. You taught me that skill and understanding. Thank you. I value manners, something you instilled in me from early in my childhood. Thank you.

I am deeply grateful for all of this. And I want to make sure you hear that I am proud of who I am and who I grow to be. I say this with humility and appreciation for the good, the bad and the ugly that life has brought my way and for what I have been able to accomplish.

I write this because I want you to know; to truly know. As my mother, you have been a part of all of this. It is important to say the things that are hard to say, and we so easily assume others already know. You taught me that. Thank you. Thank you for all of this and for letting me lick the spatula when you would make your Candy.

In my mind, you shall always wear purple – a favorite color we share.

I love you.
Amelia

It was nearly
two months too early,
but I felt a distinct impulse
to put to paper what
I wanted to say to
my mother…

Mom's Celebration of Life

My dad, sister, Angela, and I sat in the Florida condo living room talking through options of how to plan Mom's funeral. Though Mom had not yet passed, she was unconscious and dying. Dad had wanted to think through how to honor her and have something planned for the coming days. We all believed it was important to do something very soon versus delaying. Dad stayed more logistics-focused, aware that high-season for the "snow birds" would be ending soon, and most of Mom's Florida friends and community members would be leaving for their other homes up north. My sister was worried about how to juggle her job, custody of her kids, and a planned trip for them all to go to Disney World. I wanted to make sure we could do something special and honor Mom soon after her death because that is what she would have said was important. We all agreed and decided on Monday, March 9 in the afternoon that the event would be held that Thursday, March 12, and if Mom were still alive, that would be okay. According to Dad, "it doesn't matter at this point if she is still alive." The point was that we do it; do it soon; do it with people who can attend; who are important to Mom, and we do it together.

Angela raced around to gather ribbons and supplies to arrange flowers and plants for decorations and coordinated with the condo building office manager to get the word out to my mom's condo friends, who arranged for coffee, and goodies to serve at the event. My sister worked on putting together a one-page invitation. I scurried around gathering photos that we could use to decorate the room and put together a photo-viewing book while taking care of Dad and navigating hospice with Mom.

This was not at all a scenario I would have expected nor could have imagined. We set out on all this planning and active preparations without knowing exactly when my mom would depart this life. As it turns out, the evening of the very next day, she died. We were all relieved that we already had made the decision about her service and plans were underway. That type of relief was something true-to-form in Mom's thinking around death, funerals, closure, and honoring people's lives so it felt fitting.

Both my sister and I spoke. Angela also said a few words. I wish I could remember exactly what they each said. My sister asked her children if they would like to say something, but the sadness and shyness was too much for them. I was surprised by how little my dad spoke although maybe I should not have been since breathing was so difficult for him. More so, I think talking about Mom in the context of losing her was something he may not have had the desire to do. Understandably so. I do recall that he kept his broad comments focused on thanking everyone for coming and how Mom so enjoyed her time in Sarasota and as part of the community there. He was impatient and uncomfortable with the length of time and pauses between music, motioning to me to speed up the music and stop certain pieces short. I don't know for certain, but instinct told me that the whole "program" part of the event was uncomfortable for him. He did well and seemed more at ease one-on-one after the planned portions.

The following is what I shared that day:

> My name is Amelia. I am Mom and Dad's youngest daughter. One of the many things my mother taught me is that it is important to say the things that are hard to say, and we so easily assume others already know. And I am grateful.
>
> This morning, Angela and I went for our morning walk and to get coffee—routine, really. The cashier asked, "What are you up to today?" After a long pause and a deep breath, I responded, "Spending time with family."
>
> Mom was born in the winter of 1943 on a Saturday. As the children's nursery rhyme says, "Saturday's child works hard for her living." She was always working hard on thinking and doing for others. "Do for others," she would say, "thoughtfulness goes a long way." Give it your best and always try. Get it right and be kind.
>
> Mom found joy in community, trying hard, learning new things and most especially in family. She treasured family

above all else.

And she was a life-long learner. She knew that you grow a bit more with each new thing you learn and experience. And she always wanted to be learning along with others and investing in us and in others. In these past days with her, she continued to teach me new things.

She used to say, "You don't understand. If I could swaddle you in cotton and keep you safe with me, I would. But I also know that would not be good for you." So, she and my father built a life together that gave us wings to spread; encouraged us to try and to take opportunities; to learn and grow. I have spread my wings in my life because of the driving force she was for me and their strength as a couple.

One thing my mother used to do is call and sing songs to me. Last week she sang the entire song "Promise Me a Rose" from the musical *Take Me Along*. I don't know why she sang that particular song but I do know it is a song she enjoyed, and while it can be interpreted as a song about disappointment and not giving up, I believe it is a song that represents a dreamer and hope.

The graciousness, kindness and generosity provided by you all and by so many for my mother and father is exceptional. We thank you from the bottom of our hearts. It is a reflection of the warmth and joy Mom found in community.

I am filled with gratitude for her beautiful life and that I am a part of it.

"Your mother knows," she used to say. And she did.

The point was that we do it; do it soon, do it with people who can attend; who are important to Mom, and we do it together.

Mom Passed

Another thing I had never thought about nor really considered is having to inform others in my life that my mother had died. I have discovered that even typing the word "died" takes strength. There is no manual for this. There is no instruction. It is an exercise that is completely new, yet taps into the core of who you are.

Below is the message that I crafted following my mother's passing. I recall so clearly: I was sitting on a pool lounge chair at my parents' Florida condominium complex, the same one where I played as a toddler and swam with my parents, sister, and grandparents. The hot sun was beating down on my skin and felt like a warm blanket. The sky was vivid blue, practically crystalline. The white clouds were few and stationary. I dare say I was on the same lounge chair I had seen my mother sit on four months prior while she chatted with a fellow homeowners' association board member. My mom loved serving on that board and the place of position it provided her in that community. It was Saturday, March 14, 2020, four days after we said goodbye:

> I hope you all are enjoying the weekend!
>
> My mom passed away at home in Florida Tuesday evening. It was beautiful with the sun setting behind her and an ocean view from her room. Angela and I have been in Florida since last Saturday and we are so grateful to have been with her in her final days and moments. We followed with a service on Thursday here in Florida with her beloved Sarasota community.
>
> I am remaining in Florida a bit longer with my father and Angela just arrived home to Charlie today. She has been amazing (as always) in support of me and our family. We are doing well and grateful, too, to be helping my father with next steps.
>
> We'll keep you posted and let you know when we have time to catch up.
>
> Love and hugs to you!

It is an exercise that is completely new, yet taps into the core of who you are.

Sharon

I try, yet I cannot. I cannot find the words. I have not yet talked about Sharon. It is so very hard to find the words.

I will try again.

It is so very hard
to find the words.

Too Much of a Good Thing

Mae West, an actress, singer and comedian among other things, said, "I've found that too much of a good thing can be wonderful." My mom used to reference that, but she would say, "You know what they say, 'Too much of a good thing is *never* enough!'" She would also say, "You know what they say, 'Things in moderation.'" She believed all of them.

Every year in December, my mother would amp up, literally amp herself up to make chocolates to give away at the holidays. She would say, "I got to get started on my Candy!" Mom's Candy was always said with a capital "C" when paired with her. I think it was to denote the celebration of it.

Mom had a complete system: heaps of chocolate chips, walnuts and condensed milk purchases on the kitchen table, lines of cookie sheets and parchment paper on the dining table, an inventory of small, medium and large-sized foil containers, reams of foil and green, yellow, and red sticky bows in mounds on the kitchen counter; and papers – lists of individuals, families, companies, along with prioritized delivery timing based upon various holiday events, my father's schedule at the hospital and my sister's and my extracurricular schedules – all stuffed into her red leather address book.

We also had Mom's Candy all over the house during the holidays—dishes by the piano, dishes on the dining credenza. Mom kept us stocked, all while attending to her holiday giveaway manufacturing line. She loved to give, and she *loved* to give out her Candy at Christmastime. "It's special," she would describe.

It brought her joy and a lot of stress: "Don't leave without my Candy to deliver!" "How am I going to get it all done?!" "I have to make two more batches of my Candy tonight," she would say at 10:00 p.m. Whenever my father, sister, or I would dare suggest she reduce the volume to ease stress, her retort was, "I cannot. People *so look forward* to it." Conversation over.

It was true. Recipients always mentioned Mom's Candy. "I just love your mom's chocolates," the older ladies at church would whisper. "Oh, how I look forward to your fudge, Nancy," the nurses would say. "Fudge? Fudge?! My Candy *is not* fudge!" This, my mother would exclaim to me and my sister later, as though fudge were moldy cheese, or worse yet, the work of the devil.

"Isn't it kind of like fudge, though, Mom?" I suggested, adding, "What's wrong with fudge?" She shot a look of disbelief and a firm scowl across the bow at my audacity. How could I make such a suggestion? "It is not fudge. It is Candy." Suggestion, consideration not accepted. Candy it was.

Folks would also say to my mom, "You *have to* give me that recipe. It is so good." My mother had a very rehearsed response to that particular statement: "No, no. It is a *secret* recipe, I *never* share."

At times, my sister and I would try to convince her that sharing the recipe might not be such a bad thing.

"What's the big deal? People like it, and it is a compliment," one of us would say.

My mom always made the point, "This is something I can do for other people at the holidays that they cannot make for themselves or get elsewhere. If I give away the recipe, I won't have something special to give."

I used to pop a piece of Mom's Candy into my mouth all too often every December. I was not a big fan of the walnut-nuttiness, but I ate it anyway. It was as if Mom's energy around her Candy made the idea of me not eating it ludicrous.

As I grew older, my sister and I confessed to each other that we didn't really care for Mom's Candy that much. It was far too sweet for me, and again, those walnuts. Plus, I think I probably ate a lifetime's worth of it by that point. But others absolutely loved it. Even after she died, people have mentioned Mom's Candy to me.

I often wondered growing up, *Will Mom ever share the recipe with me?* I watched her make hundreds, maybe thousands, of batches over the years, so you would think I have it memorized. I don't. I can come up with the entire ingredient list and the methodology for making Mom's Candy, but I don't know the ratios by heart.

She never did offer that secret recipe to me.

After weeks of combing through my parents' home following my father's death— sixteen months following my mother's death, and working with the estate sale team to prepare for the sale at my parent's home—I was standing in the kitchen, leaning on the very counter where, as a young child, I would lick a large, wooden spoon of chocolate my mom would offer after having made a batch of her Candy. It was late evening, and I was beyond exhausted. I picked up a black box from the counter that was next to a stack of recipe books from the 1960s and 1970s. It was filled to the gills with index cards of recipes curated by my mother. Each was carefully written by hand in blue ink, and I could immediately envision the exact pen she would have used to produce such ink. I paused for a moment and recalled the sound of that clicking pen.

As I flipped through, I found myself reading each recipe. One after the other, I was transfixed by her handwriting, each card representing evidence of my mother. I didn't even recognize most of the recipes and even questioned whether she ever made them. I wondered what sparked this practice of writing out recipes so neatly and alphabetically organized. Was this a trend of most moms in the 1970s and 1980s? A few recipes I recognized—the "anniversary hotdish" casserole that was a staple over the years that she would bring to families grieving a loved one, and the ball of cheese that she would roll in nuts and serve at her neighborhood bridge parties. I came to the "C's" and there it was: "Candy." There in plain sight. My mother never gave me the recipe, but there she left it, alphabetically organized in her recipe file. The "secret" recipe was there all along.

Mom certainly had a point about her Candy and it being special. To this day, in the far reaches of my soul, Christmas will always carry a memory of Mom's Candy. And more so, her point about giving a gift that was special. Too much of a good thing, I suppose.

I cannot tell you the last time I tasted a piece of Mom's Candy, or whether I would like it now. Perhaps I will whip up a batch.

The "secret" recipe was there all along.

Sharon

Nope.

Sharon

I am channeling Sharon's strength.

Sharon had an exceptional strength of spirit and was a giant of personality; *a joie de vivre* that cannot be matched.

I can still hear her laugh, and at the very same moment, I ache so badly because it is far too faint and I want to hear it once again.

Sharon craved and enjoyed decadent, delicious things like fancy chocolates. Have you ever had Vosges chocolate? If not, do it. I started purchasing Vosges chocolate because I discovered that they have the most beautiful purple packaging while on a work trip that took me through the Chicago O'Hare airport. They have a dedicated Vosges shopping nook! I bought some truffles there for Sharon and thought, *Sharon will love this! Chocolates and purple packaging?!* She would appreciate both the indulgence of the chocolates *and* the packaging, particularly because purple was her favorite color, just like Mom. In retrospect I think, *Wouldn't it have been neat if Sharon had the chance to taste Mom's Candy?*

Sharon knew how to work hard, how to do her best, and how to indulge. I learned that last bit from her. She would exclaim, "Fuck it! Life is too short." She was right. It is short. It was all too short for her, and for me, and for all those who had the magnificent opportunity to know her.

One spring, she organized a girls getaway weekend to Delaware beaches for us and another friend. We indulged in Cinco de Mayo lunch margaritas before going for a long walk together in a nature preserve. There, Sharon shouted in awe about the colors of unique birds we saw while peering through binoculars she had brought along. "Look at those blue stripes on its wings! Aren't they incredible?!" She was the force that made the trip happen and a master at communication and balancing group activities with individual desires.

She was also an artist. Sharon crafted beautiful pieces of stained glass and was an active member of the art community near her home. She was generous too, offering to make us a custom stained glass of our choosing one year. We immediately took her up on the offer but then delayed moving forward as other minutiae of life took over. It was Sharon who persistently badgered us with her generosity, "Seriously, you two, I need a project for my next workshop, and if you want one, you need to get me a design!"

With her urging, we got to work investigating designs and colors, kicking off a most special collaboration with Sharon. She walked through our house with us and highlighted the pros and cons of various window locations, helping us settle on the large transom window overlooking our side garden. Perfect. It would be visible from any point in the back of the house and a one-of-a-kind location to suit a one-of-a-kind piece of art. Sharon showed us the tools she would use and magnified our design onto large sheets of graph paper before any glass cutting would take place. She was methodical and precise.

After breakfast at our house one morning, we all leaned over the to-scale graph paper rendition she brought over that she had coded by color using our design, and we reviewed Sharon's glass placement recommendations.

She introduced us to the glass store she used for projects, and we took a three-hour outing together, carefully picking out each color and piece of glass for the design. Sharon knew which hue of green may look too opaque or which texture we may want for the clear pieces.

I think the whole project took six to eight months. And a lifetime's worth of Sharon's expertise.

What we have today is a bright, magnificently-crafted representation of Sharon, her strength of spirit, and *joie de vivre*. It is inexplicably meaningful.

Breakfasts, lunches, dinners, coffee outings were dates we loved putting on the calendar with Sharon. She loved offering comments about a menu, making reservations somewhere new (or familiar) and serving up ideas for meals we could all enjoy together.

I remember sitting across from Sharon during one of our dinners together. She and her husband, Brian, made a delicious roasted chicken. She held her belly, excusing herself saying she could not eat anymore. She asked us for a gastrointestinal medical doctor recommendation because she was experiencing trouble with her digestion. We didn't think much of it.

That was April.

In August, she was gone.

I don't know if I can ever fully appreciate the magnitude of such memories. I can only tell you that I will forever be grateful for every belly laugh, every smile, every joke, every martini, every piece of advice, every scowl, every recommendation (she had the best ones), every glass reflection, every hug, every "Fuck it! Life is too short."

The truth is, the loss of Sharon is one I cannot really wrap my head around. I like to think I cherished every moment, but I think in the case of Sharon, my heart cannot catch up to the stark reality of losing her. I never took her for granted, but I do not think I fully embraced the present force of her in our lives—in my life—and what an incredible void losing her would leave.

She was my go-to friend for advice, a sounding board, and a reality check. And suddenly, she isn't here. Aside from my partner, who has been with me in every moment, every ounce of this and who, too, has suffered this loss deeply, Sharon was the one other person I wanted to go-to. And suddenly, that go-to is no longer here to call or share a story over a delicious cup of coffee.

I miss her.

And yet, I experience Sharon's strength of spirit nearly every day. She shows up in the cardinals who perch momentarily on our patio chair and in the beautiful colors of light that reflect onto our living room walls from our beloved stained glass. She shows up in every bite of delicious Vosges chocolate.

"Fuck it! Life is too short."

Celebration of Sharon

Nearly nine months after she died, a group of friends and family who were united by Sharon gathered to celebrate her on May 22, 2021. Because we were not all able to be together face-to-face due to COVID, a small group united in Virginia while others joined in parallel at their own locations. We had colorful, raffia ribbons that we used to reflect upon memories of Sharon: purple was for a happy memory with her; rainbow was for our gratitude that she was a part of our lives; and red, white and green for the Mexican flag to honor she and Brian's Cinco de Mayo wedding and to send well-wishes for him. The ribbons were biodegradable so the idea was for each of us to quietly reflect while we found a tree or plant to tie them to - leaving a colorful mark, as she had done on our lives. What I did not know then and only now know in retrospect, is that the crafting of such a celebration (which was done in concert with the same friend who joined us at that Delaware beach girls' get-away) was ritual in action.

Below is what I felt compelled to share on that day in remembrance and celebration of Sharon:

> Sharon was a non-gentrified super-hero, and I know I could not ever find a sentiment that would fully capture her. I celebrate the tremendous, lifelong impact she has had on me.
>
> I have to dig deep to find words that adequately serve in what has been unimaginable yet real, and find I must channel Sharon. And forge ahead.
>
> Sharon loved the arts, and I loved going to events with her. She convinced me to join her for Matthew Bourne's Swan Lake last year, which was not a tall task. And, she convinced me to splurge for the box seat, which *was* a tall task. She exclaimed, "That was phenomenal!" It was a perfect summation. I loved accompanying her. Dancing and belting out a lyric at Wolf Trap National Park for the Performing Arts was one of my favorites.
>
> Sharon was emphatic and always at the most opportune

moment. “To hell with the consequence” as Melissa Etheridge would sing; Sharon would utter “You gotta let that shit go!”

She savored good food and great cocktails. Whether deviled eggs, lemon cake, seared scallops, beet salad, or a perfectly-chilled cocktail, Sharon would ENJOY it. Thank you for introducing me to Grey Goose and a fantastic martini, Sharon.

Sharon loved to plan trips, travel and experience new places.

She was expert at details and planning. Whether dedicating her stained glass workshop to our transom window with 177 pieces of glass, or helping me figure out how to turn my mother’s wedding dress into mine, or jumping in to help us redesign our office, Sharon could think of every last detail and really think through things. “You don’t want to be worried about that,” she would say.

She was dedicated to self-care and understood it was a key ingredient to showing up for other people.

Sharon was a bird watcher. I appreciate birds because of Charlie, but I found a new way of noticing them because of Sharon.

And, she always had the best recommendations and advice. Evermore channeling her, I ask, “What would Sharon tell me to do? What would she say?” She was such a champion of spirit; I know the answer.

I am thankful because she made me laugh; she made me rethink my hesitancies, and she demonstrated living life to the fullest.

My spirit is sore but my love for her is as strong as the pragmatic presence of Sharon.

I found her referencing a passage from a poem of Kahlil Gibran, a Lebanese-American writer and poet, in celebrating my birthday one year: “And the sweetness of friendship, let there be laughter and sharing of pleasures. For in the dew of little things the heart finds its morning and is refreshed.”

We also had paper sky lanterns that each of us took to a spot of our choosing to release in honor of Sharon's bright, vivacious spirit. My partner and I chose to release ours on one of our favorite hikes with our pointer, Charlie (who Sharon always showed so much generosity toward—he got a brand new set of tennis balls one Christmas from "Aunt Sharon"). We made our way to the beautiful quietness of the river and lit her lantern. Releasing it, we watched it fly—for all of five seconds—before it plummeted into the creek bed and floated away. We were mortified but then immediately burst into the deep belly laugh of our dear friend, Sharon. It was just as it was meant to be.

Alongside the creek bed, after watching the lantern float away in the gentle current, I took a deep breath and said to myself, "Fare thee well, Sharon. Goodbye."

I have to dig deep
to find words that
adequately serve in
what has been
unimaginable, yet real…

Afternoon Doze

Dad was sleeping soundly, taking his afternoon doze. This time, his brow was furrowed, and the skin creases on his forehead danced a tango. His oh-so-shallow breath became hollow and stuttered.

Connie was Dad's favorite caretaker in South Dakota. Every morning that she was scheduled for a shift with Dad, which was always on weekdays, she would pull up the driveway in her large Chevy Silverado. It was barely identifiable as a white truck since it was covered in dust and dirt from the gravel roads on the outskirts of town where she lived. "MS KITTY" appeared on her license plates, front and rear. MS KITTY would walk through the front door holding Dad's Wall Street Journal in one hand that she had picked up from the driveway. In the other hand, she would carry a large soda from a fast-food taco chain. She would lay out Dad's newspaper on the tray table in front of his wing-back chair just how he liked it so that when he hobbled—with her help—to the den an hour later, he could see the front-page headline even before bracing himself to sit down. She knew how to make Dad's eggs "just how I like them," he had told me on the phone in May 2020 as he was preparing to leave Florida and head back to South Dakota.

On this particular afternoon, now in early July 2021, Connie stood beside Dad's hospice bed, just to his right, and rested one hand on his delicate, thin forearm and the other on the cold, metal railing of the bed. I stood to Dad's left, staring at the dreaming animations playing out on his face. I was transfixed, watching the flutter of his eyebrows.

Then Dad winced, eyes fully closed.

Connie looked at me squarely, noticing my questioning look of concern. "He knows what he has to go through, and he doesn't want to have to do it yet."

Her words came effortlessly—so clear, so plain, so precise, and correct.

Turns out, MS KITTY was able to describe the thing that was most true and present in that very moment. She gave words to it, shared them with me, and encircled the moment with a perfect description for what I did not recognize and for which I could not find the words. I could simply be in that circle of time and complexly feel the dance of Dad's forehead creases while her words cascaded through my being. It was the moment when I fully recognized the conviction inside myself for being present for him on his journey toward death. The reality of his medical wisdom—his knowledge as a clinician—married with the reality of his being the patient, the very patient to walk this walk intersected.

Just like the evening my mother died, when I watched my father double over in tears, this became another I-could-never-have-imagined moment, and yet there it was, right in front of me. Again, I found myself feeling unprepared and so perfectly raw.

I gave his sleeping face a smile, rested one hand on his shin, and slid the other into his right hand, the same hand that had written me so many scribbles of great postcards over the years and taught me how great receiving a postcard is. The hand that had sewn stitches in my cut eyelid when I was four years old after a tree branch had snapped back on my face. The hand with which he would delightfully hold a puppet (usually Punch from *Punch and Judy*), presenting the character to a young child and demonstrating his prowess with puppetry.

I breathed in and whispered, "I'm here, Dad."

He woke up a couple hours later, and I felt closer to him than ever before. I got to know him in a beautifully new and vulnerable way. I witnessed him take on the struggle that lay before him, a struggle to include contemplating what would happen in the all-too-short time ahead of him, in the days before he took his last breath—to contemplate facing death.

That afternoon doze will stay with me forever. What a gift. What an honor. What an outrageously tough, human thing. For him. For me.

Dad died three days later.

I got to know him in a beautifully new and vulnerable way.

The Old Pro

When I was a kid, I went to golf camp. One summer, I even won a contest as "best putter." (It was the precision of putting that I really liked.)

My dad golfed. He really liked golf and walking the course. He enjoyed meeting up with his doctor buddies on Wednesday afternoons to talk shop, smoke cigars, and play a round. He liked convincing my mom to play with him on the weekends.

Playing golf on weekends was always a point of contention as well as a family activity to enjoy. It was a duality. My mom always felt the pressure to join and play, exclaiming "I don't have time for that; there is so much to do!" That was countered by my dad's relentless spirit and recognition that "play" is just as important as work. It was a never-ending tug of war between my parents. And I see both sides. One thing I absolutely adore about my father and my childhood with him is his sense of play, his ability to play with children and be absolutely present. At the same time, I understood my mom's position—there was always so much going on and so much they both were managing that getting things done felt better than pausing to "play."

It was almost always emotionally-charged when we would go play golf. I would get pissed off at frustrating shots. My mom would get pissed off at the people "breathing down her neck" behind us. Then, there would be the celebrations for a great shot down the fairway and a two-putt. Dad took on the roles of cheerleader and coach and careful husband and father. He used to explain how to approach a shot based on his latest Jack Nicklaus reading, or tell me to imagine a roll of toilet paper from the ball to the hole, drawing it out by waving his putter over the grass. It was helpful (not really) most of the time. But he loved it, and a part of us, I think, ventured to the golf course because we *did* want to do something fun, we *did* want to be outside, and we didn't want to disappoint him. For me, it was mostly the latter. As an adult, I now tend to share the view of Hannah Gadsby when it comes to golf—

that it is simply "a monumental waste of land, time, and water."

It was the 1990s, and my dad decided that the vehicle for him was a minivan. I remember the first time he described his excitement at purchasing one. What?! I was so confused. This man who drove large, boat-like sedans, Lincoln Town Cars, and Cadillacs, was overjoyed to be getting a minivan? I didn't get it until one day years later when I was visiting my parents and headed to the golf course with my dad. He opened the back of the minivan. There I found his golf clubs, a brown duffel bag bursting at the seams and filled with socks, sneakers, golf shoes, extra sweaters, rain jackets, an umbrella, and every accessory you could imagine for heading out to the "range." My dad popped a squat on the bumper and started getting ready to change his shoes. It was in that very moment that it crystalized, and I understood the draw to the minivan. Ding, ding, ding! Here it was: A vehicle *and* a personal, outdoor "locker room" for getting ready to play golf. It was perfect for my dad. Never again did I question why he was driving around in a minivan.

The night my father passed away, while standing with him before the morgue representatives arrived, I was suddenly caught off guard when I noticed, through my thick tears, the blanket cleanly draped over him. It was a throw blanket that used to be in my parents' den that the caretaker had covered him with that night to keep him warm. It was navy, cream, and maroon and had the weaved design of a male golfer with knickers and what appeared to be a wooden golf club from the early 1900s, and the words "The Old Pro."

Fitting, I thought. In a moment of deep sadness, I chuckled, *Perfect*.

In a moment of
deep sadness,
I chuckled, *Perfect*.

Goodbye

Around 3:00 a.m. on July 4, 2021, my father talked to me about persistence. He was tired and weak, struggling to breathe with his oxygen concentrator set to level eight (out of ten).

"You have to understand," he said, "Persistence is what makes life worth living. If you aren't persistent, you give up on yourself, and you *never* give up on yourself."

He said it so emphatically. Because of his fibrosis, he really had to muster the energy to emphasize the words as he did. And I can still recall the deep and striking look of his eyes into mine as he spoke.

Saying goodbye is one of the most empowering things you can do. It represents the distinct recognition of what you truly value. By letting go and taking the action of "goodbye," you take ownership of that action, your priorities—you offer to others what you no longer need or want and create space for something new.

There have been so many "goodbyes" in the past months. So many things I have had to say goodbye to, let go of, make a decision about and to set free. And like many actions, saying goodbye takes practice. It is not something you can do once and replicate easily. It takes thought and involves degrees of emotion. Saying goodbye is powerful—it is an opportunity to honor what or whom you are letting go. The pang of the aftermath felt is proportional to the degree of emotional investment, the vibrancy of the memories, and the raw feeling of knowing it will no longer be as it has been.

I said goodbye to my mother on March 10, 2020. I kissed her on the forehead, squeezed her hand and said, "I love you, Mom. This is my goodbye." At 6:23 p.m., with a pelican gliding by outside the window, my mother passed away.

And on the night of July 7, 2021, I said goodbye to my father. I kissed him on the forehead and said, "I love you, Dad. Goodbye."

At roughly 1:20 a.m. on July 8, 2021, he let go and passed away.

Set her free. Set him free. I like to think I may have helped set them both free.

Saying goodbye is one of the most empowering things you can do.

Dad Passed

In July 2021, I once again found myself needing to let others know about a parent dying. Turns out, practice does help. I would not say it makes it easier, but it does help. It offers a familiarity and a knowing that you will come out the other side. The following is the message I crafted following my father's passing to send via text message. It was July 8, 2021.

I hope you are doing well!

I want to let you know (because you are so dear to me and because I am working on sharing):

My dear father passed away at home in South Dakota in the wee hours of this morning. It was just as he wished: to be at home resting in his beloved home, in his community where he established his career and nurtured our family.

Angela and I have been with him for the past few weeks and are so grateful to have been with him in his final days and to have had the privilege of a final goodbye.

We are remaining in South Dakota a bit longer (and Charlie is pleased to have a longer reign of the yard here!)

Angela has been amazing (as always) in support of me and our family, and we are doing well.

We'll keep you posted on our travels and let you know when we have time to catch up.

Love and hugs to you.

Amelia

It offers a familiarity and a knowing that you will come out the other side.

Don't Cry Out Loud

Peter Allen wrote a song called "Don't Cry Out Loud." One of my mom's favorite Broadway shows about his life was *The Boy from Oz* starring Hugh Jackman. She and I went to it three times during the period he was headlining the show in New York City. It was also during the time when I was going to school in New York for performing arts. My mom loved to shake her shoulders and unabashedly belt out the lyrics from the show.

I have a distinct memory of her sitting to the left of me at the theater and seeing the glassy tears in her eyes during the song "Don't Cry Out Loud." My mother was a very proud person, and she did not want anyone to see her sweat or cry out loud.

It has been hard for me to cry out loud. And crying comes at some of the most unexpected moments. I have cried while writing this story. I will be feeding our dog and suddenly burst into tears. The oven repair man will bring over the new igniter that was sourced from my hometown—more tears. My phone will pop open with a memory from four years ago—a sigh plus tears. But in each of these moments, I am crying alone, hiding sadness: "Don't Cry Out Loud."

Contrary to this song, crying out loud or showing emotion isn't a lack of pride or falling—it is actually a window opening for further connection.

I finally cried in front of someone the other day and apologized. She asked, "Why are you apologizing?" I explained, "Because I don't want to put sadness on you." She responded, "But it makes me feel closer to you." I stopped short. In that brief exchange, she offered me a most significant *aha*.

"Don't Cry Out Loud" is for the birds. Stand tall and proud for sure and share with others that pain is real, that it is present, and that you are navigating through it.

…crying out loud or showing emotion isn't a lack of pride nor falling, it is actually a window opening for further connection.

Dad's Memorial

Dad's celebration of life consisted of a family dinner the next night at a local steak house including me, Angela, my sister, and her two daughters. My nephew was not present because he did not make the trip from Florida to see Dad those final days.

Dad wanted us all to go to dinner together. He loved knowing that his children and grandchildren were eating "a good steak." He didn't want a funeral, and he didn't want pomp and circumstance. He wasn't connected to the church and even questioned religion, particularly late in life. He was a thinker, a kind of philosopher. Funny, since I chose to study philosophy in my undergraduate work. He loved to tell stories, inflate them, and for all his periodic boasting, he was a humble man and carried himself so. He was incredibly accomplished—a brilliant physician, scientist, and art connoisseur. "Your father *knows*!" my mother would exclaim.

I have often thought about how the family dinner following his passing is mismatched with the magnitude of his life, his accomplishments, and the impact he had on others. He was revered by so many former patients, neighbors, mentees, caregivers, community members, and family. Yet, the private family dinner matched *him*. The remembrance of Dad and the celebration of his life has happened in the beautiful anecdotes and stories others have shared about him and will continue to do so.

He didn't want a funeral, and he didn't want pomp and circumstance.

Obituaries

Obituaries are tough. If memory serves me correctly, the only time one really learns about obituaries and writing them is a brief assignment in a high school Writing or English class when a teacher assigns the homework to write your own obituary. You might read a short book of epitaphs and learn some of the key structural elements that make up an obituary, and then you set off to finish your homework and write what could become a future obituary. "Think of it as a letter to yourself for a later date," is what my Writing teacher advised.

Letter to myself?

What the assignment doesn't consider is that most people don't prepare their own obituary. Most people don't write a letter to themselves or record the facts of their life, nor do they typically do so in a way that captures unique, descriptive qualities in a concise manner. And most certainly, they don't do so under the weighted sorrow blanket of their still living loved ones. Rather, writing one's own obituary would be part of offloading that from loved ones and preemptively avoiding the distillation of your life from the perspective of those closest to you.

After my mother passed, I remember my sister was sitting on the 1970s reupholstered couch in the condo. She looked across the room at me and asked, "Do you want me to come up with a draft obituary for Mom?" It was the first offer and a solid one.

In hindsight, I am even more grateful for that offer. At that point, I did not even know where to begin with crafting Mom's obituary. I had already written my card to Mom, read it to her, and written words for her celebration of life. My focus now was on ensuring everything was taken care of relative to her affairs for Dad, and making sure to care for him.

It worked out great because my sister could recall details and things that I could not, and vice versa. So, she wrote a draft, had me read it to offer edits, and then we would post with the newspaper-both newspapers: in Florida and in South Dakota. Since my parents travelled to Florida that preceding fall without any inkling she would get sick and pass away, there were friends, neighbors and community members of my parents in South Dakota that would be stunned to learn she would not return to their home there.

This obituary drafting worked so well for my mother's obituary that we did so for my father's too. When he passed away and it was the wee hours of the morning, my sister and I were sitting at the kitchen table (the same glass table where he would give us fruit at every breakfast growing up) in South Dakota, my sister looked over at me and asked if I wanted her to "take a cut at a draft obituary for Dad." I grasped my hot tea mug and readily took her up on the offer. This time, there was more coordination on my part to bring it across the finish line and posting it in the local newspaper. Regardless, it was a big help. Plus, it was beneficial to lean on the details she recalled and those that came to my own mind. My parents' obituaries were the one thing in all of this that my sister and I got to approach together.

Collecting content, editing, and reviewing obituaries brought a sense of obligation, tears and quiet smiles while recollecting their accomplishments and the amazing lives they led. In the end, I think obituaries are precisely intended for those still living to create because they serve as an immediate exercise to recognize the gravity of your loved one in your life and their life as a whole. If I saw my former Writing teacher, that is what I would tell her.

Brian wrote Sharon's obituary, which he chose to share privately versus making it a fully public notice. It was a beautiful tribute that conveyed the impact of her life and the amazing life she led.

All three of their obituaries make me cry and pull on my heart and my soul, as if I am six years old, pounding piano keys with the tune *Heart and Soul*. I used to think obituaries needed to include a laundry list of accomplishments - a resume of sorts. Now, I believe them to be notices - notices of a person having died, so that others who knew them can know they died; an invitation to consider that person's life; and a tribute. In my mind, the tribute part lives forever. It reaches far beyond the obituary and shows up in the form of shared stories, tears, laughter over a joke Dad told that made Mom scowl, smiles in reverence of Sharon's stained glass, and the sensation in my heart left behind.

…the tribute part
lives forever.

Alexander

When I was little, my mom used to pull out the book *Alexander and the Terrible, Horrible, No Good, Very Bad Day* by Judith Viorst whenever I was having a really tough time. She would ask, "Is it time for Alexander?" Almost certainly, I would respond "yes" through rocket tears, and we would sit together while she read the story of Alexander's troubles on his most very bad day. Somehow, I would feel better, or at least comforted by this. My tears would dry, my sniffles gradually subsiding.

Today, fast-forward forty years, I found myself standing in my former childhood room, staring out the window where my mother always told me to draw the curtains. I was surrounded by copious amounts of items from my childhood: my rocking horse piggy bank, the "This is a fierce bad rabbit" needlepoint pillow, and the most amazing doll house that had electricity running through it! Suddenly, my eye caught *Alexander and the Terrible, Horrible, No Good, Very Bad Day* peeking out of a plastic bag filled with children's books. Without hesitation, I picked it up and started leafing through Alexander's no-good-day and immediately felt the phantom pain of my mother's warm arm wrapped around me as she read me the story.

I wrote earlier about this whole season of loss feeling like a life hijacked. So too, it has often been a terrible, horrible, no good, very bad day. On repeat. On this day, there was no further sound of my father's oxygen concentrators humming, no voice of a health aide pouring him 7-Up. It was me, my partner, and our dog amidst all of these things that I grew up with, along with the gravity of handling the estate and executing my parent's wishes.

I thought, *I am taking this book with me.* Because maybe just as it did while I was a child, it will bring me comfort when I pause to read it - to read that Alexander too has had a rough time. It will remind me that I am not alone and that tomorrow *is* another day. Or perhaps simply, it will serve as a reflection of my mom's care and hearing her voice in my mind's eye.

No matter the remedy or memory, moving forward is within reach.

Plus, Alexander may have hated lima beans, as told in Judith Voirst's book, but I have grown up to like them.

So too, it has often been a terrible, horrible, no good, very bad day. On repeat.

In Omaha

I am in Omaha today cutting brussels sprouts to roast. I grew up not liking lima beans or brussels sprouts. What I knew of these was my mom cooking these frozen vegetables in the microwave. Now, I love the tiny cabbages—roasting them in olive oil, salt, and pepper and then drizzling them with lemon juice. Yum.

I am here in Nebraska today- we are here. And this week. Not enjoying it, rather, staying here and working from a rental apartment because the estate sale team reached a point of needing *all* the rooms in my parents' home to complete preparations for the sale. Plus, we could find no place in my hometown available to take our dog. So, here we are, in Omaha.

Today, I called a few of my parents' friends. Finally. Finally, I got the energy together to make those calls to thank them for the final messages they left my father, and to personally let them know he had passed.

No one tells you that is part of the duties. No one tells you what that feels like.

I will.

It is both unimaginable and taxing. I was nervous! At the same time, it is very energizing and beautiful. These are people, in many cases, who you know from childhood. You remember their voices but have a very distant recollection of their demeanor. They have stories of your parents and loved ones. They have shared experiences with them, and they, too, have lost them. You have to extend a hand and close the loop. Well, you don't *have to,* but it is the right thing to do. These people were important to your parents and loved ones, and they have a shared understanding of the people you love. And, in most cases, you end up having the deep pleasure of hearing a story or a nugget of information that you did not previously know, which inevitably brings a smile. For instance, Melanie said, "It was an amazing connection we had. We truly became family." Now, I know Melanie and her husband, Terry, to be close friends of my parents. I even found joyful photos of their travels together over the years. I remember my mother calling to tell me, "Your dad and I are headed to Terry and Melanie's for the weekend. We're going to the dinner theater together!" Then there were my parents' friends, Kitty and Quido, who lived in Florida. They used to meet Mom and Dad for lunch or dinner at a halfway point between their places and it was Quido on the phone who helped me understand when Dad's research lab was built.

It is so very hard to do this, yet it brings unexpected comfort to hear their voices and to listen to their stories.

No one tells you
what that feels like.

Don’t Let the Bed Bugs Bite

In carrying the responsibility for Dad’s care in those last sixteen months of his life, I carried the weight of the nurse schedule, instructions for the medical professionals, maintenance of his house, paying bills, and all the detailed management of his life. It was a weight I didn’t scoff at nor feel slighted by. I was pleased to do it. It was like trying on my dad’s massive, long sheepskin winter coat that had heavy snaps and massive pockets when I was eight. I felt the weight enfold me as I put it over my shoulders.

In doing so, I also got the benefit of knowing my father without my mother living. It is not something I would wish for, but given the circumstances, I discovered so many amazing and new things. And I got to learn and experience them in the short window before losing him.

I remember the magnitude of emotion in his tears as he wept by my mother’s bedside once she was pronounced. They had been together since the fourth grade. I cannot imagine knowing my person that long and losing her, and yet, I saw it right before my eyes.

I also got to witness the moments in my father’s grief when he tapped into his sense of humor. “Well, honey, don’t let the bed bugs bite.” That is exactly what he said when the men from the morgue came to roll my mother away the night of her passing. I recall it so clearly. My father, Angela, and I were sitting at the dining table rather than the living room so as not to have a clear view of my mother on a gurney while they prepared her to leave. It was a gentle and firm suggestion from the kindest of hospice nurses. My father, ever the clinician, initially dismissed the suggestion, stating, “It’s no big deal,” waving his hands in the air. Yet, after some caring coaxing from the nurse, he moved to join Angela and me at the dining table. The three of us sat there, chatting about everything and nothing at the same time. It was a perfect example of suspended, awkward time. All three of us were acutely aware of the activity happening in the other room and equally determined to stay present in the environment surrounding the dining table.

After about thirty minutes, the two finely-dressed men began to wheel the body bag containing my mother through the condominium to exit. As they wheeled just by my father's peripheral view, he gave a side glance to her and blurted out that statement, "Well, honey, don't let the bed bugs bite." It caught us all off guard, and it was a perfect representation of his own style of humor in order to break the ice. It's as if my father's empathy for Angela and me, the hospice nurse, the gentlemen from the morgue, and the seriousness of the moment invited laughter. I think it was both his way of easing the stress of such a circumstance while caring for us.

On the first of my mother's birthdays following her death, I was speaking to my father on the phone. We were enjoying one of our typical telephone conversations and trading stories. I mentioned how much we all recognized Mom's love of birthdays and celebrations in particular. His usual stoic self, mid-way through the conversation, he said, "It's times like this I miss her the most." It stopped my breath. "I know, Dad."

He told me old stories and new stories. He let me draw pictures for him and play records. Angela and I moved his large record player and speakers into the den so he could listen to his vinyl records. I was the only one who could get the thing to work; I attempted to teach some of the health aides, but that proved futile. I remember seeing him smile when I got the player working with a Noel Coward album.

One of my favorite things from the final weeks with him was holding his hand while he told the hospice nurse and me about his most-loved vacations. I got to listen to him describe road trips and colorfully explain to her about traveling to Mackinac Island in Michigan. I would join in on the stories and memories—we laughed and smiled.

I got to read the opinion column of the Wall Street Journal to him each day in his final weeks—he was always curious to know what the topic was.

My dad confided in me. He demonstrated his trust in me. And he came to me for help.

On top of this, I also bore the responsibility of carrying out his wishes.

I got to follow through.

It was a perfect
example of suspended,
awkward time.

Follow Through

Time is strange. The hours and days following my mother's passing felt long, extended, suspended slow-motion. There was so much to do and figure out. My father was not independent. He was sick and elderly and needed care. My sister once said of my parents in the months prior to my mother's illness, "Somehow, they muddle through together." With Mom's passing, that "muddling through together" was no longer an option.

Before my mother died, I knew that she managed most of my parents' affairs. But it was not until she was gone that I became acutely and immediately aware of the one hundred percent degree to which my mother managed everything for my parents. My father didn't know how many bank accounts they had, where their wills were located, or even how to pay the bills.

On the evening of January 3, 2020, my partner and I had just wrapped up a lovely, restful get-away, and I was looking ahead to some final winter holiday recharge time before jumping into the new year. My phone rang. "I have to go to the hospital." My mom exclaimed wildly. "My doctor called. He said that because of the blood work results, I need to go to the emergency room!"

I was on a plane the next morning.

When I arrived, I made it to the hospital just in time to pick up Mom as she was being discharged following a blood transfusion. Her blood cell and platelet counts had been critically low. I spent the next few days with my parents, navigating calls with doctors and cooking them food while noticing how incredibly fatigued my mom was. I took her to her first oncology appointment where they explained that she was at severe risk of bleeding to death if she were to fall or get an injury. A bone marrow biopsy was in order.

When I was making the decision to fly to Florida for that January trip, I recall the voice of a colleague who once advised, "Never hesitate to visit. We cannot know how long our parents will be around." I am so grateful now for that advice.

I am also happy that I could be there for my parents, to be there for them together while mom was sick, and to be there for them as individuals during those really tough and final times. I am happy that I could be her health advocate, and then my dad's.

During that time in January 2020, because of Dad's illness, he was not strong enough to join Mom on doctor's visits or blood transfusions, of which she had many. He was too weak to drive and was relegated to their condominium 24/7.

It was on that trip that I learned the password to my mom's phone and iPad. I wheeled my mom into the lobby of the oncologist's office and gathered the clipboard of paperwork from the front desk before settling onto a chair next to her. We sat together while filling out the medical paperwork for my mom to prepare for this first oncology appointment. It was a role reversal from when I was a young child at the doctor and my mom sat beside me filling out medical forms for me. Just as my mom had taught me how to complete these forms, talking me through each question, I now did the same for her. "On a scale of 1 to 10, how tired are you?" "Do you have kidney disease?" One by one, we walked through the questions. We had to gather some information saved on her phone, and it was then that I asked, "What is the password to your phone, Mom?" After she told me and we turned in the forms, my mom shared that she had a password document saved on her iPad, and the code to open the iPad was the same as her phone's.

On January 10, my mom was diagnosed. We lost her exactly eight weeks later, to the day.

Everything I had to figure out, investigate and solve in order to take care of my father and manage my parents' affairs was made possible by having that single phone code. It was the key that opened the pathway of a treasure hunt.

In the days following my mother's passing, this massive hunt of "figuring things out" and tackling endless "to dos" began.

My father needed to be cared for. His health aides' schedules and long-term care needed to be managed. My parents owned two properties: the condominium in Florida and their home in South Dakota where I grew up. I needed to pay his bills, close out my mother's final bills, understand his financial situation, and keep the ship sailing, so to speak. This led to a full-court press focused energy on keeping his routine and care in place while putting things in order to support him and attend to his affairs.

Every day was consumed with searching for paperwork, organizing papers—papers and more papers—searching for their wills, scheduling my dad's care, rescheduling my dad's care, picking up groceries, cooking him nutritious meals (I saw before my eyes how nutrition played such an important role in his awake hours and his sleep), picking up prescriptions, doing laundry, making instructions for caregivers, and sifting through yet more papers…

One evening I remember kneeling on the cold tile floor triaging paperwork that my mom had stuffed into a reusable grocery bag. It was a sign that day-to-day management had been getting too tough for her, too, though she never would admit it.

Because my parents never shared the details of their financial situation and did not have estate documents clearly organized and accessible, I was starting from square one - wait, square zero.

Ultimately, I had to shepherd my dad through a decision on whether he wanted to remain in Florida or if he wanted to return home to South Dakota. He had failed to an extent that made it apparent that traveling back and forth twice a year was no longer possible. I drafted the financial profile and presented it to him. We weighed the emotional aspects too. My dad loved the home in South Dakota and the community there. He too loved the decades-worth of memories from visits to the condominium in Florida to see his parents with my sister and me, as well as with his grandkids, and most certainly, with Mom. It was not fiscally possible nor reasonable for him to retain both properties, and he understood that. The condo in Florida had a steep monthly homeowners association fee, and Dad was concerned about an impending special assessment. Plus the bylaws prevented capitalizing on the property by renting it. He also understood that traveling back and forth between the states was no longer an option for him. He was the one who first offered that realization. "It's best to choose," he said. I would support him with either, but he needed to make a choice.

He chose South Dakota.

Angela and I continued to work remotely full time through it all. We spent May 2020 in South Dakota, setting up my father with his care there. Angela figured out how to get him medically transported from Florida to South Dakota where he would have his round-the-clock oxygen and nurse care during the drive. Essentially, it was a hospital room on wheels. Impressively, she arranged all of this in the middle of the COVID-19 pandemic.

We then spent October 2020 in Florida sifting through my parents' condominium and preparing it for sale, then selling it on behalf of my father. He wanted it sold "before the presidential election." I told him that I would do my best.

We then spent June and July 2021 in South Dakota caring for my father in his final weeks of life.

We were back again to South Dakota in September and October 2021 to work with the estate sale team and prepare for emptying my parents' house, my childhood home. This was followed by months of estate management and work to close out the estate, carrying out my parents' wishes, and putting a bow on the beautiful package of their life as we knew it.

I felt completely unprepared at the outset, yet resolutely confident for what had to be done to honor them and their lives, to carry out their wishes and follow through.

It was the key that opened the pathway of a treasure hunt.

Old Masters

My parents surrounded themselves (and my sister and me) with many things, one of which included an art collection in our home. It was a mix of paintings, portraits, sketches, posters, sculptures—you name it—procured from an eclectic variety of venues my parents visited over their many years together. A portion of that collection included Old Masters Paintings, a term and description I only later learned by way of art and auction houses when I was researching and avidly trying to determine the best way to handle the collection and find them new homes following my father's passing.

My father used to say, "This is very valuable. And this one, this one is *extremely* valuable." As a young child, I would think, "Wow!" During the most random moments, such as leaving for a walk, my father would grab a pen-light nestled from his jacket breast pocket and hold it up to a painting with his right hand while his left hand held the dog leashes in our front hall. He would zoom in with his eyes and get his face and hands centimeters from the paint, gazing closely at the piece. I, on the other hand, would zoom in on my father, watching him interact with the art before modeling his behavior and gazing at the paint, too. "Look at the detail on her fur. Look at how the colors come to the forefront under light," he would quietly exclaim as though the dim light of the hall and subject at hand required a whisper. "This is why we mustn't keep this painting under direct light. Good thing we have it in the front hall." I would respond with different versions of, "I see" or "uh-huh" or "yep." Then, before I knew it, he would stand up straight, put the pen-light back in his breast pocket, and we would head out the door to walk the dogs.

This type of interaction with the paintings happened often. In the dining room, it was the details of the background the artist so perfectly painted and the baby's foot that my father would call out. "Look at how the child's foot juts straight out at us," he would say. By the piano, it was the gaze of the mother and the trees in the distance. My father would always add a comment about the artist, or in most cases, who he believed to be the artist. He would take photographs of the paintings and photocopy art history books with similarly-styled paintings. He would fixate for minutes at a time while visiting an art gallery, such as the United States Portrait Gallery, the National Gallery of Art in Washington D.C., Mauritsthuis in The Hague, or the Uffizi in Florence.

He procured most of these paintings early in my parent's marriage. To me, they were fixtures in the home, always there. Except for one. There was one painting that my father purchased later, and I got to hear the story of how FedEx delivered a massive crate to the driveway. The painting and frame filled an entire living room wall. Clearly, it was meant for an art gallery where a bench would typically be placed opposite it. My father saw it as a living room piece.

As I got older and I learned more about the world, goods, trade, markets, and business, I came to believe that something is as valuable as someone is willing to pay for it. So, my childhood thought of *Wow!* when my father would reference how valuable a painting was turned into, *It's only as valuable as someone is willing to pay for it.* I didn't tell my father this; rather, I went along the journey with him in his wonder and belief in the collection.

Figuring out what to do with my parents' collection of art came with a heavy weight—a weight of more than forty years of seeing it through the eyes of my parents and the belief that everything was extremely valuable. "You must not let any 'old schmo' try to deal with these. You need to find a real expert," my mother would say at dinner. My father would agree and launch into another story about the sketch on the wall, how that piece may actually be the most valuable one they owned. It went on and on and on. When it came to the fate of the Old Masters after my parents passed, the focus was always on the mechanics of handling them, never on the emotions involved.

In reality, it turned out to be just as much about emotion as it was about mechanics.

I spent hours and hours researching and making phone calls. I took photographs, dug through copious amounts of unorganized files to investigate details about each piece of artwork. I spoke to countless art appraisers, reached out to universities and auction houses, even Sotheby's. I spent endless wakeful nights thinking, *What am I going to do with these? What if I don't find an expert? I just cannot sell them at an estate sale; they are not fit for that...*

I became the real-life detective I played as a child when we gathered for a game of Clue. But this wasn't a classic "whodunit"—no Colonel Mustard in the study with a knife. Instead, it was: What are the pertinent facts about the art? Who is the expert? And, what is the best way to let them go in a manner that suits the art and honors my parents?

Finally, after months of research (on top of the time I had spent previously investigating this for my dad), I found an art auction house from Minneapolis, my parent's hometown, and where they went to the university together. It was fitting—not just because of its location in the Midwest where my parents, grandparents, and great-grandparents hailed from; but also because the auction house was extremely capable, deeply knowledgeable about Old Masters Paintings, and confident in gathering the necessary information, finding appropriate new owners, and posting the pieces for auction. I found them through a letter from the 1980s that my father had received from the Gallery of Art in Minneapolis regarding one of the paintings he had previously inquired about. This letter, of course, was found late at night during the investigative phase, stuffed into a random manilla folder that was in a packed file drawer in the basement. On the phone with me, a woman from the museum described the auction house in Minneapolis. It was like finding a needle in a stack of needles. In hindsight, my father was very much part of this investigation. While he did not leave specific notes to help me find them, it was because of my father's outreach to the gallery way back when I was five years old that ultimately led me to them. It made sense.

The day the auction house owners came to retrieve the art, I felt such a sense of relief. Finally, after years and years of conjecture about how this would go, how anyone would possibly find or know what to do, I had found them, and it fit. I also felt trepidation: Was I really to this point? Were these paintings actually coming off the walls and physically moving out of the house? (Something I, nor quite possibly anyone in my family could ever have imagined.) And here it was: another moment of something new.

Once the paintings were gone, I saw walls I had never seen before because they had always been covered. The most profound discovery was that the house even smelled different. "Well, of course," I said to Angela ("of course" in that it truly was a new discovery). "Think of all the scents and odors they must have absorbed over the years. And Dad smoked pipes and cigars!"

A few months later, each Old Masters Painting sold at auction and each had multiple bidders. Every single one found a new home and a new journey.

What I have come to realize is that these paintings *were* very valuable—extremely valuable. They were so to my father. I think when he said, "This is extremely valuable," he meant, "This is likely worth a decent amount of money but more importantly, it is extremely valuable *to me*. It carries a lot of meaning *for me*." Each carried a story for him: how he procured it, where he was, how he perceived the subject of the painting, the environment depicted, and most importantly, his wonder about the artist. He didn't ever share much about how or where he procured these paintings—facts that clearly would have come in handy. His focus was always on the painting itself and the sense of wonder surrounding the artist, their techniques, their life, and how they compared to other artists.

These paintings were also very valuable to our family—to me. They were the subject of so many meals and moments—they were fixtures of our life and our home. My memories of growing up are set against the backdrop of these paintings, so to speak. Just like the detailed trees in the background of that painting by the piano, these paintings were details in the background of my childhood. They will always be extremely valuable to me because they were an extension of my father, because they meant so much to him, and because he means so much to me.

Whenever I feel the distinct pang and thoughts arise about the many things of my parents' I had to "handle" and make decisions about, I recall my father peering at the paintings and telling a story. I recall the beautiful memories I have with him, my parents and my sister in a wonderfully overstuffed home. Most importantly, I recall the moments of wonder and I gain strength. And I find myself wondering: *Where is that painting now? Who is enjoying it now? What is its story now?*

I bet it is an incredible one.

And here it was:
another moment of
something new.

Colorful and Dynamic

My parents were colorful and dynamic people—as individuals and as a couple. "Your parents were of another world," one of the estate sale ladies told me. I knew exactly what she meant, and she was spot on. She didn't mean that they were quirky in a science fiction type of way; she meant they were eclectic, boisterous, and from another era. Having never met them, she gathered this by combing through all the things representing a life curated together. They were the plosives of linguistics, the strength in a whisper—exuberant, vibrant and exceptional people. They loved to tell stories, listen to music, entertain, and be entertained. They worked hard, fought hard, and laughed hard. They were Renaissance-type of people, leaders of exceptional lives. Growing up with my parents was messy, delightful, and loud; more arduous than it needed to be at times; beautiful and exactly as it was supposed to be. I am confident that they loved me with all their might. And I am confident that they felt the might of my love for them.

Sharon also was colorful and dynamic, eclectic and boisterous. She was loud and loved to laugh with a really good-hearted, deep belly laugh. She appreciated the beauty around us and wasn't shy about diving into the appetizers before everyone else at a dinner party. She demonstrated so many admirable qualities that I carry with me today and I consider to be the ever-presence of Sharon.

They all appreciated a tasty cocktail, and all three of them were early for everything, always. Including death.

I think it is neat that they all met each other. Mom and Dad knew how dear Sharon was to me, and Sharon too knew how dear my parents were to me. My hope is that they are telling stories together, exclaiming and belly-laughing over a delicious cocktail.

It is good fortune that I have had each one of them in my life.

I am confident that they loved me with all their might. And I am confident that they felt the might of my love for them.

Music

Music has played a significant role in my life. I started tap dance lessons in second grade, piano and ballet in third grade, violin in fourth grade, continuing them all through high school graduation. I was in musicals and theater (school and community), played in orchestra (school and community), and I still play violin today although not as often as I would like. My grandmother used to say to my mom about me, "Everything she does, she does with a dance." I hope that is still the case.

I am a feeler. I feel things deeply; I think and lead through feeling.

During the past (what has now been) twenty-four months, I have seen and learned that about myself. I was the kid who sat at the symphony and cried, my imagination going wild while humming along. I am still that kid. A few notes of music can make my heart sing. They can make my heart cry…and dance.

Along with this journaling, I am offering music that has played a role and been ever-present for me during this time of my life.

They may be songs you already know or new to you:

"Little by Little"

Vocals by Clare Bowen | Composition and Lyrics by Clare Bowen, Amy Wadge, Brandon Robert Young

"Shiny"

Vocals by Sara Bareilles | Composition and Lyrics by Sara Bareilles

"Before You Go"

Lead vocals by Lewis Capaldi | Composition and Lyrics by Lewis Capaldi, Peter Kelleher, Ben Kohn, Phil Plested, Tom Barnes

"Someone Who Loves Me"

Vocals by Sara Bareilles | Composition and Lyrics by Sara Bareilles

"Younger Me"

Brothers Osborne | Composition and Lyrics by TJ Osborne, Kendell Marvel

"A Million Dreams"

From *The Greatest Showman*, vocals by Ziv Zaifman, Hugh Jackman and Michelle Williams | Composition and Lyrics by Benj Pasek, Justin Noble Paul, Rob Mathes

"The Other Side"

From *The Greatest Showman*, vocals by Hugh Jackman and Zac Efron | Composition and Lyrics by Benj Pasek, Justin Noble Paul, Rob Mathes

"Never Enough"

From *The Greatest Showman*, vocals by Loren Allred | Composition and Lyrics by Benj Pasek, Justin Noble Paul, Rob Mathes

"This Is Me"

From *The Greatest Showman,* vocals by Keala Settle and Ensemble | Composition and Lyrics by Benj Pasek, Justin Noble Paul, Rob Mathes

"Rewrite the Stars"

From *The Greatest Showman*, vocals by Zac Efron and Zendaya | Composition and Lyrics by Benj Pasek, Justin Noble Paul, Rob Mathes

"Tightrope"

From *The Greatest Showman*, vocals by Michelle Williams | Composition and Lyrics by Benj Pasek, Justin Noble Paul, Rob Mathes

"From Now On"

From *The Greatest Showman*, vocals by Hugh Jackman and Ensemble | Composition and Lyrics by Benj Pasek, Justin Noble Paul, Rob Mathes

"Doors and Corridors"

Vocals by Clare Bowen | Composition and Lyrics by Clare Bowen, Brandon Robert Young, Amy Wadge

"While You Still Can"

Brothers Osborne | Composition and Lyrics by John Osborne, Travis Meadows

"She Used To Be Mine"

Vocals by Sara Bareilles | Composition and Lyrics by Sara Bareilles

"Edelweiss"

From *The Sound of Music*, vocals by Charmian Carr and Bill Lee | Composition and Lyrics by Richard Rogers, Howard Lindsay, Maria von Trapp, Oscar Hammerstein II, Russel Crouse, Irwin Kostal

"Wish You Pain"

Vocals by Andy Grammer | Composition and Lyrics Andy Grammer, Tom Meredith, Ryan Met, Jack Met

"You Haven't Seen the Last of Me"

Lead vocals by Cher | Composition and Lyrics by Diane Warren, Matt Serletic

"Only You"

Vocals by Sinead O'Connor | Composition and Lyrics by Ilan Eshkeri, Nikki Hassman, Pam Sheyne, Scott Shields

"The Best"

Lead vocals by Tina Turner | Composition and Lyrics by Holly Knight, Mike Chapman, Tina Turner

"The Best Day"

Vocals by Taylor Swift | Composition and Lyrics by Taylor Swift

"Supermarket Flowers"

Vocals by Ed Sheeran | Composition and Lyrics by Ed Sheeran, Benjamin Levin, Johnny McDaid

"A Safe Place To Land"

Vocals by Sara Bareilles featuring John Legend | Composition and Lyrics by Sara Bareilles, Lori McKenna

"Warrior"

Vocals by Clare Bowen | Composition and Lyrics by Clare Bowen, Justin Halpin, Brandon Robert Young

A few notes of music can make my heart sing. They can make my heart cry… and dance.

Renewal

The real voyage of discovery consists not in seeking new landscapes, but in having new eyes.

– Marcel Proust

It's February 2022, nearly twenty-four months (one year, eleven months and two days exactly)— since my mother's death. The timeline from that monumental change in my life will remain crystal clear even as "time marches on," as she would say. And today, I am experiencing a sensation of renewal—one that feels newer than any prior sense of renewal I have ever experienced in my life. And one that has quietly crept in over the past couple weeks in slight and sporadic moments—like a popped popcorn kind of feeling—until the full presence and recognition of the sensation is known in my being on this day.

Angela and I are visiting friends in California, where they generously invited us. Of course, we are working from this most magnificent location during our stay, but being here and saying "yes" to the invitation represents for me actively participating in a refreshed moment in time. I am giving myself permission to be here unencumbered by the past twenty-four months, yet transformed by them. The sun is shining, the birds are chirping, and I feel myself growing by giving myself the gift of these moments.

I have come to learn so much about life, death, living, dying, heartache, joy, and pain; about my mother, my father, Sharon, my grandparents, my aunt, my partner, my family, long-time friends, new friends, and strangers; about the world. I have learned new recipes and excavated my love of cooking and using spices; new baking techniques and the thrill of seeing a smile upon delivery of warm scones to a neighbor. And mostly, I have learned about myself: how to grieve, how to distance then move closer; how to experience new feelings, how to ache, how to accept an unexpected hug, how to ask for help, and how to let that help arrive.

I have also learned that the sense of renewal may fade and that I will need to remind myself: there will be tough days, tough moments, and sad days. There, too, will be bright days and new memories.

I have continued to learn in a way that makes my mother proud. I can hear her say, "I am so proud of you."

I have found ways to indulge in life that Sharon would applaud. I can see her smiling.

I have discovered, re-discovered, and begun to look at life through new lenses. It is funny to say that, given my father's specialty as an ophthalmologist, his expertise of eyes and love of art with their ability to create perspective. Sitting here with the sun bathing my legs and the green views of the countryside in front of me, I am only now coming to realize—to know—that perhaps these new lenses of mine are the very ones my father endeavored to create. His quest to produce artificial corneas and help others regain sight is something he not only succeeded in while living, but gave to me after his passing. They are not artificial, nor do they take the place of my prior lenses, but they are new and have given me new sight.

"With Design Foresight" was the tagline of my father's medical manufacturing business–whether intentional or unintentional, design and foresight, indeed.

I am forever changed. And I am forever grateful for it all.

I am giving
myself permission
to be here unencumbered
by the past
twenty-four months,
yet transformed
by them.

Act I Curtain

Act II: You Cannot Make It Up

Crazy Sh*! Happens

When Your Heart Is Breaking

For Angela.

Scenes

Crazy Sh*! Happens
Makeup
Disney World
Takeout
Pan Con Queso
My Face Is My Mask
Needlepoint & *Alice in Wonderland*
That Damn Van
Skeleton in the Living Room
Everyone Needs a Boris!
Uncomfortable Cot
Rosé and Rocks
Pall Mall
Your. Job. Is. To. Keep. Me. Alive.
Title Burn
Gravity
Is There Breakfast Included?
Sara and Stacy
Keep Moving. Keep Doing.
Doug
You Can Just Mail It USPS
White-Girl-Wasted
Biohazard Bags and Bone Cement
Can I Help You?
Facebook Marketplace and Tap Dancing
Creepy Clown
Joy of Giving
You, Me, Hector, Miguel and Neso (…and Larry)
Photos
Playboy, Pipes, and How To Turn On a Lamp
Piano
Skull
It's Not About the Skates
Most Exceptional Emotion
Music

Crazy Sh*! Happens

Today my heart is breaking. I can feel it. I can feel it in my chest. It is deep and it is dull. Pure heartache. And it stings.

I knew that tough days would continue to show up, even with my newfound growth after losing Mom, Sharon, and then Dad. Yet, when your heart breaks and you feel loss again after losing *and* recovering, you come to find that the dull ache is as piercing as a misguided needle.

I was sitting on the couch and deciphering paperwork with Angela, late in the afternoon and about ten minutes shy of joining a call for work, when suddenly, a text and photo popped up on my phone. It was from the neighbor next to the house where I grew up. An immediate flood of sadness rushed to my eyeballs, my lids welling with tear drops. A photo of the backyard revealed a vacancy where two beautiful spruce trees once stood—something was terribly awry. Apparently, the tree service team hired to trim and remove a different, sickly tree had mistakenly also cut down these two tall spruce trees.

The decision to keep or remove these two trees had weighed on me for the four weeks leading to this day. "There is nothing wrong with them, and they are not at risk of falling, but they are not thriving, and they are way too close together," advised the arborist, who had also worked with my father on the many trees in the yard of my childhood home.

I was beside myself. This was not my plan! The evening prior, I had made the decision *to keep* these two trees—I was not ready to let them come down. The arborist's words—"nothing is wrong with them" married with my childhood memories of planting them with my father, had steered my decision. Yet, the outcome was not of my making.

I frantically went to confirm my authorizations to the tree service company. While I had requested an estimate for removing the spruce trees and noted that I *might decide* to have them taken down, I had clearly stated, "I will get back to you to confirm" whilst clearly detailing what *was* the authorized work for other, sickly tree.

How could they know how much meaning these two trees held?

Trees coming down is very hard for me. *These* trees coming down is very hard for me. The fact that I did not decide this or opt for this, nor was I prepared, is very hard for me. It was yet another unexpected loss. These spruce trees represented so much: the joy in being outside with my father, learning to appreciate plants and nature, and the curiosity in watching them grow. One had been planted for my sister, and one had been planted for me—representations of our very lives.

A tree foreman had taken down those two beloved trees by mistake. What are the odds? And, it broke my heart.

I have discovered (and just today, am rediscovering) that crazy shit happens all the time. But most profoundly during profound moments in time, such as life and death. And after death.

It happens in life. It happens in death.

Crazy shit happens that breaks your heart.

And, crazy shit happens *when your heart is breaking*.

Everything in the following pages actually happened.

As my mom would say, “You cannot make it up.”

Once again, she was right.

Makeup

Sometimes you find yourself doing things you never thought you would do—things that do not enter the scene or your thought process. You do not even imagine doing them. You find yourself doing things or being asked to do things that simply never enter the orb of your being. Yet, you do them. You find yourself doing them because of the circumstances—because of the love you have for another. You do them without hesitation because of that love.

After my mom was pronounced, we were waiting for the gentlemen from the morgue to arrive when my father turned to me and said, "Go put some makeup on your mother. You'd better go dress her up a bit."

Pause.

"And take some photos."

I think I blinked twice and said nothing. I stood up and proceeded to my parents' bathroom to find my mom's makeup kit.

Mom loved celebrations, and she always wanted things to "look pretty." I remember often times when she would ask my father, "What's wrong with wanting things to look nice?" This question was posed as they were having a spat about the flag outside the front entry, the flowers (to which she never tended; my father was the gardener), or the tidy-up-the-house-night before the cleaners would arrive. She believed in the power of being "presentably" prepared. She would advise, "Even though you are feeling low and do not want to do the thing you need to do, make yourself look nice. You will feel better. You will feel more prepared to tackle the thing you don't want to do. *You* will feel better about *yourself*."

I took that advice so many times: I don't feel well and I need to present to 300 people the same day. I shower, take a Tylenol, drink water, and look nice. Make myself feel how I feel nice. Thanks, Mom. Maybe I need to lay off somebody at work. Take a shower, wear that favorite blue shirt, straighten my posture, and make myself feel how I feel nice. Thanks, Mom. I took her advice without even thinking. And afterwards, I nearly always thought to myself, *Mom taught me that.*

There were times throughout the years when I would purchase Mom a face cream or eye shadow or lipstick for Mother's Day, her birthday, any day. As she aged, and at times had an unbalanced cosmetics application (mostly around her eyes), I loved to help her. I would say, "Mom, I would love to do your makeup. May I?"

I am not a makeup artist, but I have learned various techniques from my performing arts training and from working with makeup artists while on set. I liked it. In fact, I had the honor and pleasure of doing our friend's makeup for her wedding in 2021. I found it cathartic, meditative, and a gift.

So, that evening after having just lost Mom, I thought, *I can make you feel better, Mom. I can make you feel how you feel nice. You are no longer here, and yet you are here. Dad wants to honor you. He knew you. He knew you better than anyone. And he needs me to exercise this action for you. For him.*

It was something I could never be prepared for, and somehow I was—she had prepared me without either of us knowing it.

I found it cathartic, a tad dreadful, meditative, and a gift.

On that Tuesday just past sunset, I pulled up alongside my mom's hospice bed. I methodically opened her face cream and whispered, "Mom, I would love to do your makeup. May I?"

And I did. I proceeded to gently apply face cream,

blush,

eye shadow,

mascara, lipstick;

brushing her eyebrows, and

taking it all in.

Taking her in. Up close.

One final time.

Then, I stepped back and snapped a series of photos for my father. She looked nice. She was pretty. And she was presentably prepared.

I did the thing I was asked to do. I did the thing I never imagined.

…you do them without pause, because of that love.
(And the sky fell.)

Disney World

When I was young, my parents took my sister and me to Walt Disney World in Florida multiple times. We were lucky kids. Since our grandparents lived in Florida, the trips to the Orlando theme parks were paired with visits to see my father's parents at their condo on Lido Key in Sarasota. Our family would fly to Orlando and soak in the magic of Mickey and friends for a few days and then drive west across Florida, over the Sunshine Skyway to Sarasota for a multi-day visit to Grandma and Grandpa. In those days, The Magic Kingdom, Downtown Disney, and Epcot Center were the three Disney areas to visit. As a child, I found it fascinating, exciting, and yes—magical.

"We're going to go see Mickey Mouse!" I would exclaim in the days leading up to a trip. I discovered rather quickly that Donald Duck was actually my favorite of the characters. His fervor, personality, waggle butt, duck voice, and large eyes—I loved all of it.

One particular trip, something happened during our flight connection in St. Louis. Our connecting flight was overbooked, and we could not all travel the second flight to Orlando as planned. My mom had to fly with us kids on our regularly scheduled flight while my dad took a later flight. I remember standing at the airport desk with my sister, looking up at my parents as they made the decision to get three of us to our destination with one parent to follow later. Mom would continue on with us, and Dad would follow about four hours later. I remember sitting at an Orlando airport restaurant eating chili while my mom explained (again) to me why my father was taking a later flight. That was a long travel day, but my parents kept us on schedule and got us to The Magic Kingdom the next morning. Well done.

The first ride I enjoyed as a young tyke was Dumbo. Then, it was Alice's Mad Tea Party, It's a Small World, Thunder Mountain, and Peter Pan. The menu of rides I enjoyed grew quickly.

My sister would join on these rides, and as the older sibling, she had to sit on the inside of the rides' cars (elephants or teacups) per my parents' rule. Every time, the centripetal force would slam my body inward to hers mid-ride and last for the duration. She would work so hard to push me away as Dumbo flew low, then high and then low again, despite the force shoving me further into her body. No matter my efforts to cling to the side of the car, I did not have the strength to avoid this shoving of sorts and so it repeated on every ride that spun in circles. I did get better at combating the force over time as I grew taller and stronger. My fingers would cling to the side of the ride's car even before it started whirring. I started counting numbers to myself to see how high I could make it before my fingers completely slid off and my body uncontrollably jolted across the bench, crashing into my sister. While my parents' rationale makes complete sense to me now as an adult, it opposed the dislike my sister had for serving as the one being slammed into and my dislike at being the one who felt the strong force smashing me into her. She would get so mad, and I would get upset. It was a recipe that caused distress for both of us. I started to identify and prefer the rides that did not go fast in circles nor jolt quickly from side to side. Snow White's ride was a good one. My sister and I could enjoy the ride without either one of us getting upset, and we shared a love for looking up at the mean Queen as she peered down while we entered the mine of the Seven Dwarves in the same car.

I once wrote a one-page essay in middle school about the time I got lost at Walt Disney World. I was four years old, infatuated by the Pinocchio Popcorn Cart, and completely lost track of my family, who had continued on to find a great spot for viewing the parade—-one of my dad's favorite Disney experiences. It was always a flurry of activity to "catch the parade," but we were not the family who waited for hours at the curb for front row seating.

We stayed at the Cosmopolitan a couple times. Then, Dad found Fort Wilderness. Once we stayed in those Disney-themed "cabins in the woods," that became a repeat spot. I loved the variety pack of miniature boxes of cereal my dad would purchase at the grocery store and the fact that we could eat breakfast on our own in the cabin before heading to the parks. My sister and I both loved Fort Wilderness. In fact, later in life, as an early professional, I joined my sister and her husband when they took my nephew to Disney, and we stayed at Fort Wilderness together. Experiencing Disney with him was magical. While I do not have children, I got to witness a toddler's amazement at The Magic Kingdom and to see my sister enjoy the environment and magic with her son.

When we departed Orlando and headed out to see our grandparents, we surely had a shopping bag full of Disney goodies from the trip matched with a boatload of joyful stories from visiting Mickey, Minnie, Donald, Daisy, Goofy, Pluto and the whole gang. One year, I was overjoyed to find a reversible sweatshirt (what a thing, a reversible sweatshirt!) that my mom broke down and purchased for me at Downtown Disney. She had also bought me a Minnie Mouse T-shirt I had so wanted. She bought both after telling me I could choose only one. I had a complete meltdown of indecision, and my mom caved. Thanks, Mom. It was generous of her, and I had clearly caught her at a weak moment. Today, I think, *You should not have caved, Mom! Hold me to the one choice!* In any event, I loved both of these new shirts. The Donald sweatshirt was puffy and featured two different poses of Donald on each of the sides so that I could highlight his happy mood on one day and his frustrated mood on another. I wore that sweatshirt many times that year of first grade, even on the hot days. The Minnie T-shirt was long and simple, depicting Minnie coyly holding a flower and wearing a red hat between her large mouse ears. On another trip, my parents got me a shirt from Epcot Center. It was way too big for me at the time, and I remember my dad saying, "You can wear it as a nightgown until you grow into it." Indeed, I grew into it, and I have that shirt to this day. It has red sleeves, like a softball shirt, and depicts the logo of Epcot Center from the 1980s. Perfectly retro, perfectly original.

We visited Disney World enough times for me to collect Disney memories at various ages while I grew up. We weren't a "Disney family," but we certainly enjoyed a privileged number of visits over the years, particularly when my sister and I were quite young and before we finished grade school. I remember being really young, my mom bringing a stroller for me, being too little to join on some of the rides, and too scared to join in on the Haunted

Mansion. Then I remember growing a bit bigger, holding my dad's hand as we waited for the monorail, closing my eyes during the first five minutes of the Haunted Mansion, and staying awake for the full Bear Jamboree after lunchtime. And then I remember growing up more such that I could not only ride Thunder Mountain, but Space Mountain too! Still then, growing up more so that the visit to Epcot's various countries of the world became just as exciting as visiting the Pirates of the Caribbean and It's a Small World at the Magic Kingdom.

It is not surprising that once my sister had children that she ended up continuing to love visiting Disney World as an adult. Once she had children and ended up living in Florida, visiting Disney World became part of their routine for fun family get-aways and vacations.

"I am so excited about our trip to Disney!" She would get so amped to tell me all the details of their plans and reservations while we talked on the phone, teaching me about the new system of reservations and pre-line booking that was now required before visiting.

When I became an adult, my fervor for Disney World waned. I discovered that I preferred nature, training our dog, and visiting other countries. I found them to be fascinating, exciting, and yes—magical. Of course, I can relate to the excitement my sister and others experience when planning; anticipating and taking a vacation to visit Mickey Mouse and all the many characters and hearing "When the car stops, step out to your left," when exiting rides. All I have to do is think about the childhood memories of our visits to the land of rides, popcorn, and parades. However, I now choose other journeys of wonder.

So, when Mom was dying and my sister was distressed that the circumstances might disrupt her planned trip to Disney World a few days later with her kids, it felt crazy to me.

"But we have a trip planned to Disney! We deserve a vacation!" she exclaimed adamantly.

"Sure, honey. Well, sure." My dad assured her.

At the time, I just couldn't believe it. "Disney?!" I self-screamed a monologue: *Really, Disney?! Vacation now?! Mom is dying; it is not the time for Mickey and friends.* I could hear my mom's voice saying from her still body, "God forbid I mess with your plans." It felt completely at odds with everything I was experiencing, that was happening around us in that condo with Dad—the zooming in of life-changing experiences that was surrounding us as we cared for Mom and Dad in those final days of her life and then for him once she passed.

It felt so wild, mystifying. It felt so unreal and real.

My sister left on Monday to get home to her kids in Tampa. Mom died the next day, on Tuesday. Her service was on Thursday. My sister returned with her kids that Thursday morning before Mom's service. She and her kids left for Disney World the next morning, on Friday, which was Dad's birthday.

This was hard. I self-screamed again: *Mom has died and you are going on vacation to Disney?!* I did not understand. I could not relate. I could no longer tap into those childhood memories and the wonder of Walt Disney World.

And I chose not to.

I did not say out loud the things I thought. It all was too much, and I believed it was not my decision. It was hers. At the time, it was something she was navigating in conversation with Dad, and he had said, "Sure, honey. Well, sure," encouraging her that it would be alright and that they should proceed with their vacation.

My focus was on Mom and Dad. The only thing I could imagine was being with Dad, taking the steps needed to care for him and making sure things were taken care of in the days following Mom's passing.

Early that Friday morning, before they set out for Disney, Angela and I grabbed some loose pieces of paper and borrowed Dad's colored pencils to draw the black circles of Mickey Mouse ears and made a sign for our nephew and nieces. The day before had been tough for us all. "Have a great trip!" Angela wrote in a fun font with a rainbow of colors. We had the sign ready for them at breakfast, just before they departed.

That evening, I sat on the floor next to my dad while we each ate a bowl of vanilla ice cream Angela had brought us from the kitchen. We watched *The Adventures of Ichabod and Mr. Toad*, the animation film based on the children's novel *The Wind in the Willows* that Dad read to me when I was a child. The story depicts Mr. Toad and his friends, Mole and Water Rat, and was produced by none other than Disney in 1949. I had found a VHS version of it at an estate sale in Virginia months prior and immediately spent the $1.50 to purchase it for my dad. "He will love this!" I exclaimed, showing it to Angela. "It will go with his birthday present this year." Of course when I bought it, it was long before my mom got sick and before I had any idea of losing her or being able to watch it with my dad the day I gave it to him.

I still cannot relate to my sister's travel to Disney World that weekend after Mom died. But I can relate to wanting to carry on following her death. In retrospect, I can now start to understand it a bit more. While it still feels crazy, I can imagine her desperately wanting to care for her kids in those moments—to carry on.

I know that people grieve and respond to loss differently. I have learned that. I have experienced that. And when I think about those sweet moments hearing my dad chuckle at Mr. Toad, Mole, and Water Rat that Friday night—his birthday—it is as if we all were at Disney together again, including Mom.

It felt so unreal and real.

Takeout

It was Asian-fusion-sushi takeout night. We all ordered something different, and our friend Erica collected the orders via text. It was a casual evening, our small friend group of six gathering to see one another. And for four of us, it was a time to check-in on Sharon and Brian and to spend time with them—to spend time with Sharon.

We all were unsure if we would even be able to get together. This was during the summer of 2020 in the throes of the COVID pandemic—which made it exceptionally uncertain. On top of that, Sharon had been in and out of treatment for cancer, traveling back and forth from the hospital, so even outside of a pandemic, being in the same place would have been questionable.

Our desire to see each other and spend time together pushed us forward. We all desperately wanted to get together, so we all confirmed ahead of time that it was a group gathering we could indeed do safely and comfortably, so long as we prioritized keeping Sharon (and us all) safe.

"No really. It will be fine." Sharon insisted. "It would be really great to see everyone." She convinced us.

With her compromised immune system from treatment, Sharon articulated the parameters that would make her feel at ease with the gathering. We all agreed to stay six feet or more from one another, no hugging, no close contact, and of course, we would all wear masks. We all were absolutely committed.

After safety, simplicity was key. We agreed that we would meet over at Sharon's and Brian's home since that would be easiest for them, taking note of Sharon's energy level. It was our friend Erica, who pitched the takeout idea, and we settled on getting food from a spot of Sharon's choosing. It was most important we chose food that sounded tasty—even edible— to her. She chose an Asian-fusion-sushi place. Done.

Takeout was not typical for us. We all loved food, and gathering to enjoy meals together was a practiced part of our repertoire. Cooking and curating meals for us all to enjoy together was a central part of that practice. Takeout hit a new surge during the pandemic. "Contactless" was the term adopted by dining establishments. And the community urged people to support local restaurants and order food to-go. While people could not dine-in and enjoy the environment of a restaurant, they could achieve a mini-getaway from the mundane virtual work, virtual schooling of children, and bleeding of daytime into evening. Takeout had become a new norm for many people during COVID. It became something for this particular group of us to try together for the first time.

Erica, Mitsie, Angela, and I sat near the table in the dining room, a step level up from and overlooking the living room. They sat at the far left front corner of the table overlooking the living room while Angela and I took the back right corner of the table. Sharon stayed seated in the super-duper comfortable chair in the living room, which we always raved about ("Isn't it so comfortable?" Sharon would exclaim so many times before.); and Brian knelt on the living room floor beside her.

The food was all separately packaged and labeled per the COVID "contactless" takeout protocol, and we each took turns picking up our labeled containers from the middle of the table. Brian made sure to pick up Sharon's and his own, while we stayed back in the kitchen.

We talked about Sharon's health. She told us how she was feeling. We asked how she was doing. And then, in perfect Sharon-form, she pivoted us to other topics. News topics, work topics, house topics, family topics—anything and everything. As we spoke, I could not help but notice how slowly she was eating. At times, she would pause to take a beat. She would say so as well. It became clear as the time passed that evening that she was pretty uncomfortable and experiencing pain. She wrapped her arm around her belly, which was swollen, then she hunched over. I remember how sweetly Brian held her arm to be with her in those moments of discomfort. I also remember that Sharon did not finish nor eat much of her food at all. All the while, Sharon verbalized what she was sensing and was there with us in it as she felt her body. That was part of Sharon's beauty—she was unapologetically real in every sense. She was real and raw and *there*.

It was not a typical late night gathering as we were previously used to. Erica, Mitsie, Angela, and I said our goodbyes and blew kisses while masked as we walked down the stairs to their front door.

"Have a good night."

"Take care."

"Let us know if you need anything."

Such were the words exchanged.

We learned later that Brian and Sharon ended up back at the hospital late that night because of her increased pain and discomfort.

I do not precisely remember the last time I hugged Sharon. When I push the double-left arrow rewind button of my memories, I know it was that warm, spring afternoon in April 2020 when we stopped by, and she and Brian told us about the strange, abnormal growth on her pancreas. We were in the courtyard of their townhouse complex. The news shot through me like an unwieldy dart. At the same time, I was pastures away from thinking anything could seriously be wrong. "We don't know yet," Sharon said multiple times. "We don't know yet what it means. Or if it is bad." Her words pulsed into the air. It was yet another instance of Sharon's grounded strength and presence shining through.

The six of us had never had takeout together. Of course, in separate segments we had, but not as a collective. We talked about it every so often, but our default was that Angela and I or Brian and Sharon would host some sort of dinner. We would say in advance a theme and what would be on the menu: tapas, or new recipes we would try. One of my favorite photos of Sharon, Brian, Angela, and me is from our kitchen when they brought over fresh pita dough Brian had made and cooked the pita on our griddle to accompany our Mediterranean-themed dinner. We also had fun going out together. We would meet at various restaurants and Sharon was always on cue with a great recommendation. We would ask about various menu items, kibbutz about the service, and laugh until we couldn't stomach it anymore. Literally, our full bellies would tell us we needed to stop.

So much joy.

There is a painful surge in my belly, my chest and my heart to think we would not be in a kitchen all together again or communing around a restaurant dining table. That we would not be chit-chatting about a particular recipe, dish, cocktail, or goings-on. It is *not* crazy that the last time this group was all together was to enjoy a meal, conversation, and connection. Given our habit of gathering to dine, of course we would be doing that! It was fitting. It was so *us*. What is bewildering to think is that that particular Asian-fusion-sushi first time takeout dinner in the summer of 2020 was our last time all together. At that moment in time, I was not thinking that at all—I was taking it all in. I was borrowing Sharon's presence and carrying hope while the unavoidable and underlying fear of what was to come for her health— her life—vibrated through me.

What's that saying? "There is a first time for everything." There is a last time too.

Of course, in the years since Sharon died, the five of us have gathered at coffee shops, gone for dog walks, and gathered in our kitchens once again to enjoy home-cooked meals together. Sharon inevitably comes to us. Her strength of presence is always among us, always carrying us along as we create new memories and hold the old ones so dear.

"There is a first time for everything.
There is a last time too."

Pan Con Queso

I like to think of myself as being nutritionally sound. Well, relatively. I try. I value my health, and Angela and I both make efforts to continuously learn about food and nutrition. We try to vary the food we eat, and we work to eat a large amount of vegetables—mediterranean. I love food. I love cooking food, shopping for food, thinking about food, eating food. I am a self-described foodie.

One of the miraculous things during all of this crazy shit was that neither one of us became morbidly (no pun intended) obese or rail thin. We maintained a routine that involved morning yoga six days a week (sometimes it was only ten minutes, but, hey it was yoga), walking our beloved dog, Charlie, and eating at least three meals a day. Through all the curves and winding roads while navigating across states and through COVID, we saw how a good, healthy, and nutritious meal could help my dad. And we felt good each time we, ourselves, had a salad or roasted vegetables. Ease was important during this time. There was so much on our proverbial plates that we were desperate to fill our actual plates with food that would be supportive.

The Columbia is a Cuban style restaurant on Saint Armand's Circle in Sarasota. In fact, there are a few additional locations in Florida, such as Tampa and Clearwater. When I say style, the restaurant is consistent with its Cuban decor, employee uniforms, and menu of Cuban dishes. They serve a "famous 1905" salad, which is dressed with The Columbia's "famous dressing" and sold at the adjacent shop. My mom really loved that salad. So did my dad. It was my mom, though, who would dramatically exclaim her thoughts of ordering and devouring the salad. "You know what I love to order? The salad, of course! And, oh the dressing, it is so delicious! You must have some." She would also order "a simple cup of black bean soup, please. That is all I want." She said this as though we had never heard about her favorite menu items before, and in a giddy, excited tone representative of experiencing something for the first time, which it was not. "Some sangria too, of course," she would add. Well, of course! That was the composition of my mom's typical order at The Columbia: the salad, soup and sangria. Mom loved clipping out coupons and newspaper articles to send along to me and my sister, and one year, she sent me a copy of the Famous 1905 Salad Dressing recipe that had been featured alongside a column about the restaurant in the Sarasota Tribune. She wrote some comments on the photocopy (she kept the original, of course). I still have that paper in my recipe file. Even though I have never made the dressing, I cannot part with that photocopy. It is an artifact with her handwriting and offers a glimpse back to those moments with her ordering Cuban food.

At The Columbia, they also bring a basket of Cuban bread for the table. It is the kind of bread used for Cuban sandwiches and cracks open, creating crumbs all over the plate and tablecloth. It is tasty with butter, dipped in olive oil, or simply as is. And certainly as part of a Cuban sandwich.

That restaurant on Saint Armand's circle was a regular stop in our family. We used to visit The Columbia at least once during our visits to my grandparents on Lido Key in the 1980s, and later when visiting my parents who spent months at a time living on the key. We even celebrated my parent's 50th wedding anniversary with a lunch at The Columbia—the 1905 salad, black bean soup, sangria and all.

Among the many restaurants my parents ventured to, Angela and I particularly enjoyed The Columbia. We appreciated the menu selection with a variety of vegetarian and fish dishes. We discovered their black bean cakes and another of their salads: the chopped tomato salad, which became a regular order for us along with the Cuban bread.

During that time in October 2020 while in Sarasota working to go through and clear my parents' (and formerly grandparents') condo, we took advantage of The Columbia's "order and pick up" curbside service that businesses were doing during COVID. It was a splurge for us to get takeout and a necessity on certain days with the grind of working full-time and remotely during COVID, sifting through family memorabilia and managing Dad's care. It was exceptionally hot that season and we found ourselves having to moderate our dog's walks, reminiscent of when we too had lived in Florida (albeit on the opposite side of the state). Charlie had arthritis, and the excessive heat was tough on him. I could see the impact of the heat on all of us by watching his dramatic panting. The high temperatures and humidity meant that we would walk very early in the mornings with short breaks during the day and then an evening walk.

Ordering takeout from The Columbia meant we were assured tasty food, relief from cobbling together a meal in the tiny, overfilled kitchen of the condo, and offered the opportunity to take Charlie for his evening walk. It was two miles round trip, so we could walk a mile there, rest on a bench while we picked up our order from the alley (the curbside for walkers was the alley) and then walk the mile back. We would take the food out to the condominium's pool patio to eat al fresco—a delight in life we so enjoy and which felt important in caring for ourselves. Charlie would stretch his nose out, sniffing the salty, beach air. And, voilà, dinner was served.

It was on one such evening, a Friday when we were thrashed with fatigue from the week, when we set out on a venture to get food from The Columbia. We were sweating buckets, my eyes stinging from the dripping sweat-sunblock mixture from my forehead. Angela had retrieved our food order and was carrying the bag. As we walked the mile back toward the condo, we lamented about our fatigue and exclaimed our gratitude for the food we were about to consume. We talked about what we had eaten recently, looking forward to the fresh tomato salad with its savory dressing. "Well, we had pizza on Monday and mac and cheese Tuesday," I recollected.

"We had bagels with cream cheese Wednesday morning, and cheese and crackers for lunch yesterday," Angela added.

Somewhere in this exchange, I asked Angela, "Did they remember the bread?" She checked the bag. "They did. Better make sure we have the *pan*! Apparently we cannot go a day without *pan con queso*!"

We both stopped in our tracks and burst into an uproar of laughter. *Pan* is the Spanish word for bread. And bread with cheese? *Pan con queso*. The lambast of hysteria our realization started had our abdomens sore from laughing. It was a welcome respite of madness, realizing that we were eating *pan con queso* all the time. Every day! In varying forms, but if you distill it down, it was *pan con queso*. Every. Day. We started thinking through every meal, every snack, and every bite we had been eating at the time and that we had been eating for months. Each time, we could name at least one meal per day that came down to *pan con queso*. For instance, a quesadilla made an excellent lunch. It was fast, easy, warm and tasted good. Then, there was the obvious, pizza. We purchased cheese (cheddar) and crackers (Ritz) from the grocery store because those made an excellent snack, or really, an entire meal. Then, there was mac and cheese—of course, *pan con queso*!

On one of our more recent long road trips, I was chomping away at Cheez-Its when Angela pointed at me and said, "Oh my gosh, *pan con queso*!" Another burst of laughter.

In the months that followed, we would regularly make reference to *pan con queso*: "What shall we have for dinner? *Pan con queso*?"

"How do those Ruffles cheddar and onion chips taste?"

"Do you mean the *pan con queso*?" (asked in a dramatic lilt). It became a welcome game to discover all the types of *pan con queso* we could potentially consume and would consume.

"Could we make this focaccia *con queso*?" I would ask. "Is that enough *queso* with your *pan*?" Angela would jest.

Pan con queso did more than feed our bellies, it offered moments of laughter and relief during deep sadness and pain. Up until that point, I think I had always experienced bread and cheese as comfort foods as most people do. But it turns out that I did not *really know* it until that exceptionally hot Friday evening on Lido Key. It was crazy to discover that *pan con queso* is indeed a comfort food. I can vouch for it. Angela and I discovered that *pan con queso* made up a huge part of our diet during this exceptional time period of our lives. Along with the vegetables, of course.

I will never eat *pan con queso* the same. I will always have a crooked smile form at the side of my lips as I eat it, reminded of those times of fatigue and delirium. How it warms my tastebuds, my belly and my soul, just as the *pan and the queso* helped comfort me during such difficult times for my heart.

Ease was important during this time.

My Face Is My Mask

Florida is a scary place for Angela and me. We lived there in 2016 and 2017 on the Atlantic side of the state. Living in Florida was not the sandy beach, salty wind-in-our-hair freedom I recall from my childhood while I ran to the ocean during visits with my grandparents. It was an adult, scary, *are-we-safe?* feeling for us. As a same-sex married couple, we directly experienced, saw, and felt the aggression toward members of the LGBTQIA+ community and toward us as humans. Being in such an unpredictably predictable place like this was foundation-shaking, to say the least, and we could not move away fast enough.

When we were back in Florida in October 2020, we were there to prepare my parents' condominium for sale on the opposite side of the state, the Gulf side. Somehow, we found ourselves there again, dealing with the day-to-day drumbeat of worry for our safety. So, we tried to mix in fun things to do. We kept our routine of early morning walks (thank you, Charlie) and yoga (thank you, online Body By Yoga). And, on Saturdays, we would try to venture somewhere in the car for our morning walk in order to "mix it up," as one of us would say, to see a new neighborhood and pass by different houses. At the same time, we had a mission: we had a job to do for my father. And for my mother.

Have you ever been to a pawn shop? Have you ever been to one in Florida? If you have - you know they are not the most comforting places. They are barely tolerable. One could argue, they are not safe. Add this to the underlying unsafe feeling such an environment embodied for the two of us, and you have a "Daily-Double" in Jeopardy speak.

Angela and I headed to a local pawn shop one afternoon because at the time, it was our best guess for where to take the two electronic keyboards my dad had in the condo. He had purchased them so that he could keep up with piano tunes when he and my mom were in Sarasota. More importantly, he could have them on hand for the grandchildren to play.

What I mean by "at the time" is that since it was deep during the COVID pandemic, the condominium building was prohibiting estate sales and garage sales of any kind and donation centers were rejecting many items, and we had to re-think options for the distribution of my parents' things. We became our very own triaging center for belongings:

- Category 1: Try to sell on Facebook Marketplace.
- Category 2: Check with local theaters and the opera house about donations to their costume and scene departments.
- Category 3: Attempt to donate or drop off items at local Goodwill and similar donation centers.
- Category 4: Trash.
- Category 5: Separate and bring back to Dad (a limited category, since his home in South Dakota was already overpacked with belongings).
- Category 6: Last resort—items that had no bites on Facebook Marketplace or at local theaters, weren't accepted by donation centers, weren't appropriate for trash, and left us stumped and thinking, *Uh, I really don't know what to do with this item...*

The bottom-line of all this effort was that we were trying to maximize what could be sold for Dad so that the funds could go toward his care. So, the two electronic keyboards that fell into that "last resort" category—that's how we ended up at a pawn shop.

The afternoon we drove to pawn the keyboards, it was like any other exceptionally hot and humid day in Florida. We had a plan, as always. Angela would go into the shop with the keyboards to efficiently negotiate the deal (she is good with that stuff) and carefully take note of the entrances and exits. I would wait in the car with Charlie, who we brought almost everywhere with us. Part of my role was to haul ass out of there if needed once Angela returned—like a heist or a scene from Ocean's Eleven. Sounds crazy, right? It was. And also necessary.

I turned the steering wheel of the giant, black Expedition into the parking lot, both of us grateful for tinted windows. We saw a few folks walk into the shop while a car with a shot-out window slowly rolled through the lot. A white low-rider had smoke pluming from the windows while music blared. A tall, lanky guy bumbled inside.

"Stay in the car," Angela said as she secured her face mask, and swiftly shut the rear door, two keyboards under her arms.

There I sat, completely vigilant of the surroundings, wet palms and sweat dripping off my brow, focused on the door to the shop while also watching Charlie in the rearview mirror. He, too, was alert—his stiff posture mimicked mine. Or vice versa. Watching, watching, watching: the right window, to our left, the pawn shop front door—watching for any movement. I moved my hands from the steering wheel to the gear shift to my phone, checking for texts in my periphery. My eyes danced: right window, windshield, left window, rearview mirror, Charlie, front door, phone screen…

Angela's first text: "A few people in here. I am next in line. One exit to the back behind the counter."

"Okay. Be careful. Should I come help you?"

"Stay in the car." Then she added, "Guy next to me is a loose cannon."

Minutes went by. More minutes. I tapped the steering wheel, eyes darting. It felt like hours. I watched more sketchy cars flow in and out of the parking lot. At the back of the building, a truck screeched its tires. I wondered for a hot minute (literally, a hot minute) if I could ever be a detective.

Then I saw her—*phew*! Finally, Angela came briskly walking—trying not to appear as though she was running, but clearly running—to the car. She opened the door and slid onto the seat in one fluid motion.

"Let's get outta here!" She breathed heavily while clicking her seatbelt. "That guy who went in before me? Did you see him come out?"

"Yeah, he came outside just a little bit before you and he was angr-"

"He was *irate*," she jumped in. "He was completely armed with anger, loaded with possibly more, shouting and shouting at the clerks. I wasn't sure what would happen next."

She explained further that they were telling him he needed to put on a face mask, attempting to explain the rationale behind the requirement: that it is intended to keep others safe, that it is COVID, that he should read the sign on the door stating face masks are required. He had proceeded to angrily shout obscenities, pointing his fingers, waving his arms, and threatening the clerks. He rounded out his tirade shouting, "MY FACE *IS* MY MASK!"

"Excuse me, what?" I muttered.

"No. I am not joking."

What?!

We believe in science. We wore masks and understood it was a minor inconvenience in the midst of the global health crisis that was still ongoing. Not to mention, it was a practice that encouraged safety for us, for others, and served the greater good.

We vowed never to go back to that pawn shop and perhaps not to any other pawn shop. Did we get money for Dad in exchange for the keyboards? Yes. Was it worth it in the end?

Once back at the condo, as I popped open an ice-cold soda, I soaked in the relief that that episode was over. Angela peeked her head around the corner from the dining room, "Hey, did you know that my face *is* my mask?"

I spit Coke Zero all over the floor.

Have you ever been to a pawn shop?
(At some point or another, we all wear a mask.)

Needlepoint and *Alice in Wonderland*

Part I

If you were to ask my dad what his favorite Disney animated film was, *Alice in Wonderland* would be in the top three, if not the top two. I shared this love with him. And to be clear, I am talking about the original animated *Alice in Wonderland* from 1951. I was enamored by the adventure: the momerats, Bill the Lizard with a ladder, how the Mad Hatter said "Musthhtard!", Tweedle Dee and Tweedle Dum skipping down the sand, and the story of the Walrus and the Curious Oysters. Is it coincidence that the mother oyster warns the baby oysters about the month of March with the "R" vibrating in bold, since it was March when my mother passed away and set off this string of loss?

The renowned story by Lewis Carroll is a delight and an opportunity to ponder transitions. I think I see something new in the story every time. When I think on it now, back in 2019, I was Alice, lying comfortably in a bed of daisies in the sunshine. Then in 2020, I fell down a massive hole, and I guess you could say all that happened from then on *was* an adventure. "Isn't it all an adventure?" I continue to ask myself.

I do not know how my mom came to start doing needlepoint. It is one of the things I wish I could ask her about. My guess is that she was somehow influenced by the lineage of it from my dad's family. But I don't know if that is true. Maybe she came to it on her own. Maybe it was a generational thing, and when she was in her early thirties in the Midwest, it was a thing to take up and do. She was talented, much more so than she ever believed. It was clear there was a talent for needlepoint in my family on my dad's side with his grandmother, my great-grandmother, and great-great-grandmother. And on my mom's side, with my mom.

Mom enjoyed it, too. Later in life when her hands had become too weak, Mom would say, "I just don't have the dexterity anymore." It also had become too hard for her to see the tiny threads. She missed taking to a hand-painted canvas to stitch a colorful design.

The collection of Mom's needlepoint was large: pillows of all shapes and sizes, wall hangings, door signs, more pillows, trinkets, purses, decorations for every holiday, yet more pillows, Christmas tree ornaments, decorations for other holidays, and glasses cases. Did I mention pillows? I knew Mom had completed a lot of needlepoint over the years. However, it was not until after Dad passed away and Angela and I were readying the home for the estate sale that I truly appreciated the extensive nature of her collection. It was massive. It was neat to look at each of the pieces and remember her working on them. She did that one on a road trip, or that one while we watched *Law & Order*. There were pieces that I recognized from my childhood but had no memory of her completing because she had done so before I was born. There was the large rectangular Bobby (English police officer) with his huge brown mustache. "You are the apple of my eye" was stitched on one of my favorite pillows. I remember she was finishing it when I set off to kindergarten. She had the pillow backed with a saturated green velvet, and the design was a border of halved apples surrounding the statement. Her favorite needlepoint store was in Edina, Minnesota, and every time we visited my grandmother in Minneapolis, a stop at Picket Fences was in order. This was a store full of hand-painted canvases, idea books, thread, accessories, and a staff devoted to the art. And so much wicker! Wicker furniture sprawled about the store. Many of the pieces my mom created showcased things from Minnesota: the Old Streetcar, Lake Harriet, and the Minnesota Twins. She had done a baseball-shaped wall hanging with their logo in 1996 when they won the World Series, and later, a one-and-a-half-foot-tall needlepoint bear dressed in a Twins uniform.

She made things for each of us throughout the years. My sister and I each had a handmade needlepoint sign for our bedroom doors. My sister's was that of a fairytale setting with a unicorn in light blues, yellows, pinks, and whites. Mine featured Paddington, with his raincoat, red hat, and boots in the center set against a cream background, bordered in navy blue to match his coat. When my sister and I fought, we would throw our door signs violently across the room, and it always made my mom so mad (I don't blame her). Over time, our signs didn't hang flat anymore and were crinkled from all the throwing. Sorry, Mom. My sister's Christmas stocking was an incredibly festive needlepoint. My mom had made it for my sister before she was born (or perhaps in her first year). Her name was stitched at the top, and it was all different colors, though predominantly red. It hung on the mantle next to mine, which was not needlepoint. My mom lamented every year in December about how guilty she felt that she never "got around" to making me a stocking. Every Christmas she said, "You don't know how bad I feel that you don't have a needlepoint stocking!"

I would always shrug it off. "It's okay, Mom. I really like my stocking."

My stocking was a festively-designed cloth stocking that displayed my nickname diagonally and vertically down the stocking in red and green, highlighted with small bells and beads. I think my great-grandmother made it, though I am not certain. When I was home for the holidays my final year of college, I opened a gift from my mom. It was my very own needlepoint stocking. It was gorgeous and meticulously crafted. It was so well-made. The backing was in a beautiful purple velvet, and it had two soft, purple tassels at the top—an ornate feature. The design was full of colors and textures. She had used shiny, almost glitter-like thread for the snow, and the scene depicted a cute family of woodland creatures (I say creatures, because they were either moles or gophers, but not rabbits) nestled warmly in their underground home, huddling cozy by a fireplace. My mom's facial expression while I ripped off the holiday paper and opened the box is etched into my memory. She was so full of pride and excitement for me to finally get a needlepoint stocking. My stomach dropped as I looked at it and worked hard to stop my face from falling. I felt my mom's excitement while my heart completely sank. This was not my stocking. It did not feel like my stocking at all. Mine had bells and beads. That is what I knew in my memory from all those Christmases growing up. Years later, when Angela and I purchased our home in Virginia, my mom shipped me my needlepoint stocking. "You are going to want your stocking," she had said emphatically. The truth is, at the time, I didn't. It was not the

Christmas stocking of my childhood. And now, years later, it also had absorbed the recognizable, musty odor of the things from my parents' home. "Mom would die if she knew this," I told Angela as I hung the stocking inside our carport during the winter months to try and get the smell out. It stayed there for a few months, but the scent remained part of the stocking. Then, I hung it on the corner of our shelving in our work shed for months. I did not know what to do with it. I never hung it on the mantle. After a few years, I finally resigned: *This is ridiculous! Someone should enjoy this. What good is it hanging in our work shed or our carport?* On a random day, long before my mom got sick, I gave that stocking away. Even as I type these words, I feel the intense pang of what that means.

Now, when I think about that needlepoint stocking, I actively work to stop my face from falling and my heart from sinking just like I did the day I opened that precious gift from Mom. I so wish I had chosen differently, that I had kept it. At the same time, I do not wish that at all. I hope that there is a family somewhere with an Amelia who adores the carefully, beautifully handcrafted stocking.

Mom's handiwork will remain in my heart forever, and I know that. I also know that it is part of my nature to give—a lesson I came to understand more deeply during this adventure through wonderland.

Part II

And there were chairs—a collection of chairs, you could call it. A good number of them were needlepoint, handcrafted from past generations in my family.

Twenty-four. That was the number of chairs in my parents' two-bedroom, two-bathroom condominium in Florida. Twenty-four. There were chairs everywhere, and it was crazy-making to see chairs lining a wall with no purpose other than to sit there (pun intended). It felt like we were tripping over chairs every time we visited and every time we walked through the condo after Mom died and after Dad moved north.

"Let's count them." Angela had said one day. "It really feels like so many chairs for the size of this place."

"I know, it feels like a lot," I joined in.

"We need to count them so that we know if it actually is a lot."

I wholeheartedly agreed. We needed to figure out what to do with all the furniture while we worked to empty the condo and get it ready to sell.

We each walked the circular layout of the condo in separate directions, silently murmuring counts under our breath. We did it twice, just to double-check.

"I got twenty-four."

"Same."

Twenty-four chairs!

There were the eight mismatched velvety dining chairs that were purchased by my mom to replace the former dining chairs from the dining set my grandparents had purchased decades prior, which were failing. My parents kept four of those former dining chairs because "they are good chairs!" I can hear my dad shouting. That's twelve. There was my dad's turquoise fabric wing-back chair in the living room and my mom's cushy, old-style swivel chair opposite his. That's fourteen. There were the two massive red-cushioned chairs in the living room, which were each more like a chair-and-a-half since they pulled out into twin beds. Sixteen. On the lanai (a veranda-type room), there were two metal-framed IKEA chairs that matched the two-top glass table my mom was proud to have added a few years before. (My parents discovered that they enjoyed sitting on the lanai to eat breakfast and overlook the Gulf of Mexico six stories below. I don't blame them.) Eighteen. And then there were the five—wait, six—wood-framed, needlepoint cushioned chairs, each with a beautiful design of flower bunches in varying colors set against backgrounds of cornflower blue, burgundy, soft pink, light green, turquoise, and deep purple. One in the master bedroom, one in the second bedroom, two lining the wall opposite the dining table and adjacent to the dining credenza, and one lining that opposite wall. And the sixth one snug against the television in the corner of the living room. Twenty-four.

All of these needlepoint chairs were in pristine condition. The colors were vibrant and there was no damage. "Excellent condition" and "perfect condition" were phrases Angela used when posting them for sale on Facebook Marketplace. Angela had come to learn from our visits to my parents at the condo that none of us used these particular stitched chairs. No one sat in them. "Don't sit on that chair!" my dad or mom would exclaim. The fear was that they would get damaged or the needlepoint would "get hurt." Thus, their great condition.

We sold the turquoise needlepoint chair on its own and the others as an odd set of five. The turquoise one was larger than the others. It was a true "sitting" chair. The seat was really wide between the arms, and since it dated back to the early 1900s, I conjectured that it was meant for ladies, wide hips, and wide skirts.

Angela and I carefully moved the larger needlepoint chair to the lobby and out the front doors of the condo building. I noted how pretty it really was while wishing it was a style I wanted to keep for myself. I imagined my grandparents' move-in day from forty years prior and where they may have put it in the condo originally. We waited for a woman to arrive who had responded to the post. A small SUV drove up, parked, and out walked a delightfully adorable older woman with soft, silver short hair, wearing a blue cotton top and gray pants. Her small frame and wide hips toddled from the driver's side of the vehicle to come look at the chair. "It's beautiful," she said in a gentle voice as she peered through her glasses, which were connected to the same type of lanyard around her neck that my grandmother used to wear.

"May I sit in it?"

"Please! Of course!" Angela and I said in near unison.

She sat in the chair, and I witnessed how perfectly it fit her. It was as if this chair—made ages ago—was somehow made just for her.

Standing up, she said, "It really is in perfect condition. How is that?"

"Well, we were never allowed to sit in them," I replied.

Then, the sweet woman before us said, "I have AML and need a more comfortable chair after I have chemo." (AML stands for acute myeloid leukemia.)

"Oh my gosh, that is exactly what my mother had!" Except I did not yell this out loud; rather, it scrolled across my inner dialogue, but I didn't have the gumption to say it. Crazy. How could this be? How could the woman wanting to purchase this chair, this needlepoint chair, be suffering from the same exact ailment that took my mother's life? How could she be suffering from any ailment at all! This woman—who appeared five to ten years older than my mother—seemed strong. She was still driving.

Angela and I gave each other a look.

Angela said, "That's what Amelia's mom had. We hope your treatment goes well. We can load the chair into your car for you."

"Take care of yourself," I encouraged as she left.
Her arm waved from the driver's window as she pulled away.

Angela and I looked at each other, awestruck.

"How perfect was that?" Angela asked me.

"Perfect." I said with a newfound comfort.

The remaining five needlepoint chairs were sold to a woman who showed up in a minivan with an Alabama plate. It was late in the afternoon on another very hot day. A middle-aged woman jostled out of the van, eager to get a closer look at the chairs. Angela and I were standing by them under the large porte-cochère of the building in the same spot where we had sold the turquoise chair to that delightful older woman.

"Gosh, these are in perfect condition!" the woman exclaimed.

"Yes… yes, they are." I stuttered. Hearing that felt good and bad. Good because of the pride I felt in the craft-womanship in the family. Bad because I felt waves of hesitation and resistance to selling them while also knowing it was the best thing to do.

"I want to purchase these for our *Alice in Wonderland*-themed bed and breakfast back in Alabama," she added.

"Really?! How cool!" I said in near-unison with Angela.

We helped her load the five chairs into the back of her van. Her arm waved from the driver's window as she pulled away.

We stood there, under the porte-cochère once again and looked at one another. Awestruck.

"How perfect was that?" Angela asked me.

"Perfect." I responded feeling another round of newfound comfort and momentary stillness.

Needlepoint and *Alice in Wonderland* are inextricably linked for me now. It makes sense when I think about the colors and the designs—the Singing Flowers who offer song to Alice and the flowers on those chairs; all the adventures my parents took together and with us as a family; the life they created together; because that gentle elderly woman was fighting the same disease my mom suffered from and gave me hope for her recovery, because that other woman drove all the way from Alabama during COVID to purchase an odd numbered set of needlepoint chairs for her *Alice in Wonderland*-themed bed and breakfast: "These will be absolutely perfect for our afternoon tea room!" And, needlepoint and *Alice in Wonderland* are associated with each other mostly because of my mom's talent for needlepoint combined with my dad's love of adventure.

In 2020, I fell down a hole into a life-hijacked wonderland. All the amazing creatures I encountered in this new wonderland mirrored those from that snowy scene from the stocking Mom crafted for me so many years ago and those from Carroll's treasured story. When I think back, indeed, there were creatures huddling together in the cold, there was Bill the Lizard with a ladder, Curious Oysters, Tweedle-Dee and Tweedle-Dum, a Mad Hatter, a Cheshire Cat, a Dodo bird, momerats (really, my favorite), Flowers, the Red Queen, and most certainly, the White Rabbit. And, my eyes were as wide as Alice's, making a pool of tears to fill a room (and beyond). I grew large at times, and I shrunk at times; I have been lost, and I have been in search. It has been light, and it has been dark—colorful and quizzical.

And most certainly, an adventure.

"Isn't it all an adventure?"

That Damn Van

The day Dad called Mom "hospice" (as in deeming her in need of hospice care—he verbalized it) was the same afternoon I made the call to the caretaker agency to initiate hospice for her. Dad said, as he gave a slight left-handed wave gesture into the air, "She's hospice." He said it so clearly, so directly, so resolutely, as if he were instructing himself and not just me.

I called the caretaker agency and left a message, echoing my dad's clarity and stating my phone number. "This is Nancy's daughter. We need to engage hospice care. Will you please call me back as soon as possible?" Then, I repeated my phone number two more times. I left my phone number for a call back a total of three times: once at the beginning of my message and twice at the end, speaking the singular digits and then the numbers in couplets, just like one of my psychology professors had advised when I was at college years prior. "Think of the person on the other end of the message trying to listen to your message *and* working to write down the number at which to call you back. Make it easy for them. Repeat it and repeat it in different formats."

Angela unlocked the doors to the van and the door handles were piping hot from the sun. The maroon minivan was a Chrysler Pacifica. My dad leased the vehicle earlier that year and my parents drove it to Florida, their last road trip in October 2019. It turns out that minivan would play a role in this rough and tumble story.

Angela and I were headed out to go to the store to purchase more items needed for Mom's care. Before leaving, we ensured the nurse had what she needed and was fully engaged with Mom (and for Dad in case he needed anything). I squeezed my mom's soft hand, offering her eye contact I did not receive back as she lay limply in the bed. "I love you, Mom. We'll be back shortly." I marched to the living room and wrapped my right arm around my dad's shoulders as I kissed him on the forehead. "We'll be back shortly, Dad. Call or text me if there is anything else you need us to pick up. I love you."

"I love you too, honey. Okay, okay. Drive safely." He said from his turquoise winged-back chair.

As I slid into the passenger seat of the van, I noticed my mom's coffee mug marked by her distinctive Estée Lauder orange-red lipstick stain on the rim. The mug was still partially full. *Oh Mom*, pierced my chest heavily. How could this mug sit here as though life were carrying on, as if Mom were going to be back in this seat with Dad, when that was so far from reality? This new reality of Mom splayed out on the bed upstairs, wavering between barely conscious and unconscious, her body fighting a massive fever, and the shutting down of her entire body on display. Surely this all meant that her coffee mug would not still be here waiting for her? This time, as I went to run errands, I was slower to move that mug to the backseat cup-holder so that I could place my cold soda water there compared to previous trips while borrowing their van.

My parents had all sorts of stuff in the van: trinkets, newspapers, magazines, a wireless hotspot, modem, books. The van was Angela's and my mode of transportation (as well as our feet, of course) while in Sarasota during that March. The trip had happened so fast, so suddenly, we didn't get a rental car. Plus, Dad had clearly told us to use it. "I'm not driving it," he had said.

Seeing my dad's state of health that March, I wondered, *How the heck had he and Mom managed the multi-day road trip from South Dakota to Florida only four months ago?* By the time my mom was sick, Dad was not capable of driving, nor did he want to. "No, no, it's too much for me," he would tell me. And by the time he left Florida that May of 2020, he certainly was not capable of getting into a vehicle or driving, nor was the vehicle equipped to support the level of oxygen he needed. Now, I think Dad knew. "Your father knows," my mom had told me so many times in reference to so many different things. I think for this, he did know. It is as if he knew that trip to Florida in October of 2019 would be his last driving endeavor.

I was in the adult diaper aisle of Walmart when my phone rang. I bent down to the bottom shelf, tapping into the resolute voice of my dad without realizing it. I said the words, "We need to engage hospice for my mom. How soon can someone arrive?" The woman on the other end of the line explained to me that the nurse would be at the condo a bit later that same afternoon to talk to my dad and get the papers signed. By that evening, overnight hospice nurse care would be in place for Mom.

Back in the van, it felt heavy and hot from the Sarasota sunshine. The ride felt distended as we drove back to my parents' condo that afternoon. Shortly after we arrived back, the main nurse from the agency, Amy, arrived. She greeted Dad then said, "I am going to check on Nancy," as both a statement and a request.

"Sure. Of course, of course," my dad waved her on toward the bedroom where Mom lay. A few moments later, Amy came back to the living room and pulled a chair up in front of my dad. She leaned over, and began to speak in her soft, clear, and kind voice, talking to him about hospice for Mom. It was a relatively short conversation. Dad repeated from earlier, so matter-of-factly, "She is hospice. It's clear."

Amy handed him a wooden clipboard with a paper for him to sign while Angela and I stood a few feet away behind Dad. She proceeded to explain to us all what was going to then happen: the hospice team's expected arrival, the medicines, the overnight care, etc. Then she said, "Tom, I will stay here with Nancy, with you, until the hospice nurse arrives." She paused. "Nancy has a really high fever; do you mind if I try some reiki to break it?"

"Yes, yes. Of course."

I had never talked to Dad about reiki before. He was a Western medicine doctor, yet it turned out that he was incredibly open-minded about varying forms of treatment despite his surgical training in the United States. I think it was due to his inquisitive nature and the research-oriented inventor that was at his core.

Mom's fever broke in less than thirty minutes. It was amazing to witness this form of treatment, watching Amy's hand rest on Mom's head as she sat on the edge of the bed and cradled my mom in her arms.

"Wonderful," my dad called out. I could hear the relief I was feeling in his voice.

We lost Mom three days later.

On Wednesday, May 11, 2020, the day after Mom died, Angela and I made a plan to get things ready for Mom's memorial, which would happen the next day. We made a list of to-do items, to make sure things were ready for the event: coordinate with the building office manager for the event room setup, organize snacks and treats kind neighbors and friends would volunteer to provide, gather photographs of Mom to display, make a music playlist, revisit the memorial service outline we had devised and had reviewed with Dad on Tuesday, and pick up decorations to add color to the rather stark first floor room off the lobby of the building. On that day, following Mom's death, we decided I wanted (and needed) to remain at the condo with Dad to take care of him and keep him company. I scurried about the condo, gathering photographs from dresser drawers, reviewing them with Dad. "Look, this is a good one, Dad." I showed him a photo of the two of them smiling in the front entry of their house in the winter of 1979. Or, "How about this one, Dad?" It was a photo of Mom snuggling "Honeybear," one of our poodles, that same year. I also reminded Dad of the music to be played, tunes Mom had mentioned years prior. "If I ever die, you need to play *Don't Get Around Much Anymore*," she would tell me. Mom had written me an email, "Postlude at church was *Wachet Auf*, which I decided I want played at my funeral. Love, Mom." She wrote that email five weeks before she knew she was sick and fourteen weeks before we would play it to honor her.

Angela took on the list of errands in order to pick up the decorative items we needed: purple ribbons, purple flowers, vases, and a picture book so we could display a memory book of photographs at the service.

My sister and her kids would arrive from Tampa Thursday mid-morning. She had made the memorial service one-page invitation flier that we had the building manager post and route to the building distribution list—the community my mom had grown to so love. My sister worked on the obituary from her apartment in Tampa and sought out photos at her place of Mom with the grandkids that would be good to add to the collection of memories we intended to display.

That Wednesday was a whirlwind for me. It was the type of day that moved in slow-motion yet felt hurried, like time was running out. I was utterly focused on the tasks at hand and keeping up Dad's daily routine: flipping through decades of photographs; putting away the sheets Angela and I had laundered late the evening before so Dad would have a clean set to rest his body; making him lunch; opening and reading sympathy cards with him; checking in with the building manager on progress for preparations the next day, including an estimate of people who planned to attend; reviewing music with Dad. "Play that one again." He told me. It went on. It was mid-afternoon before I even realized how long Angela had been gone. Five hours. Is she okay? I texted her. *Traffic on and off Lido Key can take a long time, but Angela is really efficient,* I thought to myself.

I found myself feeling a sensation foreign to me. It was an overwhelm of loneliness coupled with a sense of being lost in a forest, a forest of a completely familiar location. My discomfort escalated, and I felt more out of balance. That of staying on-task for what needed to be done that day and worry for needing the love of my life by my side. Now, in hindsight, I realize I was in need of comfort and consoling—I just could not name it or recognize it at the time.

When Angela finally walked into the condo, it was nearly four in the afternoon. "What happened?"

She scrambled to the living room with bags full of delightful decorative choices and pulled out the book for photographs. "I want to show you. I thought this would be good to make a memory book of photos of your mom." It was perfect. "Hi Tom. Are you doing okay?" She checked-in with him. Then, she grabbed my hand and pulled me to the guest bedroom.

"Everything is fine. I am okay, and everything is sorted out."

Oh god, what? My face shifted.

"I need to tell you that I got into an accident." Tears welled in her eyes, "I know it is the last thing needed on a day like today."

"What?! Oh honey. Are you okay?"

We hugged.

"Yes, I promise. A bit shaken, but I am okay. And, I have all the paperwork and the stuff with insurance for what we need to do sorted out. I didn't want to tell you until I was back." Her voice was a speeding roller coaster on descent.

"I am so glad you are okay, that you are back, that you are here. I needed you." I hugged her again. "Is there damage?"

"A little. Minor, and I will make sure to get it fixed."

"Do we need to tell Dad?" I lobbied aloud, posing the question to us both.

"No. I don't think so. I have everything figured out, and I will take care of everything so it will go to our insurance, not his."

"Right, I don't think so."

It would have been so upsetting to Dad, and we had no desire to upset him further. He had just lost his wife.

It was that whole thing that happens during times of stress that I learned about over the years: people are simply more prone to accidents during times of stress. It played out in a real-life way for us on that day.

That damn van.

In the weeks following Mom's death and during the triage, detective-worthy sleuthing and management setup we were doing to take care of Dad and his affairs, we discovered that my dad was paying a horrendous monthly amount to lease the van. I held the monthly statement in the air and exclaimed in disbelief, "Look at this!" Angela and I were both appalled and completely dismayed by the monthly cost. As we worked to downsize Dad's costs to prioritize his care, getting rid of the van and getting it off the books was a priority, particularly since he had no feasible use for it. He physically could not drive it. Dad also had no concept of what he was paying for it. "What??!" He exclaimed to me as I told him. "That *cannot* be right!" It was clear he had no idea what was in his lease agreement.

Angela and I talked to our friends who used the phrase "elder abuse" with us when we described the structure of my dad's van lease. We could not be certain elderly abuse played a role in the situation, but we were worried Dad had been taken advantage of, got swindled or simply agreed to a bad lease. This set us on a mission to relieve my dad of the lease and get rid of the van. Since it was leased and licensed in South Dakota, we needed to first get the vehicle back there. We contemplated driving it, but with our full-time jobs, our need to get back to our home in Virginia, and the van not being our vehicle, we decided driving it the 1,900+ miles across state lines might not be the smartest option. We landed on shipping the van back to its state of origin. That was going to be the safest, smartest, most efficient, and most frugal thing to do. Then, we could really tackle getting Chrysler to take the vehicle back. We had no concept of how difficult our mission would be or how unhelpful, disrespectful, and inhumane the leasing company would be.

The first time following Mom's death that I truly broke down—lost it, you could say—I was huddled on a wooden floor in a pool of my own tears. It was the floor of our kitchen about a month after Mom died. Angela and I were back in Virginia, and it was a Friday. I had taken the day off work and was attempting to bake scones at our house. I had an unspoken self-goal to take off the day *from everything*: from work, from managing Mom's stuff, and from managing Dad's stuff (while staying on call, of course).

"I just wanted one day," I yelped in tears, my face increasing in red hue from crying.

I had sunk to the floor, my back sliding along the wall, my tank top scrunching up and my skin pressing against the drywall, until my head fell between my knees. I was in a perfect tornado-threat protection pose that I had learned as a child at school. The tornado this time was the complication from the damn van leasing company, who was refusing yet again to be helpful and work with us on a solution. *Why does e-v-e-r-y-t-h-i-n-g have to be so…hard?* I asked the universe. "WHHHHY?" My hands rubbed my forehead as my face became cherry-red with large tear globes streaming down my face. I could feel the damp, mother-of-all headaches setting in. This was a question I asked of the universe so many times. If only I had known what I was going to face in the months ahead. If only I had known that dealing with that damn van— that van my dad was paying way too much for, that he could not even drive— if only I had known the nightmare it would be to deal with the vehicle leasing company or that all of what was that van was going to end up a mere blip on the screen of many more hard things to come. If only. If I were able to stretch my limbs out and make a giant leap into the future, I would have consoled myself in those moments on the floor, soaked in my own tears. I would have let myself know that there is another side to the tornado, and that this, too, will be in the rearview mirror someday. Someday. But, that was not today. That was absolutely not something I could contemplate at the time. I was neck deep in all of it and scrambling to tread emotional waters that crashed all around me, and face into the forceful winds of that epic tornado.

One day, months after refusing to pay the monthly leasing fee, the sun came shining through the windows, and my beautiful partner, Angela, came running into the kitchen after having spoken to Chrysler for the billionth time. "They agreed to take the van back." Given the circumstances, Chrysler had finally agreed to take the van back.

"Really? Really?!" My eyes welled with a different sort of tears this time.

"Really."

"You are the most beautiful person I know," I wrapped my arms around her. She had taken the baton for dealing with Chrysler for me after that day on the floor. She showed up, yet again, as the most amazing partner.

The Chrysler dealership in South Dakota is called Billion, so it is not surprising that after having spoken to (and exchanged letters with) Chrysler nearly a billion times, we had a resolution. We were instructed to get it to the local dealership the following Tuesday. Done. That we could arrange. With our being in Virginia, it was Doug, my parents' trusty handyman, who agreed to transport the van from my dad's house to the dealership and send us the confirmation receipt he would get from Chrysler.

The universe never answered my question why things had to be so hard. I think maybe, it was the universe teaching me a hard lesson, that while hard is what it is meant to be, it does not have to be *that* hard. And in the end, I may never understand that vehicle and its journey to Florida in 2019, back to South Dakota in 2020 and back to Chrysler later that same year.

To this day (and I think it will be this way forever) when I see a Chrysler Pacifica minivan on the road, I think to myself, *That damn van.*

"WHHHHY?"

Skeleton in the Living Room

Something that was part of my environment growing up was not a thing at all. It was all the things, including the medical accoutrement—the devices, equipment, and paraphernalia that were part of my father's collection. These things included delicate, historical surgical instruments, sterilizing equipment, and machines with complicated functions I was absolutely not versed in. It also included models. There was a cool, faceless human torso model that was meant for learning the various intestinal organs of the body. Each organ had a different color. I recall my father lifting it off the top shelf of his study when I was in the "human body" chapter of 6th grade science. And I liked pulling out the liver so I could see the gallbladder. To me, it was a 3-D puzzle that was fun to take apart and put back together again.

Growing up, I was often at my father's ophthalmology practice—after school, before school, on weekends—helping my mother drop something off, doing homework between extracurricular activities, or stopping by to simply "say hello to your father," as my mother would direct. I recall being quite young, probably about four years old when this started. If you could ask my parents, they would know that would be my age estimate. It was a running joke in the family that 'everything happened when I was four years old,' according to me. "Were you four years old?" they would ask. But, for real in this case, I *was* about four years old, and I would run to my father's desk at work, which involved running past piles of Scientific American magazines and skipping over medical articles and books while passing the long wooden conference room table that was covered with more books and papers. As soon as I made it to his desk, I would either hop into his lap, or if he was still with a patient, I would lean on his brown leather desk chair and gaze at the photos he had along his desk, peering at the people in the frames, which included my mother, my sister, and me. If he were there, as I jumped into his lap, he would put his dictaphone down and wrap his arms around me, "Do you know what this is?" He would show me some medical instrument from his desk and explain its uses.

His medical office, which was also part of that long conference room, was filled with all sorts of things. He even had a marble bust. Yep, that's true. I only later learned via the auction house personnel that it was early Roman or Greek. The bust had a remade nose. "A shame," Dad would say. "Too bad about that, but it's a nice piece," he would add. "Uh-huh," I would respond.

There was a unique floating shelf that hung about two feet from the ceiling. It had brass ends forming an intricate pattern with a wooden surface. Dad put his *Wasserbar* ("water bear" in German) hat on it along with his Scottish cap that he would adorn while ice skating in the winter, and his fishing caps were stored on that shelf in the spring and summer. The table's eight chairs were really hard to pull out since there were papers stacked beside them, on them, and on the floor surrounding them. True to form, there was way too much in the room. He and my mother (who was the administrator for his business and ran the optical shop, a role she was very proud of) would hold staff meetings in that room. I used to wonder, *What does everybody else think of all this stuff? How do they hold meetings at a table that is packed with stacks of articles and books?* I asked my mother about it one day, and she said, "Well, you can imagine the effort to move everything before each meeting." What?! Somehow, I accepted her answer as sufficient.

The other thing in that room, in the far corner, to the left of the bust, was a skeleton. A human skeleton, to-scale model, hanging on a stand that had wheels, just like you would see in a lab. Sometimes it was in the hazy, medical-grade plastic bag zippered up. And sometimes it was "naked," outside its sack, so to speak. Each bone was painted with a label. Most times, I passed it without pause. Other times, particularly when I was taking biology class in high school, I would take moments to study it. *Ah, there is the 12th thoracic vertebra!* When I broke my wrist—the first time—I held my casted arm with my uninjured arm while Dad spent time showing me exactly which bones I had broken by holding up the hand of the skeleton and pointing to the wrist.

Years later, the skeleton was one of the many things (along with the bust) that my father had moved to my parents' house after he retired. Much to my mother's chagrin, dismay, and frustration, the copious amounts of office things got mixed into their home web. Why not put a skeleton in the living room? My father stated, "It's as good a place as any."

Following my mother 's passing in Florida, and after my father decided to make his final home at my parents' house in South Dakota, it then became time to move him there. It was May of 2020. Angela and I arrived at the house in advance of his arrival. There were so many things we needed to prepare for to make his arrival go as smoothly and as comfortably as possible. We got there on a Saturday, and he would be arriving Monday evening. Due to his condition, he was not fit to, nor able to fly. He needed to be medically transported via a vehicle from Florida, which meant he was being transported in a private ambulance with a twenty-four-hour nurse and driver on-board. Discovering, identifying, and arranging this type of transport during the pandemic was a feat for which Angela can take one hundred percent credit.

Prior to this 2020 arrival at my childhood home, the last time I had entered my parents' house was in June of 2019 when I was surprising my parents for a visit after Mom had her second knee surgery.

This time, the entrance felt longitudinally, latitudinally, magnitude-i-nally different. Life had shifted. Death had shifted life.

When Angela and I, along with Charlie, staggered into the house after the twenty-two-hour drive with our Yeti cooler (remember, this was COVID, so we had road-tripped with all our food and drink, stopping for fuel only), the skeleton was one of the first things we saw as we walked past the living room to the kitchen.

While I knew its origin and it was somehow familiar, its new location in the center of the house made it, well, *ghoulish*. My parent's house was built in the 1940s and did not have any ceiling lights—rooms were lit by lamps. My parents had several, but overall, the house was a rather dark place. Plus, they had done things like paint the living room walls a deep red and kept the draperies closed which made it even darker.

So, there in the center of the home, among the darkness, shadows, and the light: a skeleton.

Angela and I opened the draperies to let in as much natural light as possible (we have heard it is good for you), and against the shining glaze of the sunshine, that hazy, medical grade plastic zipper bag cast a glow on the boney shoulders and spaces between the ribs. It was dour, to say the least.

Another thing about my parents' house is that you could not walk to the kitchen without passing the large entry to the living room. So, when I say the living room is central, I mean central. You could not walk from the kitchen to any other part of the main floor (the den,

the back hallway, the bathroom, the bedrooms, and back the other way), without passing the living room. Do you want to go to the basement? Well, you must pass the living room. Do you need to use the restroom? Well, you must pass the living room. And there it was, a skeleton, each and every time. All times of day. For instance, at noon on Sunday, while getting my father his 7-Up or at five in the morning in my pajamas stumbling to the kitchen to make coffee. Who wants to pass a skeleton in the dark at one o'clock in the morning when all you want is a glass of water? Not me! And, trust me, probably not you either. (I speak from experience.) The skeleton was part of the family scenery that made sense to me. It belonged and did not belong at all. It was bizarre, and it was crazy.

After a week, Angela asked me while we ate eggs on the back porch (a respite of fresh air in the early mornings) before my father awoke, "Can we pleeeease relocate the skeleton?"

"Why?" I asked in jest.

I was all in—or, as Mom would say, "in like Flynn." I only now know from looking it up that that is a phrase with direct reference to Erol Flynn, who starred in a number of Hollywood movies. I am not sure the phrase is aptly used here, but it is what came to mind as I wrote this, probably because I can hear my mother's voice.

My parents' house was large, and they found a way to fill it. I suppose all the navigating I had learned to do in my dad's office conference room was training for navigating their house as an adult: skip, slide, hop, stop short… A clear path was something my mother longed for, yet one was not to be found. Relocating things was something Angela and I had been doing since the moment we arrived at the house. We needed to make room for my father's care (caretakers, supplies, accessories), for us, and for our things since we would be there for at least a couple of months. We needed some space to simply operate and make our way through the days. The relocation of items—"shifting," you might call it—was done out of necessity, simply to navigate daily life. It was always more involved than it originally seemed. Need a spot to do early morning yoga because it is the only way you will manage to get through the day? Well, that means you will need to move that super heavy machine that does who-knows-what, from below the antique coffee table, because you need to move the coffee table in order to move the chair. And in order to have an open path to the dining room, you need to move the chair… You get it.

Relocating your loved ones' things is a delicate dance. While you need to prioritize things in the near-term, you also operate with a sense of deep respect for the personal artifacts that belong to your loved ones. And at this point in time, all the belongings were now my father's, since he was a widower. (I had to fill that out on so many forms, writing "widower" on behalf of my dad—yet another thing I had not thought of until I had to do it.) Plus, in our situation, Dad was anxious about *ever* moving or getting rid of anything. "What are you doing with that? Why are you moving that?!" It stressed him, and stress was the last thing he needed when he was working so hard simply to take a breath. Given his condition, it was important he did not have elevated worries, so it was a priority to help him remain at ease, to be able to take a good breath. Couple this with the fact that most of my parents' things were delicate, antique, or just really old, and it made relocating things around the house a task that required great care. To relocate the skeleton (or anything for that matter), we had to either delicately explain the reasoning and justification for the relocation or try and relocate said object without Dad's awareness. The latter was imperative for something such as, I don't know, a part of his medical collection—the skeleton.

It is important to note that my father lacked mobility at this point in his life. He was nearly outliving his prognosis (which he ultimately did), and his limited movement landed squarely on the shoulders of his lungs. He could not breathe—he was unable to get air on his own. Breathing had become such a difficult activity, (I struggle to find the right word here - "function" "activity" "process"- none sound appropriate), he was now on oxygen 24/7 using electric-powered oxygen machines almost at their full capacity. We had to have oxygen tanks on hand in case of emergency—such as the power going out—and later in the summer of 2020, I learned all about full-house generators because I had to negotiate with Generac, Briggs and Stratton, and the local install company on Dad's behalf for a full-house power generator to be installed. The only time Dad was not connected to the oxygen machines was in the *very brief* moments of switching his cannula (the small tubing, in this case, connected to an oxygen machine that wraps across cheeks and nestles just below the nostrils, carrying air to the respiratory system) from one to the next in order to change machines. The inability to breathe on his own limited his movement more so than the atrophy from non-movement. The main culprits were his lungs. This meant that where he spent his time was governed by connection to oxygen machines. So, at this point in time, he spent his waking hours in the den, which was arguably the smallest room in the house but had the advantage of being just to the left of the front door (which he liked, and it also allowed him to know when a caregiver would arrive or depart). Plus, the den had the winged-back chair he wanted to sit in and a television with a built-in DVD *and* VHS player. He loved that TV and how it was "all-in-one." At night, he slept in the master bedroom at the back of the house. He would make the trip from the bedroom to the den once in the morning after getting ready for the day and once in the evening when he would set off to bed. It was also during this timeframe that he was still using the bathroom during the day. In other words, making the trek to the bathroom during the day when he had to use the toilet. I came to learn he only did that about once or twice a day, and that soon after Angela and I left town to return to our home in Virginia, he ceased making the trip to the restroom altogether. "It's just too far," he told me. Yet he refused to let me set up other arrangements or move him out of the house. He would die in that house. I knew it. I also knew it was his wish, and so I hoped he would be able to remain there. I did everything in my power so that he could remain there.

When it came to relocating the skeleton, the first question to answer was: where? Where do you put a skeleton? If you had to, where would *you* put a life-size, true-to-scale, human skeleton model? My father, clearly, would put it in a living room. Not me. Angela and I both immediately decided on the answer: the garage. This answer came to us after a quick assessment about whether it would get harmed by unregulated temperatures and remain in good condition in the garage. Our assessment also included two facts: there really was no space for it in the basement (that was packed with more of my parents' things), and relocating to any other room on the main level would not solve the multiple times a day creepiness issue. The garage it was. I heard my father's words ring in my ears, "It's as good a place as any." This time, in my voice.

The next question to answer was, how? Well, one of us would have to carefully steady the skeleton body while wheeling the stand it was attached to, while the other one of us would have to look out and serve as mission control. Of course, making sure to do it in a way that Dad would not hear or see such a mission taking place.

More on the layout of my parents' home—this is important. The front door was located squarely between the den, where my father spent his waking hours those days, and the hallway to the bathroom and bedrooms. From the outside of the house, there was a window smack dab in the center of the front stoop, which was the window in the hall bathroom. To move the skeleton from the living room to the garage, we had two options: the back route and the front route. The back route would involve the following: rolling it from the living room to the back door near the kitchen (a path completely *out* of my father's view), wheeling it across the back breezeway, which ran alongside a very large window of the den (completely *in* my father's view), then through a large door at the back of the garage, down concrete steps (blocked with, you guessed it, more stuff) to the garage. While that route had the great benefit of avoiding wheeling a skeleton across the front entry of the house and across the driveway and avoiding crossing the internal viewing threshold of the den to get to the front door, it had two major drawbacks: navigating the back breezeway (completely *in* my father's view), and the six, concrete, unlit, blockaded stairs of the back garage. That left us with the "most direct" route: from the living room, past the den door, through the front door, outside to the front stoop, past the hallway bath window, down the front brick steps to the driveway, and into the garage through the main door.

Got it? If not, read that paragraph again.

Next came timing. Remember that part about a delicate dance? In a dance, you have to know when to move fast, when to move slowly, and when to pause. Well, we couldn't just wheel the skeleton to the front door while my father sat in his chair in the den. He would see it. And we could not wheel it across the front stoop and carry it down the front stairs while he was in the bathroom. He would see it. Our most opportune time would be *during his transit* to and from the hallway bathroom. While my father shuffled from the den to the bathroom, we had to get the skeleton outside to the front stoop, just to the left of the bathroom window yet out of sight. Then, while he was in the bathroom, we had to wait on that front stoop until he exited the bathroom to head back toward the den. Finally, we could wheel and carry the skeleton down the front steps and into the garage. What a plan!

Angela and I always believed we would do well on the Amazing Race—that television competition show where teams of two adventure-compete at various locations across the globe, executing crazy challenges. This was our own personal version of it. I was in charge of skeleton movement, and Angela was command central: "Go, now! Go, go, now! STOP. Wait! Don't move. Okay, go! Go! *Go*!" The commands coupled with the object—a skeleton— yielded quite the image.

During this timeframe, a friend of ours had convinced us to start watching *Schitt's Creek*. The twenty-minute episodes were perfect for what we had the capacity to manage in the late evenings. We were so tired after work, juggling WebEx, Zoom, caring for my father, investigating longer-term caregivers, shifting belongings, and more. I think we were able to watch about two episodes a week with everything going on. A big shout out to Daniel Levy and Eugene Levy for orchestrating such a heart-warming comedy. What occurred next in real life for us was my very own *Schitt's Creek* moment.

It was a sunny day. Dad was wearing one of his favorite shirts. I remember it vividly because it was a brilliant shirt, and it was also one of my favorites of his. It was a bright cornflower blue plaid button-up that he looked really great in. My mother was a fan when he wore it, too. I mostly remember it because, as I toppled over in laughter while waiting on the front stoop, adhering to Angela's commands of "STOP. Wait! Don't move," I was about to pee my pants with my two hands clinging to the skeleton stand's pole, and I watched as my father looked out the window of the bathroom—a direction where I (and the skeleton) could not be seen. That's when I coined it: My *Schitt's Creek* Moment. *Am I really trying to hide a giant (okay, life-size) skeleton from my father while I stand on the front stoop of the house I grew up in? Yes. Yes, I am. And I will do it confidently and successfully.* I watched him stand up and take another look out the window before shuffling in the opposite direction toward the den. "Okay, go! Go! *Go*!" I heard Angela's voice, and I jumped into action. I moved with as much speed, ease, and finesse I could muster (you know, for relocating a skeleton). Once in the garage, I closed the door and high-fived with Angela. *Phew.*

I don't know if any neighbors witnessed this. For their sake, I hope so.

You know that saying, "skeletons in the closet?" Well, for us, we had a skeleton—a literal skeleton—not in the closet, but in the living room, because as my father said, "It's as good a place as any." Sure, Dad. Sure. We had it in the garage too because—to echo my father—"It's as good a place as any." Just like on so many other occasions, like when we did all that research for the Old Masters paintings, I wondered if other people dealt with this crazy stuff after recently losing a parent and caring for another parent. They must. Really? *Really*? Angela always murmured, "Ummm, I don't think so. Not to this scale." Did she mean, not-to-the-life-size-scale-of-this-skeleton-I-am-about-to-roll-out-of-here?

The truth is, everyone has skeletons in the closet. Some have one in the living room. In our case, I know we had both.

Death had shifted life.
(I want to laugh. I need to weep.)

Everyone Needs a Boris!

It was deep in the winter of 2020, just following the holiday season, and Angela convinced me to go see an energy healer. I exuded my typical skepticism, which was now combined with curiosity after the experience of watching reiki effectively break Mom's fever. Over the past few years, the window of my skepticism for non-Western medicine was closing, and my interest in alternative ways of healing was growing. The situations in which I witnessed positive outcomes from such alternate forms were adding up.

"We can just go and give it a try. I think we have to try something," Angela offered.

We both were wrought with fatigue, unable to sleep, and suffering from various forms of physical pain. This was a compounding negative effect of everything in 2020: Mom's illness, Mom's death, figuring out Dad's affairs, Sharon's illness, Sharon's death, managing Dad's caretaking, two massively long road trips, clearing and selling my parents' condo—oh, and COVID. It all settled into my being, revealing itself as a constant awake-ness and automatic propelling of myself into everything except the care of my body, mind, and emotions.

"Okay, I'll give it a try," I agreed, the hesitation evident in my voice, stemming mostly from the internal thought, *Do I really need help?*

"Listen, we'll just drive there, and I can go first to check it out. Then you can decide."

In true Angela form, she took such care in gently leading me to a conclusion: to try something new, to try to heal. She showed me the somatic therapist and energy healing website she found by doing research and asking for recommendations. It looked interesting. It looked professional. It looked worthy of a try on my part.

The healer's name was Boris, and he was located in Maryland, a forty-five minute drive from our home in Virginia.

Angela booked us each an appointment back-to-back on a Friday morning. We decided to take the day off work and use this self-care experiment as a lead-in to the weekend. I had stashed in my tote a few of the *Real Simple* magazines that had arrived at our house over the past ten months, which I had yet to open. I decided I could use the time during Angela's appointment to browse some of the recipes. I figured that aimlessly flipping pages of these magazines would force me to sit still and serve as a time-passing form of support while I waited to hear the outcome of Angela's appointment. We decided to bring Charlie with us since we did not know what our exact timing would be. We knew it would be a long adventure, a minimum of three and a half hours including travel time and appointment time.

We arrived in a small Maryland town, pulling into the tiny parking lot of a house-turned-business location. Angela parked and we looked at the outside staircase of the house, leading to the top floor "suite" of Boris's office.

"Well, what do you think?" Angela gazed up at the strange-looking therapy location.

"Hmmm… I don't know. It looks…" I couldn't come up with a description. "It's kind of strange, but probably totally fine."

"Here's the deal: I'll go first. Once I get inside, meet Boris and see that everything is okay, I'll text you within five minutes, so check the clock." Angela said this in the same rhythm as when we were out front of a pawn shop in Florida.

"Okay. I hope it goes well and is positive." I said in an uncertain tone.

Angela leaned over and gave me a sweet kiss on my cheek. "Here I go. See you soon!"

Two minutes, twenty-five seconds later: *Ping!* "All good," her text read. "See you after."

I think Angela's appointment lasted about ninety minutes.

In the meantime, I took Charlie for a walk down the block and around the corner to a church's plot of land. Back at the car, the magazines with recipes kept me occupied for about twenty minutes. I had to move again. I drove to a nearby gas station and fueled up the car and used the restroom. I walked every aisle of the station's tiny convenience store section. Then, I got back in the car and drove to a parking spot across the street from Boris' business. I got out and walked Charlie up and down that part of the block five or six times, adding in some training drills with him.

"Sit. Good boy."

"Stay."

"Spin. Good boy."

"Down."

He executed all of them perfectly. Charlie had a PhD in us, and I could tell he knew this was a new adventure that we were on. His eyes told me he would perform these drills perfectly and assured me of the consistency and familiarity of the drills in this unknown place and time.

He and I then got back in the car and parked in our original parking spot. There I sat, flipping page after page of the magazines again, consuming no information and looking up at the rearview mirror image where Charlie was sitting poised and inquisitive in the backseat.

It was Charlie's gaze that shifted to the staircase and caused me to notice that Angela was walking back to the car. She walked steadily and purposefully. She looked calm and relaxed. Her shoulders appeared to be resting at least three inches lower than before her appointment.

"How was it?"

She took a foreign-to-me deep breath. "That was incredible. Boris is great. I feel so relaxed. And tired. I might take a nap."

A solid wave of relief passed over me. More data supporting the decision to try this new form of caretaking.

"Okay, I'll see you after. I love you." I gave her a soft kiss on her cheek as she nestled into the front passenger car seat, reaching an arm back to give Charlie a pat.

"We'll be here. Have a great appointment! See you after."

I walked up the stairs, opened the creaking door, and entered to find a small room that had been transformed into a tremendously welcoming Zen space. I barely stepped over the threshold to the inside when a slight man greeted me.

"I am Boris."

There stood a man the size of my pinky finger. I immediately felt like a giant Amazonian woman standing in front of him. He motioned for me to sit on the massage table in the center of the room. As I walked, I tried to invisibly tower less into the space with my height, countering his small stature. My toes grazed the floor as I sat on the edge of the table, Boris now sitting on a soft stool across from me.

He bore deeply into my eyes with the kindest, most present gaze that startled me. Then, he uttered four words: "How are your emotions?"

BAM!

Instant tears. Instant full body emotional release. I trembled. I sobbed. No one had ever asked me that question—not in those words. No one had ever sat so presently with me and put attention *first* to emotions. This was new to me. I sat there on the edge of a massage table in the middle of Somewhereville, Maryland and realized I was carrying so much emotion. The dam I built to hold them back broke. And Boris was there to take care of me.

I had never contemplated tending to my emotions nor my emotional health before then, except for in a very analytical, academic way where I essentially intellectualized them. Boris introduced me to somatic healing with his expertise. It was soothing, full of calm energy, tranquil, and hard. I came out refreshed, stunned, exhausted, and undisturbed.

My appointment with Boris lasted over two hours.

"You look different," Angela said, astounded by my changed appearance.

"How so?"

"Relaxed. Tired. Almost like there's a different aura about you."

"Good thing we brought Charlie with us." I told her.

"Good thing we took the day off work."

Angela drove us home, and we recounted the details of each of our sessions with Boris: how they were different, how they were similar, how we both felt changed by the experience. By the time we made it back home, we both were exclaiming, "Boris is amazing!"

Once home, we fell asleep for a few hours, barely managed a dinner and short walk for Charlie, and then went to bed early that night. In both instances, I slept more deeply than I had the past ten months and most certainly than I ever had before in my life. It was as if my being rested for the very first time.

The experience convinced us. Boris convinced us. Energy healing and somatic therapy was a firm "add it to the list" form of taking care of ourselves.

Those two sessions with Boris were clearly positive for us. We felt it. And by feeling it, we knew it. The feeling part came first, before the knowing part. I was now on board with energy healing and somatic therapy. What's more is that I was now on board with trying different forms of therapy. It only took me two weeks after that appointment in a strange-looking house in Maryland to finally seek out and start regular sessions with a therapist.

The positive impact from the appointments with Boris was surprising, supremely notable, and baffling in three dimensions.

Dimension one: it was astonishing to be introduced to a form of caretaking that felt so powerful and effective yet so foreign—so *not* mainstream. Dimension two: it was astounding to take care of myself and to venture into the land of learning the importance of that. Dimension three: it was nutty to think about how hesitant and skeptical I originally was to try this form of therapy. I realize now that my own skepticism about it was less about the form of therapy and more about hesitation (and fear) for what it might reveal: the unmasking of my emotions and the state of my emotional health that so desperately needed time, love, and tenderness. By me.

I started learning *to* take care of myself, *how* to take care of myself, and that taking care of oneself is *vital to well-being*. I started exclaiming regularly, "Everyone needs a Boris!"

**The feeling part came first,
before the knowing part.**

Uncomfortable Cot

"The caregiver indicated that the cot is not comfortable. If there is something you can do about that, that would be great."

The administrator at the caregiver agency emailed that unsolicited feedback to me the day after we had set up a bed, or a "cot," in my father's bedroom so that the caretaker scheduled to work overnight shifts could have a place to rest her eyes between addressing my father's needs. Providing such a cot was labeled as "nice-to-have," which is how it had previously been described to me during the intake interview with that same administrator.

Excuse me?! I self-screamed. *You have got to be kidding me!* My energy, rumbling like lightning, shot through me out of frustration amplified. I was seething. *Seriously? Seriously?!* I self-screamed harder. *My father is in hospice, struggling to breathe, in the last stages of his life, and the caretaker is going to complain about the comfort level of the family-provided bed!* Ugh. "This is nuts," I firmly stated out loud to the universe, throwing my hands in the air.

I declined to respond to that email.

When I first heard the middle-aged woman with dark brown hair from the caretaking organization mention that in most cases it is really helpful if the family can provide a cot for the overnight care, I rationalized it while empathizing. The overnight shift for caretakers is their work *day*, and I also understood that deep in the dark night between the needs of my father, it would be beneficial to have a comforting spot to rest nearby. My empathy was drawn from my own experiences of wakeful, exhaustion-filled nights during my mother's care and in the recent weeks with my father. I thought about his early career in medical residency when he worked in an emergency room. He would take advantage of the "rest rooms" (not bathrooms) to squeeze in any bit of shut-eye during those excessively long shifts. "Your father can fall asleep and wake up on a dime. It's all those nights working in the ER," my mother would tell my sister and me. So, I figured that it now made sense to provide something like that for his caretakers.

After learning about such a perk, Angela and I decided the same day to do yet another furniture shift to make space for a twin mattress in my father's bedroom, which was full of dressers, a bench, a large chair (winged, of course), and armoire. Fitting another bed into the room seemed impossible at first.

"How are we going to get another bed in there?" Angela asked from the kitchen. We both knew the answer: "We'll figure it out." We borrowed the twin mattress from my old room across the hallway and were able to squeeze it in front of two of the large dressers across the room from the foot of my father's hospice bed. Even though it was cramped, we made doubly-certain to carefully situate it so that there would be enough room for anyone to safely and easily walk around the foot of the bed to each side of the hospice bed. That was critical in order to properly care for him: to shift him, administer medicine, roll him, clean him, sit him up, etc. And, to be with him.

"What are you doing?" My father inquired while peeking one eye open and peering over his square-shaped, wire-rimmed glasses.

I tugged at the side of the mattress, wisps of my hair stuck across my sweaty forehead. Angela pushed forward as we slid the mattress around the corner toward its destination.

"We're bringing this in here for the overnight caretakers, Dad," I said, winded.

"Hm-hmm," he muttered with his approving nod. I had come to learn over the years that this was a firm sign of approval from Dad. He definitely would let his disapproval be known if that were the case.

We made up the twin mattress with freshly cleaned sheets and a blanket. I remember looking back at it and feeling a sense of success. "That should be nice," I whispered to myself, claiming victory. During all this time since my mother got sick, I would take in and relish any and every small success. Claiming a mini victory was pumping any possible fuel to refill my mental, physical and emotional batteries, which were running on fumes.

In no way will I diminish the wonderful care that was provided to my father and how incredibly amazing the community of caregivers and hospice were. They were exceptional and I discovered, no - I lived, how critical their roles are in people's lives, including ours, during such transformative times.

Still, something struck a chord that morning while reading the email from the agency with feedback about the bed we provided. It was dissonance amidst everything that was going on and everything I was focused on. It was *so low* on the huge list of priorities. And yet, the next day, I found myself tugging the sides of a twin box spring while Angela pushed forward for it to slide along the floor from my childhood bedroom into Dad's room. The box spring was so much easier to slide across the carpet!

Dad peered over his glasses at us once again.

"We're bringing in the box spring for the twin mattress, Dad," I informed him before he could inquire.

He did not say anything and offered that nod.

While at the time, the nutty part was receiving such feedback during what felt like a fragile time, it was also odd to think about the fact that my childhood twin bed, where Dad tucked me in and where he had to give me at-home stitches on the edge of my eyelid, had now turned into an overnight "cot" for his caretakers. "Are you comfortable, Tom?" my mother had asked him, as he prepared to weave thread through my eyelid those years ago. If he was comfortable, he would be better positioned to offer me his best care. I was able to make the link now: if Dad's caregiver was comfortable, she too would be better positioned to give him her best care.

It was operating off this principle that spurred action. It was firmly rooted in the quality of my father's care. I learned that moving a very heavy, old twin mattress and responding with an added boxspring to "the cot is not comfortable" was something I could do to help ensure the best possible care for him in his final days and hours.

I self-screamed harder.
(I am uncomfortable too. I quake in sorrow.)

Rosé and Rocks

Côte de Rosé is a wine you can purchase at most wine stores. The bottle is long with a slender neck, a wide base featuring a grooved rose pattern on the bottom. The cork is glass (therefore easy to open with a crank of your hand), and it tastes delicious (enough). Angela and I started buying this wine at Costco because it was a decent price point, a fun bottle to look at, and went down easily after a long day of work, phone calls, caring for Dad, cleaning, shifting furniture, walking Charlie, and getting by.

A couple nights after having flown to South Dakota in June 2021 to get to my ailing father as quickly as possible, Angela and I sat on the back porch of the house drinking Côte de Rosé and discussing how to handle the next few days. It was apparent that a longer stay with my father was in order, and that it would most certainly be our final stay with him. He was declining and clearly on a path vectoring away from stability. We had tossed aside summer plans, canceling a trip to Bermuda that we had booked on a whim to try and get some sort of vacation since my mother died. Once I got the phone call that June from Dad's most trusted caregiver, we knew our plans would be different.

"Your dad has taken a turn," she said with a strain of sadness in her voice.

This was coupled with a conversation with my father.

"I'm not doing well. It doesn't look good," he told me as I stood outside with Charlie, briefly feeling the ease that Dad was letting me know just like he said he would.

I was on a plane the next day. Angela followed one day after, since our dog sitter could only arrive on such short notice to take care of Charlie.

There we were once again, problem-solving. Our dog sitter in Virginia could only watch Charlie for a couple days, and we could not know how long we would need to remain in South Dakota with

Dad. We did know we needed to get Charlie there with us so that we could be available and prepared to stay as long as needed for Dad—together. This was not going to be a fly in, stay a week, fly out scenario. We also recognized our own needs and wants: we did not want to separate from each other, and we did not want one of us doing the long twenty-two hour drive from Virginia to South Dakota solo. Our friend, Erica, generously offered to drive Charlie the entire distance or to do so with Angela so that she could fly back to Virginia and road trip together with her. We gave those two options serious consideration; however, for the former, we knew at least one of us needed to make a stop at our home in Virginia to gather more things of ours (besides Charlie) that we would need for the temporary relocation. Another temporary relocation. A stop back in Virginia was needed as a grounding of sorts for that transition. Of course, we were well-versed in these temporary moves, temporary relocations. We had done many of these over the course of my career, as I took strategic leaps, accepted new positions and almost all of them required some type of move. However, it was the three most recent relocations (to Florida when Mom died, to South Dakota to move Dad back, and back to Florida to prepare and sell my parents' condo for my dad) that offered a PhD education in Temporarily Relocating. Plus, these three most recent relocations related to the current situation more intimately. Ultimately, we deduced that our friend's generous offers seemed too much to ask. As for us both flying to Virginia to retrieve Charlie (and so on), only to turn around and hit the road—it did not seem like a solid option. I did not want to, nor could I, leave Dad. As his healthcare surrogate, it was clear I was needed to help navigate any changes in his care. More importantly, I did not want to leave. I did not want to be apart from him. Angela did not want to leave him or me either. Yet we both knew we needed a longer-term plan, and Charlie was part of that. He was part of us, part of our daily routine, part of our very essence of being. Not to mention, Dad always liked seeing him and kept asking about him. "Where's Charlie? Is he coming?" Dad liked that Charlie could have the run of the large yard and watch the wild turkeys from the windows of the house. He had become accustomed from the past May when we settled him back in at the house; he had gotten used to Charlie's presence, our routine with him, and Charlie coming into that small den some evenings to sit with me across from him.

We contemplated making the trip together multiple times. We could both fly to our home in Virginia and then both drive back. The options kept running in circles around our thoughts. And our wine glasses. And, again: we could both fly back to Virginia, pack up the same afternoon, and head out on the road trip the next day. Since it was around eight o'clock at night, in that scenario, the soonest we would be back to Dad would be four days, if we were lucky. Four days was too long to be away. In addition, that type of flight plus packing up plus turnaround on a long road trip seemed extreme the more we talked about it. On the other hand, neither of us thought a twenty-two hour road trip solo was safe, particularly in our current wrought, stressed out, and fatigued state.

The problem-solving activity escalated. We both became increasingly upset as we talked through these options over and over again, each scenario coming to a dead-end. I cried tears of frustration and overwhelm, taking giant swigs of wine (super helpful). Angela was also in tears, her face turning darker shades of pink while knocking back the rosé (super helpful). Suddenly, she stood up, marched from the table, picked up a couple rocks from the surrounding landscaping, and threw them into the yard a few feet in front of her.

My tears stopped. My voice stopped. I sat there shocked. This was so unlike her. And perfectly representative of the level of wits-of-all-ends, the level of sadness and emotional fatigue we were feeling. I could not name it as that at the time, but that was precisely what it was. There was an underlying feeling of having the wind knocked out of us repeatedly while life's punching bag continued swinging towards us hard and we were desperately trying to do the best we could. And Dad… Dad was failing.

I do not know if we laughed in that moment. Wait, I take that back. We did, we absolutely did. We totally barrelled out laughter, as if the rocks spewing through the air thrust ridiculous levity in such a hard series of moments, and their rock-weight revealed the answer we could acknowledge as the solution we could now accept.

I raised my glass of wine. What else to do? Angela raised hers.

Holy shit, I thought, our glasses gleaming from the lightning bugs in the dark. "Rosé and rocks. We can call it rosé and rocks," we agreed. The "it" being the trigger to a decision, to a realization of the best and only seemingly-feasible and seemingly-obvious path forward.

The conclusion? That path forward? Angela would fly to Virginia solo. I would remain with Dad. She would then get back to South Dakota as soon as possible with Charlie via escorted road trip. That's right. That night, Angela found a service (she is such a great researcher!), where a driver would pick her up on a Monday morning in Virginia and deliver her to South Dakota the next afternoon. This would allow Angela and Charlie to arrive back in South Dakota within a much tighter timeline, enabling her (with Charlie in tow) to return as quickly as possible, *and* prevent her from the responsibility of being behind the wheel for such a long distance herself. We had to pay a hefty price for such a service, but once determined, we did not hesitate. It was the best option determined by none other than Côtes de Rosé and rocks.

Charlie and Angela arrived back at the house around four in the afternoon three days later.

As I stood up from the chair where I was sitting next to Dad, I said, "I'll be right back. Angela and Charlie just arrived."

"Oh that's tremendous, that's great!" Dad smiled.

Now when I come across a bottle of Côtes de Rosé in a store, I cannot help but shake my head, cringe, laugh out loud, feel a cavernous pang of sentiment, rush to all the hard decisions we had to make, and know we did the absolute best we could under impossibly emotional circumstances.

We figured it out with the help of rosé and rocks.

More importantly, I did not want to leave.

Pall Mall

What is that thing some people say? "There are no coincidences in life." I have to wonder about that.

MS KITTY (also known as Connie) was a tall, robust woman, whose cackle made it clear she was a cigarette smoker. Over the course of mid-late 2020 and early 2021, combined with the recent weeks with Dad in the summer of 2021, I had become so familiar with MS KITTY's cackle, both in person and over the phone. For the times when Angela and I were back at our home in Virginia, she served as a key source of helpful information. She and I stayed in close contact; I would reach out to her, and she would reach out to me with information, updates, and helpful details to let me know how Dad was doing and with things that he may need. It was MS KITTY who validated what I was gathering from Dad in early summer 2021 when it became evident his health had taken a nosedive.

That raspy chuckle of MS KITTY's made it clear she was a cigarette smoker. Although, I never really smelled the scent of cigarettes on her (I am not sure how she achieved that).

It was just past noon a week before Dad died. Angela and I were walking up the driveway after having taken Charlie for a short walk. Caring for and walking our dog, Charlie, helped keep me on point. It provided a much-needed respite from everything through required movement.

Angela and I both looked at Connie's Chevy covered, per usual, in dust and dirt and let out a quick laugh yet again at the now familiar license plate: "MS KITTY."

"I'm going to ask her," Angela said. "I'm going to ask Connie what "MS KITTY" is about."

"Yeah, I would like to know the story behind it, too," I nodded.

We walked through the front door. I unleashed Charlie with

perfect muscle memory, and we followed him to the kitchen where we all got some water to drink. A few minutes later, after putting Charlie in another room, Connie came into the kitchen with Dad's soup bowl.

"How did lunch go?" I asked.

"Oh, pretty good, you know. He's resting now."

"Connie, I have a question for you." Angela leaned on the counter just to the right of the sink.

"Shoot." Connie put Dad's bowl in the dishwasher.

"Why the "MS KITTY?"

Connie let out her infamous cackle once again. "Oh, that was a nickname from high school, and it just stuck." Her eyes widened as she said it, yet another indicator that this jovial and robust woman carried traits similar to my mom.

"We noticed your license plate," I offered, realizing as soon as the words exited my lips how ridiculous it was to state the obvious.

"Oh yeah, the nickname stuck, so why not have it on my truck?!" Another cackle while I wondered, how long had it been since her last cigarette?

It was crazy to think about. Here was a smoker, caring for a man with a terrible lung disease. She was witnessing the awful state of a disease that hinders—no—*prevents* the very exchange of oxygen and carbon dioxide. MS KITTY never smoked near Dad, near me, near Angela, or near the home. That was such a hard no, such a hard requirement, that it never even had to be addressed by us.

The next day, Angela and I were once again walking up the driveway returning from our walk with Charlie. We were curious how similar the interior features of MS KITTY's Chevy were to our own white Chevy truck that was back at our home in Virginia. We peered into the front driver side window, and my eyes zoomed in on a small box leaning on the dashboard, just in front of the fuel gauge and behind the steering wheel. The slender box was a pack of cigarettes: Pall Mall.

My breath stopped. "Oh my *gawd*!"

"What?" asked Angela.

"Those are Pall Malls!"

"*What*?"

"My mom smoked those! You know… years before I was born, and when I was young."

"Woah."

Breath in. Breath out.

Before seeing that pack of "ciggies" (as my mom had called them) on MS KITTY's dashboard, I wouldn't have been able to tell you the brand name of cigarettes my mom used to smoke. She quit in the early 1980s with a lot of pressure from Dad to do so, when I was quite young. Still, I remember her driving me to preschool with a cigarette balanced between her right pointer and third fingers, beautifully coral painted nails while she held the steering wheel.

Is it ironic that Connie was a smoker taking care of a person with a lung disease? Absolutely.

Is it a coincidence that my dad's favorite caretaker exhibited similar traits to my mom? Maybe.

Is it a coincidence that she drove the same model truck Angela and I did?

Maybe.

Is it a coincidence that she smoked the same brand of cigarettes my mom did?

No. That's bonkers. That felt bonkers.

Hmmm, I really do wonder about the statement "There are no coincidences in life."

I have to wonder about that.

Your. Job. Is. To. Keep. Me. Alive.

Wendy had short dark hair and wore makeup to highlight her dark brown eyes. She always brought a frozen meal with her to eat during her long overnight shifts taking care of Dad in his final weeks. The day I met her, she explained to me that she preferred working overnight shifts, that she liked being there for the person she was taking care of during the wee hours of the night, and too preferred longer shifts versus shorter ones.

"It helps me understand the routine and needs of the person."

I immediately liked her. It was a "blink" moment: when your first impression provides a sense of conviction about a person that is confident and positive. I loved that she referenced my dad as a "person." It sounds funny, but when someone is sick and dying, words seem to shift and become more distanced, like using the word "patient." I think it is part of the natural distancing that occurs when there is an unknown (or known) timeframe for the presence of death's door.

Wendy had just been assigned several overnight shifts with Dad, and I was grateful. After a few nights of her being with him, I remember telling Angela, "Gosh, I hope Wendy is here when Dad passes." Aside from the circumstances and situation, it seemed like a strange thing to wish for; yet because of the circumstances and situation, it was not at all.

Through the process of coordinating Dad's care and in caring for him, I learned how hard healthcare agencies have to work to keep good in-home caregivers on the payroll and to keep them scheduled with some consistency to ensure they are available to people and families. It is hard to avoid experiencing a revolving door: different caregivers who enter a home and have to learn on-the-spot about the person, their routines, where things are in a home, what the medication instructions are, what the person eats, how and when they sleep, and so on. To aide with this, Angela and I created labels—(so many!) sheets of instructions posted in the bedroom, the bathroom, and the kitchen. We included Dad's likes and dislikes, how to cook the eggs just how he likes them, where the journal is to record the timing of his medications, and more. We were well-versed in this, having done it for him in Florida and now doing it in South Dakota. Our being present in Dad's home was helpful in order to offer a crash course for each new health aide, allowing us to give them a quick tour and tutorials. All of this effort with an aim to increase the consistency of great care for Dad. Plus, we needed to be available for when there was a delay or gap in caregiver coverage which occurred on most days. With everything Angela and I were managing, we could not be certain that we would be at the house every hour of the day. There was too much to arrange, errands to run, work meetings to attend, phone calls to make, documents to find. The lists never ended. We also knew it was vital that we got sleep (or tried to get sleep). We needed to make sure we stayed as healthy as possible so we could be at our best when caring for him.

So, whenever we met a really good caregiver who preferred longer shifts, we knew that the revolving door would pause or stop. The idea was to create an environment for Dad that would provide him the routine and consistency he craved and that would meet his medical needs.

Fortunately, Dad had amazing insurance that covered his care. Dad always was good at foresight and this was a perfect example. Years earlier, even before his diagnosis, he had the prescience to purchase a unique (and now most likely unavailable) insurance policy that would cover the costs of his in-home care without term limit. It was a primo policy that my mother had scoffed at when he purchased it, thinking it was over-the top and too expensive for the risk that it would not be necessary. Turns out, it *was* primo and it *was* necessary. It also ended up being a saving grace for the care we were able to arrange for him.

On the afternoon that we met Wendy, I brought her into Dad's room.

"Hi Dad," I said with a cheer. "I want to introduce you to Wendy."

He turned his head as we entered the room, "Okay. Hello."

"Hello, Doctor." Wendy stepped in front of me and stretched out her right hand to shake his hand.

Phew! In that moment, my nerves took a rest much like the way Dad was resting, dozing in and out of sleep. This was going to go well. I knew they would get along.

From that moment forward, she always referred to Dad as "Doctor" when addressing him. It was a formality that is not required nor typical for present day, but it is a sign of respect from my dad's generation that he appreciated. I know it gave him a sense of comfort and trust in her.

"Dad, Wendy is going to start coming over tomorrow night and will be here during the nighttime with you." I put my hand on his shoulder. "She wanted to come meet you this afternoon."

He looked up suddenly from his resting state, surprising us all, his eyes squarely meeting hers.

"Your. Job. Is. To. Keep. Me. Alive."

He said it methodically as if each word served as its own sentence.

Wow. Okay. Wow. Take that in for a second. I took it in as the oh-my-gosh-Dad's-body-is-failing-and-he-wants-to-stay-alive (of-course-he-does)-I-want-him-to-too series of words. He articulated clearly exactly what her charge was in his mind. It was the foundation of what his principle was at the time: stay alive, keep me alive.

I could see the weight of his words fall across Wendy's face as she fixed the sheet draped over him.

"Okay, Doctor, I'm going to take the best care of you that I can." She said it with a confidence I knew Dad needed. I noticed she did not promise anything she could not deliver, and I admire that in her to this day.

And she did. She took such great care of Dad on those long

nights. I could tell in the hour before I would head to sleep, and I could tell in the middle of the night when I would get up to use the restroom and peek in the room. And I could tell in the mornings when Dad would say "good morning" with a smile. At times throughout the days and nights, Dad needed to sit up or lie back or turn to one side or the other. He did not have the strength or ability to do these things on his own. She was the only health aide who could effectively shift him physically on her own.

"Doctor, it's time to have you sit up a bit more. I'm now going to help you sit up." She let him know what was going to happen, and then she talked him through what she was going to do to help him. Then she did. It was treating him as a person first, then a patient.

A few days after their first meeting, Wendy told me the story of her first few moments alone with Dad during her first official shift. She put her hand over her face as she described trying to roll the hospice tray that reached across his bed in order to adjust his bedding and accidentally knocking over his glass of orange juice. She scrambled to get a towel and wipe it up quickly so he would not get drenched in juice. She mentioned how silly she felt in that moment: "Geez, my first shift with the doctor, and he's going to think I am a dunce." She told me that he did not get upset, and he was not concerned about the juice spilling at all. He simply looked at her with a slow glance and calmly asked her, "Are you going to be alright?" She knew they were going to get along just fine after that. I told her that I knew that was the case the moment he met her.

The night Dad passed away, Wendy was there. After he died, she exited his room while Angela and I spent a few moments with him, then me solo with Dad. When I left his room that night, I walked down the hallway toward the kitchen, "I have to call my sister," I said out loud. My sister was at a local hotel and would be heading over to the house right away. I called the hospice nurse just like I had learned to do a few weeks prior for when this moment would come.

In her role as health aide, Wendy had to remain at the house with us until the hospice nurse arrived to officially pronounce Dad.

Only then could she be relieved of her duties. Wendy peeked around the corner of Dad's bedroom at Angela and I who were standing in the hallway.

"Would it be alright if I sat at the kitchen table while we wait?"

I immediately burst into laughter. I was standing in the dark corner of the hallway and my entire body convulsed in laughter. Both Wendy and Angela stepped back, utterly surprised by my reaction. I may have even scared Wendy a bit. It was not what they expected. Nor I.

"Are you okay?" Angela asked me.

I nodded as my head shook with laughter.

"Of course!" I looked at Wendy, tears running down my face while my belly vibrated. "Of course, you can come sit at the table. You don't need to stay in the room with him now."

I do not know why her question made me laugh so hard. At the same time, I do. It was a complete release of emotion. For me, her question was perfectly timed. Dad died, and she said something that made me laugh. It seemed ridiculous to expect her to sit by Dad's body while we waited for the hospice nurse to arrive. I loved that she asked. I would not have known to offer her that answer without her having asked the question.

A few weeks after he passed away, I received a hand-written sympathy card from Wendy. At the very end, she asked if I would provide a letter of recommendation for her so that she could continue to provide care to elderly veterans. Over my career, I have written and provided a number of references for various people. Wendy's letter of recommendation was my favorite to provide. She said she would give Dad the best care she could, and she did. She took her job seriously and with a sense of humor and only made promises she could keep. She immediately built trust and demonstrated the earning of that trust. I wrote the letter for her the same day I received her request. I felt a soft smile come across my face as I dropped it in the mailbox.

Stay alive, keep me alive.
(Sometimes we react in the truest possible way.)

Title Burn

The last car my mom owned was a 2005 Lincoln Town Car. It was a "pearl essence" color with a cream leather interior. My parents owned Lincoln cars long before Matthew McConaughey's sultry voice was used to help boost brand sales. We had a variety of Lincoln Town Cars over the years, or "boats," as my sister and I would refer to them. They were very large cars. The sedans of today, I would argue, are a mere third the size of the generation of Lincoln's from the 1970s and 1980s.

The first Town Car that I recall my mother driving was a gray "boat" with a maroon, velvety interior. It had a sunroof, which was a big deal at the time (or maybe just to my three-year-old self). There was a weirdly-shaped cream blob—a sticky blotch on the interior ceiling next to the sunroof's manual sliding door, courtesy of yours truly. It was planted there one hot, summer day by my vanilla soft serve ice cream cone. I had accidentally flailed it into the air while attempting to climb forward to the front seat from the back seat while my mom drove from the ice cream stop. This was before the law mandated wearing seatbelts, and I am certain I was not in a booster seat. *Squish*. "Uh-oh. Sorry, Mom!"

I remember the rides to preschool in that car, pick up from Kindergarten, and the rides to the Sunshine grocery store, where my mom would pay a penny so I could ride the mechanical horse at the front of the store. There was the stop at the MilkyWay ice cream bar too, of course. Eating ice cream cones in that car felt decadent—well, until the stain incident when I was no longer allowed to order cones. "You have to keep licking," my mom would instruct. The speed of ice cream melting always out-paced my lick-frequency and consumption speed. It was only later in life, probably when I was in college, that I reverted back to ordering cones. My mom was all too pleased to get rid of that car, upgrading it after several years because of the sunroof. It was not because of the ice cream stain; rather, the continual leaks after every rain shower or storm. Water would drip from the back left corner of the window and run toward the front driver's-side corner, cool water plopping directly on top of my mother's head, hair, and right shoulder before running down her back while she attempted to focus on the road. "Don't open the sunroof!" She would demand, after one of the many repairs for which my dad had taken the vehicle into service. Still, it leaked. It didn't matter the repair, if it rained, that sunroof leaked. As a result, Mom carried disdain for sunroofs until the day she died.

In later years, we had a tan "boat." It was just as large as my mom's gray one, but all tan. Tan exterior and interior with the same velvety textured seats. There was even a cigar smoke hole in the driver's seat, evidence that my dad smoked in the car, which he, of course, did not deny and which my sister and I were abruptly reminded of each time we entered the vehicle and smelled the lingering potent scent of cigar. I drove home from the Department of Motor Vehicles (DMV) with my dad in that tan car when I got my learner's permit at the age of fourteen.[1] I think the tan Lincoln was the vehicle we were driving when my sister and I coined the term "boat" for these cars. This one *truly* felt like a boat. It was as if with our growing older and taller, and these cars still feeling so big, made the cars seem that much larger.

Lincolns were not the only type of car my dad procured. I returned from the DMV after having taken the written exam in the tan boat, but it was our Ford station wagon, wood-paneled and with a heavy, long swinging back gate for a door, in which I learned to drive. To this day, I gratefully attribute my parallel parking skills to the wide-ass, long-ass Ford. Who needs a back-up camera? Who needs a side rear camera? I got this with the rearview mirror, side mirror, and looking over my shoulder move. Thank you, 1970s Ford.

Over the years, my mom drove a red Cadillac sedan and my dad drove a goldfish-bronze one. Those were cool cars. I recall enjoying driving the red "caddy" to high school when my parents would travel out of town, borrowing Mom's car, so that I could take a break from the tan "boat" or the Ford station wagon. I fully recognize and appreciate that I was a lucky kid to not only have a

[1] At the time, fourteen was the legal age in the state to get a learner's permit and start driving solo during certain hours of the day.

car to drive, but also to have a choice of vehicle from time to time.

There was also the sparkly blue convertible Oldsmobile with white leather seats that I drove my summer home after freshman year of college. I loved exiting my shift in the wee hours of the morning from Perkins (a popular midwestern diner), where I served "all-day breakfast platters," chicken-fried steak, and ice cream sundaes to locals and travelers before marching to that Oldsmobile. I would pull up on the small silver lever to the left of the steering wheel while I watched the roof mechanically fold back behind the back seat. I would clip my seat belt and look up at the night sky, taking in the crisp, starry night before jolting the gear shift to reverse and embracing the night's wind that surrounded me as I drove home. This was the same car I referred to as "the fast gray car, except it's blue" when I was little.

The "fast gray car" was my dad's convertible Jaguar, which he sold in the early 1990s. "Good riddance! That car is nothing but trouble," my mom frowned. She disliked the maintenance and upkeep of that Jaguar. To me, it was the coolest of cool cars, the one I adored riding in with my dad and sister on the way to the pool in the summers, feeling the warm summer breeze blow across my face while a yellow, red, and green beach ball stuck to my belly as I held it in my lap. It was the car my sister and I practiced leaping in and out of like we were the *Dukes of Hazzard*. It was the car that Dad rarely used—once or twice—to drop me off at school on a warm spring day.

On those rides, I asked him all sorts of questions over and over again about the car while I repeatedly opened and closed the tiny glove box, watching his hand fold over the center gear shift, which had interchangeable spherical ornaments you could swap in and out depending on your mood. My favorite was the ornament molded to that of a jaguar's head. So cool.

Over time, many years after my sister and I had moved away, my parents were finally in possession of only two cars. My dad had—you guessed it—the minivan, and my mom—you guessed it—the 2005 Lincoln Town Car.

As my parent's aged, it became apparent that they

predominantly used my dad's minivan to get around together. Mom did drive the Lincoln around town (fitting, since it was a Town Car) occasionally when heading to the church for a Tuesday morning meeting or to and from the nail salon. However, it mostly stayed parked in the garage. From Florida, Dad would call their handyman, Doug, in South Dakota to go "run the car" (Lincoln) for a bit, "Just to keep the thing working."

Even before Dad left Florida to return to South Dakota after Mom died, we had a heart-to-heart about the Lincoln. He understood that a decision needed to be made about that car. He came around: "I suppose there's not much use for it. I can't drive it." He had not been in the garage at the house for months, maybe years, and he certainly had not driven that car in more than a year.

"Dad, who actually owns the car? You? Or Mom? The Trust?" I sat criss-cross-applesauce on the carpet of the living room in Florida, a child looking up at my father, while he sat in his turquoise chair.

"Well, let's see," he pondered, "it could be your mother. It could be me…" He thought about it for minutes upon minutes before stating plainly, "Well, I don't know. What does the title say?"

"That's the thing, Dad. We need to get the title. Do you know where it would be?"

"Somewhere in your mother's files."

Oh, gawd.

I needed to understand how the car was officially titled, to whom it was titled, and I also needed the title in order to do anything with the vehicle—to sell or to donate or do anything with it aside from letting it sit and rot in my parents' garage.

Since my mom was a resident of Florida, and since she held multiple pieces of property (a condo plus a couple of bank accounts) in sole ownership, her estate had to go through Florida probate. This created a fourteen-month delay in my dad receiving property and funds they considered theirs as a married couple.

Going through Florida probate with my mom's estate generated attorney's fees, court processes, document signatures, notary coordination, copious amounts of (additional) paperwork, additional worry and headache for me, not to mention additional stress for my ailing father. All of which took place during the COVID pandemic. *And*, it was completely unnecessary. If only my mom had named additional owners for the Florida condominium and on multiple checking and savings accounts, all this could have been avoided. She held them as sole owner, which meant, no matter what her Will stated, no matter the law of the land that ownership transfers to a spouse, sole ownership of property (real estate, banking accounts, etc.) must go through the court system in order to actually get transferred to a spouse or the person named in the deceased's Will. This is important, and I think most people do not understand it. My mom didn't understand it. My sister tried to explain this to her many times. So did my dad. Although, after Mom died, it became readily apparent that Dad did not know, nor understand, how much Mom had kept in sole ownership. To his credit, neither did I. So, when I had to explain to him that he did not have access to certain accounts and that the condo was not yet in his name and could not simply be transferred to him (despite her Will and his being her spouse), his sunken figure sunk even further into his chair, and he grasped his forehead with a massive cringe, "*Why* did she do that?!"

"It's okay, Dad," I consoled. "We'll get it sorted out. It'll take time and work, and I'll help you."

I had just watched Dad lose the love of his life while continuing to struggle to breathe, so the last thing I wanted was more strain on him.

As if the shock and grief of losing Mom was not enough, or that figuring out my dad's care, keeping up with his bills and needs, and sorting through my parent's things just to understand the state of my parents' affairs was not enough, add probate. In hindsight, I learned a lot. I learned in the deep waters of COVID how to interview attorneys, how to get documents filed, how to convince a notary to make the trek to Lido Key from Bradenton on a Friday at 7:00 p.m. just so she could witness my dad sign documents she would notarize and so I could get the document filed to the attorney and court on time. I re-learned that having multi-colored file folders to keep things organized, easily recognizable, and easily accessible is a necessity. I learned and re-learned the importance of having a separate filing system for managing my mom's estate and managing my dad's affairs.

It is not that Mom did not want Dad to have these things—the property, the accounts—it is that she never imagined them not being in her possession or the actual transferring of them. She also never imagined her not being there—she could not see beyond her own mortality. Thinking, contemplating, and planning beyond her life was outside her desire and possibly beyond her capability. She simply could not imagine it. If I were to provide a single piece of advice to others, it would be to think beyond your own mortality, to imagine beyond it. I do not by any stretch mean to imply that this is easy. This is hard. This is hard, real stuff. I am still figuring it out. It can be done, and it can provide a manner of soul-searching, self-awareness, and human enlightenment. It will also provide a tremendous gift to those you love and who love you. I wish I could tell my mom this again and in this way.

So, after probate in Florida, if the Lincoln was owned by my dad and/or my mom as individuals, it would be the one remaining item of my parents' outside of a Trust. If that was the case, that meant it was important to get rid of it while Dad was still living. Mind you, the county and estate attorney confirmed that "It's not the end of the world if it is still in possession after his death. It just takes a 'simple' affidavit" to file at the court due to the value being below a certain threshold. I do not care how convincing an attorney, paralegal, or county administrator is, nor how much emphasis they place on the word "just" or "simple." What these professionals do not advise or mention is that filing a "simple affidavit" to the court and the 1-2-3-4-5-6-7-8-9-10+ steps in between and after are exactly not what you want to add to the heaps of tasks and actions you have to do following a loved one's death. Let alone while you are reeling from shock and grief, having just said goodbye to people who have known you your entire life. Not to mention, if you have just gone through probate in another state.

When we moved Dad back to South Dakota and got him settled, the initial A-number-one-and-two actions on the to-do list were to find the title to that 2005 Lincoln Town Car and get rid of the car. Of course, this after moving furniture to accommodate Dad's safe movement within the house, buying groceries, negotiating caregiver schedules, picking up prescriptions, checking on the Florida probate status, paying Dad's bills and working full-time.

The car title. My father's words, "Somewhere in your mother's files" played in my head like an audio tape on repeat. Hmm… the title. Angela and I spent hours searching. No, we spent *days* searching for that title. We were focused. We were adamant. In May of 2020, we were set on locating that dang title before Dad arrived at the house in South Dakota from Florida. We knew, we just knew, that once he arrived at the house, our focus would have to shift and there would be much more to juggle, that a fervent all-out search for a document would be harder to execute. Stuffed, and I mean stuffed, in one of the massive fire-proof file cabinets in the basement of the house was a file marked "Cars." The label was written in blue ink by my mom, that same blue ink I knew all too well from her recipe card file box. Surely the title would be in that folder, right? Nope. What about a tax file? Nope. Desk drawer of papers? Nope. Glove box in the Lincoln? Good idea! Nope. Ugh! The hunt continued. Angela and I spent so many brain waves trying to sleuth our way to locating that title. We did not find it during that spring of 2020.

The day came late that May when we implemented a new tactic: file a lost title form with the county and get a duplicate. Angela and I marched into the county administration building a couple days before heading back to Virginia that summer and got a new title printed.

The clerk at the county administration building smiled, "Where would you like the duplicate title mailed?"

"Ummm. Let's see," I looked at Angela. We nodded and responded in unison, "Virginia."

"I'm going to give you my address in Virginia," I continued.

Angela and I both knew that if the duplicate arrived at my dad's house, it would create a new wave of searching. It would be lost or shuffled in a large pile of other mail in his den, despite our efforts to leave organizational tools for him and the health aides. It was too important to risk losing this copy.

The duplicate title arrived at our home in Virginia about four days after we did from the near 1,300 mile drive from South Dakota. We slipped it into a clear plastic protector and placed it in the blue "Lincoln Town Car" hanging folder in the file box for Dad's paperwork. We added "Lincoln title" to our South Dakota packing list as we filed it so we would be sure to remember to bring it with us on our next trip to Dad.

Fortunately, that 2005 Lincoln was officially owned (as in how it was titled) by Mom *and* Dad. (It should have been Mom *or* Dad, which would have made selling, disposing, or donating it easier. What I mean is that it would not have required proving my mother was deceased nor having to file more paperwork. Having to state over and over again that she was deceased and submitting death certificates over and over again is not a comforting activity after the death of a loved one. Have I mentioned paperwork yet?) It meant that, given the approximate value of said property—under $5,000—and with Dad's agreement, I could offload the vehicle with one signature, Mom's death certificate, and the title, and avoid the entire post-mortem, attorney, affidavit, delay mess.

We dissected the priorities at the time and adjusted our timeline too. New plan: we still would get the Lincoln sold or donated as soon as possible while also juggling many other priorities (many of which became a higher priority), but it would have to be at a later date when back in South Dakota with Dad and before he passed away.

So, that is what we did. After loads of other priorities attended to and during our last trip to South Dakota while Dad was still living, we put effort—once again—into offloading the Lincoln Town Car.

That trip, it became even more apparent to Angela and me, given the car's current state, we would be lucky *if* someone would take it. It would be best to donate the car and then Dad could get a tax deduction. I had another heart-to-heart with him, and he thought donating the car was a great option given the potential value of the fifteen year-old "boat." I had to explain to him the current state of the vehicle, that we were not sure we could get it started, that the tires were so deflated, we were trouble-shooting how to get them jacked up and inflated enough so that we could roll it out of the garage to the driveway for potentially more work just to get the thing running. Thankfully, Dad was on board for the donation.

Angela carried the investigative baton for identifying the best and most appropriate donation entity, as well as figuring out how to get the "boat" out of the garage. That meant checking the contents of the car, sifting through the trunk, and bringing to my attention belongings of my mom's that I had forgotten about. Like the Powerbar ball cap that I had sweat in while rowing in college and later had gifted to Mom. She was not one to wear a ball cap, so I recall being surprised when she was pleased to take it from me and surprised more so when she told me she would "sport it" after going to the gym. "I like to wear it after AquaChi class," she had told me on the phone in 2019. "You know, to cover my wet hair!" So, on that particular day in 2021, there it was. The ball cap peaked out of her gym duffle in the trunk of the Lincoln. "Awe, Mom." I took a deep breath as Angela showed me the contents of the trunk that afternoon. On another morning, I found Angela laying on the filthy garage floor alongside the passenger side of the car, working to inflate the tires with a portable pump. *Geez.*

Then, on another sunny, hot day, we found the *original* car title. What?! It was stashed in a random pile of papers, somewhere between my 1st grade artwork, my uncle's funeral program, and my parents' 1982 tax accountant receipt.

"Oh my gosh, I found it! I found it!" Angela wailed while leaping up the stairs to the main level of the house.

"You did? You did! You did!" I exclaimed.

We hugged a familiar we-just-figured-something-out-found-a-missing-link type hug we had only recently learned was in our treasure chest of hugs.

Dad looked up from his book as I ran in to share the news. “Well, that is great, honey,” he cheered.

A day or two later, Angela told me confidently, “I’ve got it.” She marched into the dining room, where I was sitting on one of the needlepoint dining chairs (not to be confused with the needlepoint chairs from the Florida condo—this dining table set was complete with eight of its own multi-colored needlepoint chairs). I had just wrapped up a virtual meeting for work, pulling the headset from my ears.

“Make-A-Wish is going to take the car.”

“Woah, that’s great,” I stuttered. “When?”

“Well, we have to submit the title along with the donation form and your mom’s death certificate as a package, and then some guy will call to come retrieve the car.”

“Wow. Okay, okay, great.”

Phew. (Or so we both thought.)

Angela filled out the form. I pulled Mom’s death certificate from our organized, multi-colored file bin created after Mom died and handed it to Angela while she held the original car title to scan and add to the electronic car-donation package. Then, I took the Make-A-Wish form to Dad for his signature.

“Thank you, honey,” Dad scribbled his signature.

“You’re welcome, Dad. We love you.” My left hand grazed his skinny shoulder.

Package ready. Package complete.

The next week, the day arrived: donation day. A blond-haired guy with a flatbed trailer rolled up the street and parked alongside the curb, *way* too close to the yellow fire hydrant that was on the corner of the yard, but I was not about to warn him. Nothing was going to get in the way of getting this car gone. Dad was living and the final remaining non-trust-owned piece of property was going to be offloaded—donated. I could barely breathe. I could barely watch from my childhood bedroom window while Angela greeted the lanky man in dirt-stained jeans and handed him the keys. I had decided to let Angela continue to carry this baton all the way across the finish line, which she lovingly agreed to do without pause. "A+ partner," as Michael from *Love on the Spectrum* (the Australia version) says.

A 2005 Lincoln Town Car weighs roughly forty-six hundred pounds. That is curb weight. That is just shy of the low-end weight of an African elephant, and right in range of a sailboat weight. It's half the weight of a speed boat and not even close to the weight it felt on my mind and body leading into getting rid of it and watching it ride away on that man's flatbed trailer.

Angela and I sat stunned that evening as bugs flitted in the air and we stared at the backyard.

"Is the Lincoln really out of the garage and donated?" I asked her.

"Yes, my sweet. It sure is." Angela raised her glass of rosé and clinked it to mine.

The next day, we received an email from Make-A-Wish, telling us that they did not have the correct title to the car and therefore the donation was not yet complete. What? Seriously! What the hell? What the actual…?

Angela received a call from the blond-haired guy that same day.

"I need the correct title in order to officially receive this car," he told her.

"Well, we had to get a duplicate title," she explained. "I guess that is what you need? I have it and you can come get it from me this afternoon."

I was already filtering through the file box, my papercut fingers reaching the blue folder. I pulled out the duplicate title and handed it to Angela. She was already off the phone.

"He's stopping by later today."

When he arrived that afternoon around four o'clock, it was supposed to be a swap of the titles, but he forgot to bring the original title to return to us. While he needed the "correct title," meaning the most recently-issued title to the car, we needed the original title in order to destroy it. We could not have a car title in my parents' names floating out there in the universe. (Hello, fraud.)

Angela instructed, "Please, you need to bring it back to us."

He was not willing to make another trip.

"Well, you need to destroy it, and I need proof that you have done so."

He agreed.

Later that evening, his number popped up on her phone.

"Hello. I have the original title here. I can burn it for you and text you a video."

Angela held her hand over her phone speaker and told me his plan. "Are you okay with that?"

"Uh—I guess so? Yeah, yes? Yes." I decided.

She removed her hand from the speaker and stated back to him, "Yes, please burn it and text me. Thank you."

She hung up the phone and we stared at each other.

A few moments later, *ping*! A new text message. It was a video. We both stared at her phone screen as a video of a man's hand held the original title to the 2005 Lincoln Town Car and his other hand scrolled a Bic lighter and burned the paper. We watched the entire paper go up in flames, burning. He had done it. That Make-A-Wish-car-pick-up guy followed through with a very strange action.

It's hard to imagine. It's hard to believe. It was real. My mom's words once again came out of my mouth, and I heard my voice,

"You cannot make this up." Then I added, "That's some crazy shit."

She could not see beyond her own mortality.
(Now, I try to.)

Gravity

One of my favorite pictures of my sister and me is a black and white photograph from our childhood of the two of us sitting in Dad's red, leather winged-back chair. I am three years old, and my sister is six. We are both wearing white tights, patent leather shoes, and dresses. My feet barely reach the edge of the seat, and my white-blond hair is wispy. My mouth is sealed shut, upper lip and lower lip pressed together, almost like a duck face. My cheeks tell you that I am happy, and my eyes show you that the flash of my dad's camera is momentarily too bright for me. My sister's brown hair is in a Dorothy Hammel-style bowl cut, and she is smiling a wide, beautiful smile.

There is more than one photo of the two of us sitting in that big chair; there is one from even earlier when I was just a baby in red pajamas and laid across my sister's small lap. And there is one from when I was a toddler, probably around a year old and my sister four. Sitting in Dad's red chair felt special and fun, and while I cannot confirm this, I am pretty sure it was an annual photo my dad would capture of us when we were young. The black and white one from when I was three is my favorite.

At the beginning of July 2021, Molly, Allison, and Bruce sat in a semi-circle facing me. We were in the corner of the living room, where I had shifted two of the needlepoint benches and one of the needlepoint chairs so that they could join me for a meeting about Dad's health decline and discuss transitioning him to palliative and hospice care. I sat in Dad's red leather winged-back chair. They each looked at me with patient, kind eyes, as a clipboard of hospice paperwork rested on my lap. They answered all of my many questions, explained the details of the impending care, the benefits, what would change, what would remain the same, and what my responsibilities would be, including in administering medicines. It was my second course in learning what is involved in hospice care. The first was in Florida with Mom just fifteen months prior. Because hospice care is regulated by state laws, there are differences in what is included in hospice and what ends up being the responsibility of the family healthcare surrogate. For instance, in South Dakota, there was not a hospice nurse with Dad 24/7. The official hospice nurse would stop in for health checks and visits two to three times per week and was on call for anything occurring in the middle of the night or outside the nurse visit window. The remainder of hours of care would continue to be covered by the health aides and family (me and Angela).

As Dad's healthcare surrogate and power of attorney, the time had come for me to finalize the paperwork on his behalf so that he could gain access to hospice care and resources he desperately needed. The evening before, it had become evident that he was too weak to move from the bedroom to the den each day and that he no longer could "use the facilities," his reference phrase for the bathroom. He desperately needed a hospice bed in his room for comfort and to aid his breathing since sitting up was important, and he no longer had the ability or strength in his abdomen to hold himself up in a chair.

I read the small print on the paperwork three times. Then one more time for good measure.

In those very moments signing that paperwork, the weight of the moment was not lost on me as I sat in that red leather chair. *This is Dad's chair*. I so rarely sat in it and yet somehow, there I was. I immediately remembered those many years prior when I was too small to fill the seat myself, my legs dangling off the edge or barely reaching the edge of the seat. On this day, I sat in the chair myself, and this time, my feet were squarely on the floor. It is the type of moment when the force of gravity suddenly enters the spotlight.

Instantly, the full weight of the moment pressed through my body, grounding my feet firmly on the living room floor. I shrank, shrank, shrank into a miniature version of my three-year-old self, just like Alice shrunk in the chair in Wonderland.

Then, as if snapped back into the present day, I noticed the pen in my hand was filled with black ink. "Is it okay to complete these with black ink?"

I had learned in the past year that certain documents, depending on the type of document and state law, require blue ink and some black ink. I was not able to follow the pattern for such requirements but had learned to ask the question for fear of having to redo important paperwork.

"Yes, black ink is just fine." Molly, the head of the hospice team, assured me.

I took a breath (barely a breath) while my hand rested on the clipboard, replaying the wishes Dad had expressed to me for his care, the prior days' significant decline in health, and increase in his needs. Comfort care was now necessary. With resolution in his instructions and confidence in my ability to serve in this capacity for him, I scribbled the pattern of my signature on the line.

Ninety minutes later, I met Nathan from the hospice organization in the driveway. He arrived with a truck full of hospice equipment. Nathan had stayed late at work that evening when he learned that it was this doctor, my dad, who needed the hospice equipment. He knew Dad as the physician who took such great care of other elderly patients in the community. Nathan set up all the equipment that evening: a hospice bed, over-the-bed tray for food, drink, and medications, bed pan, and extra oxygen tank for emergencies. We had received the wheelchair, but Angela and I both knew that was not going to be of use. Dad was no longer able to sit in any chair.

The first time we put the railings up on the bed and hit the automated button to show Dad how we could get him sitting up in bed, he said, "Slick. That's slick."

"Hey, this is comfy!" It was the immediate thing Dad said to me after his first night sleeping in the hospice bed. Angela and I witnessed the relief and almost surge of energy he had.

Countless moments have felt crazy like that—feeling an absurd, newfound gravitational pull and force that comes into sharp focus. On that day when I signed Dad's hospice paperwork, I no longer was the small child looking at the flash on my dad's camera from that big chair. I no longer was the child dancing through the living room while my dad read his newspapers and books from that red chair. I was the one serving in his capacity, for him. And I was sitting in his chair. It wasn't my plan. I simply looked for a place to have a conversation with those three hospice team members and found myself there in his chair. It was wild to think about it. And not. In so doing, I set in motion his wishes—what he needed for care in his final days. And I did it from his chair.

I took a breath (barely a breath)...

Is There Breakfast Included?

"It's time." I said. "I think it's time."

I sat on the quartzite stones that originally hailed as pavers from the city's streets in the late 1800s and that were put in the backyard of my childhood home (probably in the 1940s when the house was built). The stones created a three-step "amphitheater" semicircle in the grass that I imagined was a giant swimming pool when my four-year-old self would play outside. On this day in July 2021, it was no longer the giant swimming pool of my imagination, cooling my body. It was a simple place to sit, crouched on a single quartzite stone with my knees to my chest, my head facing the ground as if preparing for a tornado to arrive. The sun was baking me once again, as was so common for the phone conversations with my sister in the days and weeks prior. Sweat dripped slowly down my cheeks, and I ignored the itch they created.

From our many conversations during the weeks leading in, it became apparent that my sister wanted me to tell her when to come visit Dad. When it was "right" for her to decide to make the trip from Florida to come see him. This was something I did not think I could do. How could I know when was the right time for her? I knew that for me, I needed to be there. I wanted to be there. Shouldn't she have a sense of when she would need to come? Shouldn't she have an idea of when she wanted to come? I was overwhelmed with managing so many things, so many tangible, logistical and crucial details, along with the tremendous emotion that was buried so deep inside me that I could not recognize at the time. All I could do was arm her with information, data, and facts of the day-to-day situation: how Dad was feeling, what he was saying, what the caregivers and nurses were saying, how his sleep pattern was changing, what he was eating, what he was not eating. I did not have the capacity to take on managing her decisions about the situation and when to arrive to see Dad. Yet, I surely wanted to be helpful to her. And I knew I had to put Dad first. I wanted to put him first. He was failing, he was ailing. And he was valiantly fending off death.

Dad had been explicit and intentional with me about my sister visiting. It was on an evening before hospice started and before the evening caretaker arrived. I was sitting closely next to him in the den, working out a word puzzle from a book of puzzles my sister had sent him for Father's Day that year. He turned to me, his eyes piercing directly into mine. "Listen to me," he said. "Your sister is welcome to come…" He went on to instruct me that in no way did he want his care disrupted.

His instructions burned into my memory with a scalding branding iron. They formed next to the memory tattoo from my mom's final days in hospice care when my sister's overwhelm, discord, and outward disruption came into focus once again. It felt raw and real all over again.

"Yes, Dad. Of course. I understand." I quietly returned his gaze.

He and I did not speak directly of the impact she had had on him, our mom, and Angela and me (not to mention the hospice staff) when Mom was sick and dying, but I saw it in him just like I saw the sadness when he learned his grandson would not be coming to see him for a final visit.

When it came time for my sister to fly in to see our dad for the last time that July 2021, days before he passed away, she told me that her daughters would be joining her. Her son, my parents' first grandchild and my father's namesake, would not be making the trip. From my sister's perspective, since my nephew was seventeen and almost a legal adult, the decision whether to visit Dad was up to him.

Her words hit me flatly: "It's his decision. He's nearly an adult."

"You mean he's not coming?" I asked, confused.

"He's an adult. It's up to him."

It was so clear to her. It was perplexing to me.

I was the one who had to tell Dad. A bounce of energy came over him when he learned my sister would be arriving a couple days later with his granddaughters. He asked about his grandson. "He will be coming, too?"

"Uh… No. No, Dad. She said it will just be her and the girls." I stuttered.

A wave of disappointment washed over him. It was unspoken yet apparent. I held his hand then saw the brilliant leap from disappointment shift to knowing acceptance. I believe it was a leap to acceptance only an expert clinician such as Dad could make. In those moments, he knew he would not see his grandson ever again, and while disappointed, he accepted it.

"He probably has work." Dad resigned and turned his head to look out the window where I had opened the draperies to let in some sunlight.

"I think so, Dad." I pivoted, "It will be great to see the girls!"

The decision for my nephew not to visit Dad one last time is one I really tried to understand. My sister's decision to make it completely about his choice as a near legal adult is something I really tried to understand. I still try to understand. While I tried so hard not to place judgment, I know that I did, that I have. They were not the decisions I would have made. At the same time, I recognize they were not mine to make. Everyone has a choice. Everyone makes decisions. Everyone makes *different* decisions. There are particular reasons and unique feelings that cause them to make different decisions. I could not see it then, I could not understand it then. I am closer to understanding now. I can see it now.

I called my sister to go over details. "We'll arrange a hotel and rental car for you and the girls. Dad said he will pay for it."

It may sound odd that they would stay at a hotel when my parents' home was large, but it really was not strange at all. Besides the overstuffing of the house my parents had done with furniture, art, and collectibles (and junk), and the lack of beds in the other bedrooms, I do not think there would have been a place large enough to house all the energy that would be together under one roof with all of us: energy stemming from the variety of strong personalities—Dad, Angela, me, the caregivers, the nurses coming and going, my sister, and my two young nieces. Plus, the very circumstance itself offered an assured intensity. Their staying at the house certainly was not the way to respect Dad's desire and instruction to keep his care under his and my control, as his healthcare surrogate. Their staying at a hotel was the best solution on all fronts: my sister and nieces would have a quiet place to stay, where they could take a break between coming to visit Dad, and his care and routine would stay on course.

"I have made the reservation for you and the girls at the hotel," I informed my sister. "It's a suite, so you'll have space for the three of you. We have a car reserved too. I will text you the reservation codes and details for you."

"Is there breakfast included?"

I nearly dropped the phone. I must have stayed silent for an extra few minutes as her question slapped me across the face in slow motion.

The sound waves of her voice bounced off my ear drum, "Well, that is important for me to know! Breakfast would be really helpful."

Really? Seriously?! Of course, of course, because all this—all of this life-transforming stuff, Dad is dying —all of this is about making things helpful for you! Thoughts rocketed through my brain. *This is crazy!* I was dumbfounded.

"Um, I'm not sure. There is a pool." Ugh. I held my composure.

I did not get it. I still do not completely get it. Maybe it hit me so crassly because of the heightened state of the situation. Maybe it was simply an example of two people operating on completely different planes. My days and nights were focused and filled with so many other significant, important details. My sister was essentially a single parent with a son and two young daughters to raise, so having breakfast included in a hotel reservation was important to her. I can imagine that. I can imagine a detail like that serving as a particular need. I can get there. Just like I imagined a large swimming pool instead of the lawn in our backyard as a four-year-old, I can imagine that having breakfast included in a hotel reservation may be valuable to know and important to have. I just had trouble imagining it in those particular life-is-about-to-change and my-heart-is-breaking-again moments in the summer of 2021.

It was such an insignificant and unimportant detail to me that July. Her response bemused me. It felt other-worldly. I think breakfast being included will forever be an insignificant detail to me. With everything that happened, how could it not be?

The silent screaming in my head gave way to the reminder that my sister and I are two very different individuals. We are sisters, I love her, and we experience the world oh-so-differently. It is only now, much later, that I can come to that acceptance. I am slower to make the leap than Dad.

It turned out that breakfast indeed was included. *Phew!* My sister played music on the piano each of the days she and the girls were in town and spent a couple times a day visiting with Dad. One afternoon while he slept and the caregiver stayed with him, Angela and I took a break to join my sister and our nieces at Grille26, a neighborhood restaurant for lunch. It was nice to get some time with them away from the house.

A few days later, their visit rounded out with Dad's memorial dinner. The five of us sat down at the nicest steak restaurant in town that Friday after he died to honor him the way he wanted: we went out and enjoyed steak together.

I held his hand then saw the brilliant leap
from disappointment shift to knowing acceptance.
(A leap from disappointment to acceptance feels far.)

Sara and Stacy

On March 11, 2020, Angela and I were walking in the wee hours of the morning. We were attempting to maintain our routine of starting the day with an early morning walk while trying to escape the exceptional fatigue and sleeplessness of the previous night. We felt the thick humid air from the Gulf of Mexico brush across our faces as we relied on movement to carry us forward from the night before: from watching my mother die, consoling my father, and watching the morgue personnel take her body away.

We walked past the rows of condominium buildings, big and small, past the small, local hotels and motels of Lido Key. A tiny black lizard scurried past my feet. We walked.

Our destination was Starbucks on Saint Armand's Circle, roughly a mile away. Coffee was in order. Caffeine—some semblance of routine and warm liquid to help bring about the day was in need.

As our feet strode step by step, suddenly and nearly out of nowhere, an older gentleman walked toward us. He was walking a dog. As they neared us, the tan and white cocker spaniel seemed to zoom in on me, trotting right up to me. Her big black eyes stared into me, as she leaned heavily on my legs.

"Her name is Sara," the man with thick-framed glasses told us. "She loves everyone."

His words were a blur as I received the unexpected and welcome furry hug. The immediacy of comfort offered by this creature was palpable. Her large, round eyes and soft but heavy lean, along with her widely spread lips of a dog's smile bore into me, telling me she knew the raw pain of my heart. She was utterly present with the state of my being, and she offered me the knowledge she held: of knowing my soul in the aftermath of loss.

Just as suddenly as they arrived, this pair departed. Sara popped up and straightened her posture while her human said, "We better be on our way. Have a nice day." And this sweet encounter ended. I turned and watched them head down the sidewalk past us, fading into the darkness. My right hand grabbed my heart as I watched them become smaller, smaller, smaller.

It was along this very path that my mother loved to take her early morning walks.

"I have to go pick up the paper," she would tell me. "It feels so good to do my morning walk," she would say. "Oh, this morning?! (this intro said as an exclamation and a question, anticipating my asking her what happened that morning), I saw the sweetest dog out on my walk. You know, I really miss having a dog."

Breath.

"And I just love seeing these dogs!"

It was these early morning walks of hers that seemed to become fewer and farther between in the months leading up to her lymphoma diagnosis and that ceased completely during her final eight weeks due to severe weakness from cancer and cancer treatment.

As these flashes of memory appeared to me about my mom's morning walks and beloved encounters with dogs, I felt the weight of my shallow breath, "Sara, thank you. I will remember you."

Fast forward to July 8, 2021, and it is once again the wee hours of the morning. On this day, Angela and I were sitting at the round, glass kitchen table of my childhood while a tall and lean woman with dark hair methodically filtered through my father's copious amounts of pills and medications.

She wore pristine emerald green scrubs and had dark, short hair in the style my mother would have liked. Her large, dark eyes were perfectly round. She was patient and quietly professional. She stood in front of the flat electric stovetop, using it as an extended countertop, as I had so often done, for her paperwork. She organized the pill bottles and medical packs, proceeding with what was a required procedure: to remove and dispose of the hospice medical substances. Her quiet presence faded into the framing of the room, and she was very present with us all at the same time. She had arrived quickly and quietly from the hospice service in order to pronounce my father.

"My name is Stacy," she said to me as she arrived and showed me her credentials. From the moment I welcomed her into the house, to the moment she held my father's wrist and listened for his heartbeat, to the moments she stood in the kitchen with us, she offered an immediate and sure comfort. Her voice was calm and soft, and her confident care was a gentle hug.

She navigated with grace the awkward, difficult, and very human nature of the circumstances, and I knew she was someone doing the job she was meant to be doing. She demonstrated the nursing qualities I had heard my surgeon father describe about his favorite nurses with whom he scrubbed in over the years.

"She anticipates and knows. She is there and out of the way when needed," he would say. "She understands her role and plays it beautifully. That is what is needed. That is what I need."

As I held the front door open for her to depart that dark morning, she looked at me with her large round eyes and the corners of her mouth lifted with a graceful smile, with a knowledge she held of knowing my soul in the aftermath of loss.

My right hand grabbed my heart as I watched her fade into the darkness of the long driveway becoming smaller, smaller, smaller.

"Stacy," I said, feeling the weight of my shallow breath. "Thank you. I will remember you."

It was only days later that I realized both of these individuals not only entered my life and created profound moments, but they also did so *during* profound moments. They had both carried significance by their manner of showing up.

I don't know why these two individuals showed up as they did, and I don't know why they showed up how they did, offering the same qualities of comfort and as representative connections to each of my parents. I don't know why they arrived as I needed.

But I do know, it felt bewildering in a this-is-utterly-awful-too-good-too-be-true sort of way.

My right hand grabbed my heart…

Keep Moving. Keep Doing.

After my mom died, my boss told me, "Take the time you need." The words were there, but the sentiment felt empty. How would I know what that is? Plus, the bereavement policy offered five days—five mere days to grieve a loved one and pack up a life. How odd. How entirely insufficient. Of course, coupled with vacation days, I could certainly cobble together more time away. Yet the culture of work I knew up until then did not support that notion. The unspoken understanding that forms within corporate climates is one of attending to work always so that you do not suffer the ramifications of lost promotional opportunities, lost recognition, or lost presence at work. Basically, the consequences of a lost career. We were on the cusp of COVID impacts to daily life, and everything work-related ended up continuing virtually. There was not an office to physically go to nor from which to remove myself. So… keep moving. Keep doing. I used the bereavement time and then hopped straight back to work, joining virtual meetings, juggling a full load managing a portfolio while triaging paperwork of my parents, caring for my dad, managing his life, and figuring out next steps.

After Sharon died, there was no bereavement left to take. The morning Sharon's husband called to let us know she had succumbed, we were standing outside the United States Postal Office in our neighborhood, walking Charlie. Ninety minutes later, I was back on a WebEx.

After my dad died, Angela and I were once again out walking Charlie for a morning walk, stunned from the lack of sleep. I staggered down the sidewalk. "Well, I guess I will go to work." My sister and I had spoken of it earlier, in the wee hours following Dad's passing while we sat at the kitchen table and drank tea before she headed back to her hotel.

"How are you going to handle work?" she asked me while I aimlessly swirled a tea bag in hot water.

"I don't know," I admitted.

We went on to contemplate the juggling of when to take time away from work. The result? We both pressed forward with work that day and the next.

In taking care of Dad and managing his affairs between March of 2020 and July of 2021, I had come to learn so much about oxygen, air, and breathing. Dad could not breathe on his own. I learned how cannulas work, how best to carefully drape them over my father and rest them on his ears while the prongs were inserted in his nostrils. I learned about the strength of various oxygen machines, how much oxygen he required and why oxygen tanks would not work for him for day-to-day use. The surge of oxygen he required each minute made it such that utilizing oxygen tanks was not a realistic option from hour to hour, minute to minute. Tanks only came into play as an emergency backup in the case of a power outage. But that too, had a timeline.

"At the rate your dad needs the oxygen, a tank will run out in one to two hours," the medical equipment oxygen specialist explained to me. That was the reason we kept two full tanks on hand, one in Dad's den and one in his bedroom for emergency backup. It was also why I became well-versed in whole house power generators. In the early summer of 2020, I did research and had several conversations with power generator companies in order to identify and purchase a power generator for Dad. He demanded one be installed at his house. He was increasingly on edge and terribly anxious until that generator was installed. I could not blame him—he could not breathe. All it would take was a single large thunderstorm, which was common in the Midwest summers, to take out a power line and remove the oxygen he required to live. He knew it. I knew it. I researched, ordered, and got Dad's whole house generator installed within a matter of two weeks.

Dad needed the electric oxygen machines that pulsed oxygen continuously into his lungs. The large stationary machines allowed for the ranges of capacity he increasingly required. The smaller, battery-operated mobile oxygen machines became increasingly insufficient with the passing of weeks and months contributing to his decreasing mobility. The smaller, rolling oxygen machine that

Dad could use to move from one room to another in the house (the den to the bathroom, or between the den and the bedroom twice per day) only allowed for a certain level of oxygen flow to his lungs, a maximum that was mid-range on the larger immobile machines. When it came time to move Dad, it was a swift orchestration of both preparation and movement to safely ensure continued oxygen flow to his lungs throughout the process:

- Go to the room of destination, plug in, and roll the heavy stationary machine into position (next to Dad's bed in the bedroom or next to his chair in the den).
- Roll the heavy, stationary machine in room of departure out of the way. Move the smaller mobile machine close to Dad, turn it on (and all the way up to the highest level of oxygen pulsing).
- Engage in an elegant and swift exchange of cannulas:
- Cannula 1 was attached to the larger immobile oxygen machine which Dad was using from his chair or bed to remain stable.
- Cannula 2 was attached to the smaller mobile oxygen machine.
- Hold Cannula 2 close to Dad's face, remove Cannula 1 while helping to gently and swiftly position Cannula 2 to his nostrils.
- Wait for "It's good" from Dad to confirm, completely breathless upon Cannula 2 being positioned.
- Turn off the departure room's large oxygen machine.
- Assist Dad in standing and beginning to shuffle to the destination room.
- Upon reaching the bed or chair and getting him seated, reverse the order of the sequence, providing Dad with an oxygen lifeline from the large machine resident in the destination room.

- Keep moving.
- Keep doing.

The process represented the necessity to keep moving and to keep doing in order to keep oxygen and air flowing. To keep him breathing.

Just like the need to ensure Dad's flow of oxygen, I kept moving. I kept doing. I had to keep moving. I had to keep doing. To me, there was no alternative, no other air. In fact, it was not even a consideration. Plus, there was so much to do! It was my own survival tactic. I know that now. The consistent, barely audible voice inside me prodded me along: *Keep moving, keep doing. Do not stop.* It went on like the phrases while playing the game Monopoly: "Do not pass Go. Do not collect two hundred dollars." Then, the hard smack: *If you stop, you may not ever start again. How could you? So keep going. Keep moving, keep doing.* After all, as physics teaches us, "an object in motion tends to stay in motion." It played over and over and over again, barely a whisper, yet an unrelenting encouragement.

There was no shred of my being that believed everything would be okay in the end. I was lost in a deep forest, wandering in a new world, in my new life. It was all entirely foreign, and I did not understand it. If I just kept moving, if I just kept doing, maybe I would understand? The moving and the doing offered a semblance of grounding I so desperately needed.

So, even though it seemed ridiculous to immediately go back to work after Mom died, I kept working. I kept moving. I kept doing. After Sharon died, I hopped on a virtual meeting. I kept moving. I kept doing. After Dad died, I joined a meeting via phone. I kept moving. I kept doing.

I was not denying the new reality I was experiencing; rather, I was denying that everything would somehow be okay. I desperately wanted to believe Shawn Mullins when he sang "Lullaby," but I could not. I could not believe that everything would be alright. I was denying that things *could* be alright in the end. That I would be alright in the end. Yet somehow that soundtrack in my mind that was urging me along must have been evidence that I had the capacity to believe that one day *everything would be alright*. That one day I would be okay. That a deeper wisdom from experience would reveal itself. That I would come to understand it all.

If I just kept moving, if I just kept doing,
maybe I would understand?
(I am grasping for air that is not there,
and all I can think of is my dad.)

Doug

"Who is Doug, Mom?"

I was sitting next to Mom in my parents' den. We were so close to one another that my left leg pressed into her. The three-seat couch was filled with a stack of blankets to my right and books to my mom's left, so what remained was a much smaller section of the furniture available for us to sit next to one another. The tray table in front of us was full. There was a ramekin of blueberries from my mom's breakfast that she had not yet "gotten around to eating," a placemat with a photo from Mackinac Island, half a dozen three by three inch papers of word scrambles from the newspaper she and Dad had been working on, her trusty blue ink pen, and a stack of stationary cards about to fall over intended for correspondence she planned to write that day.

My dad sat across the small room in yet another wingback chair, reading from the day's Wall Street Journal. The TV had been blaring the local news and I conveniently muted it upon my arrival.

Mom had just mentioned a guy named Doug to Dad, suggesting something with reference to the vents in their bedroom.

I leaned over her shoulder as she brought up Doug's contact on her phone.

"Oh, it's Doug. You know Doug!"

"Mom, I don't think I've ever met Doug. Who is he?"

"It's Doug!" My dad interjected, barely looking up from the newspaper.

"Yes, Doug," my mom continued. "He is so handy. He helps us out with all sorts of things. The house, the car. He is very handy."

"Ah, okay. Is this the same Doug you call from Florida to check on the house and the car?"

Mom nodded.

"I'd like to meet him one day. Can I have his contact information?"

"Sure." My mom was getting ready to write down Doug's information on a scrap of paper next to one of the word scrambles.

"May I see your phone, Mom?"

"Sure!"

I shared Doug's contact information with myself right then and there, texting it directly to my phone.

It was June of 2019—nine short months before Mom died. I had surprised my parents with a visit since my mom was recuperating from knee surgery. That morning, we were awaiting the arrival of her physical therapist, who she was all too eager to introduce me to and even more excited to show me her physical therapy exercises.

"You have got to see what she is having me do!" Mom exclaimed proudly. "And, I can do it from home!" She was extra impressed that her physical therapist came to the house for sessions following surgery.

"That's really great, Mom! I'm looking forward to meeting her."

Her therapist arrived and we stood in the front entry of the house to greet her. She was tall and lean with a calming smile. It was clear to me that my mom was completely enamored and perhaps more excited for the attentiveness the physical therapy session would grant her than the actual exercises.

I had no clue that eleven months later, I would be standing in that same entryway, shaking Doug's hand because the ivy had grown out of control, up onto the front of the house and the retaining wall. Angela and I were about to move Dad back to the house from Florida.

Doug met me at the house on a Monday that May of 2020, the day before Dad was scheduled to arrive at the house. He was tall and lean with a calming smile just like Mom's physical therapist. It was a friendly-to-the-core type of interaction that I came to find would always be the case with Doug.

"Oh geez, ya know, I'm so sorry to hear about your mom," Doug said in his northern midwestern accent where 'o's are really *long* 'o's.

Dad had called Doug from Florida and let him know about Mom's passing.

"Thank you, Doug. It all really happened so fast," I managed.

"Oh geez, ya know, it sure did. Your parents just left for Florida last October!"

"Yes, that's right." I gave him a warm smile. "Dad will be back here tomorrow, so we'll get him settled. I'm wondering if you could help us with the ivy on the front of the house and the wall? It has really taken over. Dad mentioned you could remove it."

"Oh yeah, sure. I'll get that done this week."

"Perfect. Thanks so much, Doug."

It turns out that Doug had helped my parents with so many things around the house. He knew his way around. And, he was reliable. "Handy," Mom had said.

It was this same Doug who delivered that damn van back to Chrysler. It was Doug who brought his "dump trailer" over so many times to fill with junk and trash we had found in the house. It was Doug who helped Angela and me lug dozens of heavy cardboard boxes filled with family photographs up from the basement so we could sort through them. (More on that later.) And it was Doug who installed the new back porch storm door on the morning Dad died. It was around ten o'clock in the morning, and I heard a newly familiar voice from outside the dining room.

"Oh my gosh, it's Doug!" I immediately spouted out loud, surprised by my own forgetfulness. He was scheduled to come over and install the door that morning. It did not require conversation. Doug had the supplies and knew what to do. We had talked about it a week prior, before Doug had gone "out campin'" with his family for a few days. Yet, I opened the door, "Good morning, Doug. Thank you."

"Good mornin'! Sure thing. I should have this done right quick."

I could not do it. I could not speak the words: "By the way, Doug, Dad died early this morning."

I chose not to utter them—I did not have the words, and I did not have the heart to tell Doug. On *that* morning.

This was not atypical for me. I had to find the gumption, the willpower, and the words first. It was almost like a new preparation I had to exercise every time and with every person I encountered.

It is one thing to write a text notifying a few close people that a loved one has died, that Mom died, that Sharon died, that Dad died. It is a completely different action to speak the words, to actually say them out loud, put them into the world, and convey the raw truth. I was not good at that. In fact, in general, I just did not do it.

After Mom died in 2020, Angela and I would see neighbors and friends once we were back in Virginia, who I typically and thoroughly enjoy seeing while out for a walk. Now, I dreaded it.

"Oh, it's _____" (insert name of friend, neighbor or friendly acquaintance here), I would say under my breath.

"Are you going to tell her about your mom?" Angela asked me on one of the many such occasions as we approached said person.

"Um… no. I don't know how."

Then, there would be a typical friendly exchange, my answering, "doing well," or "just fine," in short spurts, completely ignoring the weight of what actually was going on in my life at the time.

And so it went so many times.

The words would not come. The sea witch of death took my voice. "My mother passed away" or "I just lost my mom" or any other manner of stating the reality was insurmountable. It was as if giving voice to the words would acknowledge the reality of her being gone. The reality of the pain. It was an acknowledgement in verbal form, from my voice. The hard scab of the loss was too difficult to articulate, too much to bear. I had another fear too that I later expressed to my therapist, "I did not want to put my sadness on others." I knew, I just knew that these losses were significant because I did not want others to witness the grief in me nor feel sadness for me.

Finally, Angela and I figured out a solution (well, really, Angela figured it out) where she would help by introducing the information.

"We just lost Amelia's mom."

I would stand next to her silently while our friend or neighbor or friendly acquaintance would provide kind and consoling words of support—all of whom were so caring and kind.

Of course, Sharon was a person for whom the words did come. I recall talking to her about the final hours with Mom while she made us martinis—the ones we so enjoyed together.
Angela and I were finally back in Virginia from our time in Florida. It was late April.

Yet, it took weeks for me to tell some of our other close friends about Mom's passing. They came over for breakfast on a beautiful Saturday morning. The sun was shining, and it was perfect weather for sitting out on the back patio.

They both sat down at the table with us. I sprung up. "I'll go get the coffee."

"So, what's been goin' on?" our friend asked in her usual excited and loving way.

Just as my feet met the second step on our back stoop, I turned around. Angela looked directly at me, her eyes questioning: you are going to tell them, right?

Every part of my being tried to muster the words. I had been nonverbal for weeks regarding the fact that Mom had died. But these were close friends. Avoiding it would not be good. For me.

Finally, as I stood on our back patio steps, feeling my grandmother's heavy blue earrings dangle from my ears, I sucked in my stomach, took a slight breath and stuttered, "Well. We lost my mom." I felt like a tin soldier, standing rock solid without emotion.

Our friend scurried over to me and gave me the longest, strongest, warmest hug. It took me by surprise. After what felt like minutes, I felt my limbs ease, and just before closing my eyes, I saw the shock on our other friend's face as she said, "Oh my gosh. We had no idea. We're so sorry!"

The hug continued.

It was that day when I learned how to state the fact of losing a loved one, of losing my mom. I learned too the power of a hug.

It was only later that I realized the sadness that might come for others from not knowing such news, about not having an awareness of what was going on. After all, if I were in their shoes, I would want to know so that I could offer my own caring, kind support. Shouldn't I give them that opportunity? That rationale only dawned on me much later, and with the help of Angela, my therapist, and those two friends.

So, I got better. I did get better at it.

By the time Dad died, I had more knowledge, more practice, and more familiarity from the experiences of losing Mom and then Sharon. Although, it still did not come naturally to me.

On that morning of July 8, 2021 at ten o'clock in the morning when I heard Doug's voice, the younger me of March and April 2020 won the day, and I did not tell him.

I knew I wanted to. I knew I needed to. The next week when Doug came over to replace the failing storm door on the front door, I walked outside to greet him. It was sunny and warm. I put the newfound rationale to practice.

"Hi Doug."

"Well hello!" Doug stood on the rockscape just outside the front porch. "I was just checking that ivy from the front of the house. There are a few more creepin' up that I'm going to pull out."

"Oh. Okay, great. Thanks, Doug. Listen, I have to tell you. Dad passed away."

I saw tears immediately well up in his eyes as he stood there in his white t-shirt and cargo shorts. His reaction to the news touched my heart. He stood facing me, his voice shaking, "Oh no. Goodness. Oh no. I'm so sorry. When did he pass?"

"We lost him last week." I did not have the heart to tell Doug it was the very day he was at the house the week before.

"Oh gosh. Well, oh my… ya know, he had the best coats and hats. His style was amazing, and he had such great stories. He really was a special man." Doug went on to tell me just how incomparable he thought Dad was, how much he enjoyed talking with him, and how much he appreciated helping him and my mom.

I had come to know Doug well in the weeks leading to that day. Yet I felt even more connected to him after that particular interaction. We connected on a more robust level: one of shared sadness.

The next evening, Doug rang the doorbell and presented me with a plate of chocolate chip cookies. "Sara made cookies for you."

I reached out and took the plate of warm cookies baked by Doug's wife and could not help but think of the warm cookies our neighbor in Virginia brought by the day she learned my mom had died. The gesture was comforting. The sweet-tasting, warm, baked goods brought comfort. Mostly, being thought of, brought comfort.

In the days and weeks to follow, Doug ended up over at the house a number of times. I would call or text him with a question or request for help and he always responded. He always showed up. During my visit to Mom and Dad back in June of 2019, I did not know how helpful it would be to have Doug's contact information. I just thought that asking my mom for his number would possibly prove useful at some point. You know, down the line. I discovered from meeting and getting to know Doug myself that next year that my parents were spot on: he himself is handy. He is also kind, caring, responsive, and reliable. He helped my parents, he cared about them, he knew them, and he appreciated them. And, he ended up helping Angela and me so much.

A few weeks later, Doug was in the driveway, hitching up his dump trailer full of old junk and trash from the house. I called out to him as I came down the front steps.

"Hey, Doug!"

"Howdy. I'm going to get this dumped. Do you think you have more? Do you want me to bring it back after I empty it?"

"Thanks, Doug. Not right now. We're headed back to Virginia in a few days and will be back here after a month or so. I'll call you then. We'll probably need it then."

"Sounds good!"

"Hey Doug, I wanted to ask you. You mentioned my dad's style, and we have all his hats and coats we need to go through. Is there something you would like of his?"

Doug leaned over between his truck and the trailer and paused cranking the hitch. "Well, I don't know… he… uh… there was that really great safari-type hat he used to wear."

"Would you like that, Doug?"

I did not wait for him to answer. I raced through the front door to the coat closet, reached up, and grabbed Dad's trusty safari hat. The one he had worn so many times, and the one he is wearing in one of my favorite pictures of him from nearly ten years before when he was sporting one of his typical and colorful plaid shirts, smiling ear to ear. As I turned to bring the hat to Doug, I stopped short of the door to look at it. I ran my finger along the inside liner that would have touched my dad's bald head and softly smiled. "Dad," I whispered to myself.

Then, just as if I never stopped at all, I raced out to Doug, my right arm outstretched with it.

"Here you go, Doug. Please enjoy it. Dad would be pleased for you to have it. I'm pleased for you to have it."

Doug's face lit up like a kid at a Fourth of July parade holding cotton candy.

"Gee, thank you," he said as he raised his hands and ceremoniously put on Dad's hat.

"Oh, it looks perfect, Doug!"

Just then, Angela came out of the house. "We should get a photo."

"Yes. Yes!" Thank goodness for Angela and her suggestion.

"May I take your photo?" I reached for my phone from my pocket.

"Sure!" Doug stood up straight and tall.

I snapped a picture while he smiled from ear to ear, a smile as wide as the length of his truck and trailer combined. As I showed him the snapshot on my phone, he leaned next to me, just as I had leaned next to my mom on the couch during my visit the year prior.

"Look at that!" he exclaimed, just like Dad would have.

I felt like a tin soldier, standing rock solid without emotion.

You Can Just Mail It USPS

Two days following my father's passing, we found an unregistered pistol in the basement of my parents' house.

Two days. One gun. Unregistered. (That last part means that the firearm was not traceable. No paperwork, no registration.)

Actually, it was my nine-year-old niece who found the gun among my father's clothing in his basement bedroom, a room my mother referred to as "his study" while my sister and I were growing up in the house.

My sister scurried up the stairs from the basement with our two young nieces.

"Oh my god. Oh my god!"

She squealed this as she shakily handed the gun over to Angela. "Take it. *Take* it!"

Angela had learned how to safely handle guns, and check them for bullets—she had grown up with a father whose profession was in law enforcement.

She carefully checked the gun for bullets. *Phew*! It was not loaded. In fact, we never found any ammunition in the house. Perhaps the estate sale team did, but there were so many—too many—things to try to uncover and find. It was an overload of collectibles and belongings from multiple generations. The mountain of stuff was shattering and overwhelmingly insurmountable. So, not finding bullets was not surprising. It was a relief.

A couple of days later, after my sister and nieces had departed for their home in Florida, my sister called me. It was a Monday afternoon, and the first Monday following Dad's passing, exactly four days later. She told me my nephew wanted the gun. "I looked it up, you can just mail it USPS," she said bluntly.

What?! I stood frozen in the backyard by the large red maple I so loved, and the tree I adored watching my father care for, and the tree he had apparently ordered in from Chicago decades before. I was dripping with sweat from the summer heat and wearing the tank top I wore the last day Mom was alive.

I had so many questions: Did I hear her right? Did she just say that? Do I have to deal with this? And, do I have to have this conversation? Now? Really? *Really?*

I had one answer to my questions: *Yes*, I thought. *Yes, I do.*

"He *wants* it!" she moaned as my internal dialogue finally ended.

"I'm not sending a gun to him. Full stop." I said this as clearly and directly as I could, the words cascading out of my mouth. I left out the part that I was not going to send my seventeen-year-old nephew an unregistered weapon. And I was certainly not sending a weapon in the mail via the United States Postal Service.

She pressed further, "Really, we Googled it, and you can just mail it."

I responded, "I'm curious why you would want your underage son to have a firearm, let alone an unregistered one."

"Well, he can be mad at you, not me." She hung up.

I love my sister dearly. And, we really do see and experience the world very differently.

My confusion grew. Why was she more concerned about him being mad at someone other than her than his having a pistol? I was now not only exhausted, but stunned, too.

This seemed crazy. This felt crazy. It felt crazy-making.

I can count on one hand the times my father would mention having a gun. It would come up in a by-the-way sort of manner while he told a story about fishing with his buddies "in the hills" out west or in Canada. Mention of it would be nonchalantly feathered into a conversation over dinner and just as easily wicked away. He never provided any details and artfully declined any answers to my queries: Why do you have a gun? When did you get it? Where is it? Do you know how to use it? His plausible deniability made it seem entirely likely that he did not own a gun at all. I chalked it up to another embellished and slightly overstated detail of his storytelling. He did love to tell stories.

Oh, the things you learn later!

He *did* have a gun. And it was unregistered. I was not prepared for this. On top of everything, I did not feel prepared for this. *And here it is*, I would think. *Here I am*. Once again, finding something else that felt preposterous and that I felt all too unprepared to deal with, married with the deep sense of responsibility that I *would* deal with it.

I came to discover, however, that I was prepared. That he did prepare me.

My father was a disciple of safety. It was a core part of his being, and he preached it. For as long as I can remember, "Safety first." "Be safe." "Remember, safety." "Stay safe." "Don't do that, it isn't safe." It was ground into my sister and me for as long as I can remember like the grinding of pepper in a pepper mill. He was playful and adventurous in his own way, and I think his devotion to science, medicine, and making things better—making people better—drove that core value of safety.

My father also shared with me the desire to care for others. Even in his final days, he was very clear with me about his wish that I do what I could to make sure my sister and his grandchildren would be okay—that they would be safe. This is what I tapped into and what showed me the way. This was core to my own conviction for what to do in those unknown moments.

Angela and I found a spot to hide the weapon out of sight and reach until we could safely, legally, and properly offload the firearm. We consulted with her father, a former police officer, who helped guide us with steps for how to surrender the gun. We contacted the local police, and based on the state's law, ultimately ended up at the local gun shop, the same one my sister and I would pass on our way to high school while listening to the local country station and mimicking the drawl coming through the speakers of that 1977 Ford wood paneled station wagon. The shop owner assessed and took in the gun just as the local police guided.

Once again, another something I never imagined doing. More conversations I never could imagine having. Yet I did. And it was safe.

Oh, the things you learn later!

White-Girl-Wasted

Molly had a twinkle in her large, spherical eyes—eyes that conveyed assurance and confidence. She could wink on a dime and used that talent at the most opportune moments. Molly was the woman Angela and I met once we got Dad moved back into the house in South Dakota. She ran the hospice care team in town for one of the two main medical organizations. As with so many people in our orbit at the time, she was also a colleague of my dad in the medical community. She knew him as a physician, caregiver, and surgeon. Now, she was attending to him as a planning-for-hospice advisor, professional colleague and a friend. Molly is one of those people who is working in a profession and doing precisely what she was born to do. She is talented and clearly educated in her field while also retaining a "je ne sais quoi" underneath it all. She has a grounded knack for her work that was apparent whenever I spoke or texted with her, and her competence was evident when she was sitting next to my father in the den and engaging in a *tête-à-tête* about his care.

Molly had been at the house multiple times to talk to Dad about next steps, more care, different care, and hospice care. She helped us tremendously and *knew* how to have a discussion with Dad without my ever having to describe him. She was patient, effective, warm and brought a human jovial sense to heavy topics. I think that mixture is what Dad appreciated, particularly with his clinical sensibility and overall data-driven approach as a physician.

The first time I witnessed her in dialogue with my father, I was amazed. It was a true heart-to-heart and pairing of two medical professionals having a discussion about a patient. This time, the patient was one of them: Dad. Molly could banter with him like the best of them, which required specific traits: medical knowledge, patience, and an ease for earning (and nurturing) his trust. She made him laugh, and she would offer me that perfectly-timed wink in between, as I leaned on the door frame to the room, listening in as a passive non-participant.

Molly served a critical role in Dad's care. She was there for him as a fellow colleague to think through and talk both about the current state of his health and his options for facing hospice. In all that, she was there for Angela and me as well.

She was yet another individual who showed up with what seemed like unending offers to help. In addition to her role as a hospice confidant for my father (and me), she had helpful ideas and suggestions for the equipment at the house. There was so much medical equipment at the house for his condition: oxygen machines, oxygen tanks, cannulas, wheelchairs, slings for moving people who are immobile, and a mechanical chair lift—all owned by my father. In the weeks following Dad's death, Molly and I were communicating with each other regularly. She would offer recommendations and suggestions for who, what, when, where, and how to offer, donate or sell the equipment to ensure it was put to use, re-used, and to the benefit of others, something that was important to Dad and me.

In one such text exchange, we were going back and forth about the chair lift from the house stairwell. This was an electric chair lift, a chair on a mechanical track that would transport a person from the main level of the home to the basement and back up again, simply by sitting on it and pushing a button. My father had insisted on purchasing this lift about four years prior so that he would be able to go to the basement for his books, puppets, trinkets—you name it. He had the foresight to plan for a time when he would not be able to navigate the stairs. But he never used it. I learned from my mother months before she got sick, that she had "given it a try" once with Dad's encouragement. For mobile people needing to use the stairs, it was actually a trip hazard and a nuisance because it blocked such a significant portion of the stairwell, and the track jutted out at the bottom of the stairs. On this particular text thread with Molly, she was identifying families in need of such a transport system. At the tail end of providing me pointers for who to call next, she added, "I'm going to a wedding tonight—they are kinda a biker bunch, but if you ladies are in need of adult beverages, you can certainly join. They are an easy, fun crowd!"

I read it twice, then once aloud. It was not what I expected to see in the context of our texts at all, so I had to look at the type to make sure I was really seeing this combination of letters.

Wait, shall I read this out loud again? I thought.

Another message from Molly: "Both of my parents are gone. I remember wanting to get white-girl-wasted and wanting to just not adult for a hot minute."

"White-girl-wasted?" Not sure I had ever heard that term before.

After some initial bantering, Angela and I decided that it was maybe, perhaps, *possibly* something to entertain doing. That it might actually be good for us provided it was real. Not the "white-girl-wasted" part, but the go-do-something-social part, the meet-new-people part, the be-at-a-different-type-of-celebration-of-life part.

But, was it really an invitation? Is it bad form to go? We pondered this.

For each of the million reasons I came up with *to not go*, there were another million reasons *to go*. So I shrugged my shoulders and stated plainly, "We should go." Angela smartly added, "There's a reason this has been put in front of us."

We decided to ask Molly two key questions:

Is this really an invitation and okay for us to join?

And, is there a dress code?

I texted her.

Her response was immediate and clear:

"Dress code would be REAL casual, like if you shower, that's cool. My boyfriend is an usher so I'll dress up, but I'd guess jeans and Harley t-shirts will be the standard. Ceremony is at four, join me at five thirty or six at the reception."

"Rough around the edges" is a phrase that comes to mind when thinking about the biker community, but really, who isn't rough around the edges? Besides growing up in the state that hosts the annual Sturgis Motorcycle Rally, I do not consider myself familiar with "bikers," and while I definitely do not consider myself as fitting in with such a community, who is supposed to fit in to anything? Up to this point, my familiarity was limited to two main experiences. The first included serving many guests midnight meals while working at that local Perkins Restaurant. Groups would come in from the freeway while making their way east or west across South Dakota, and I always found them to be straight-forward, kind, and generous tippers. The other experience was after moving into our house in Virginia when Angela and I had neighbors across the street who, while unstated, showed evidence of being part of the biker community. The couple was welcoming, kind, and matter-of-fact. He would work on his bike every Saturday afternoon out front of their house, and nearly every Sunday afternoon, they would head out for a ride. She wore one of those helmets with Viking braids attached to it. They were great neighbors.

"Well, okay. I guess we are headed to a wedding this evening." I turned to Angela.

First time for everything, I guess?

When I let Molly know that we would join, she texted, "Great! I will send you the address shortly. Dinner and dancing start around six."

I had nothing to wear. Shorts and tank tops seemed out of form, even for a "biker wedding" with no dress code. As if I would know, but I was going with my gut on this. So, we squeezed in an afternoon stop at the local sporting goods store, efficiently combing through the clearance section where I found a new outfit. Nice, not too fancy and not too casual: a sundress, a jean jacket, and sandals.

Once we made it back to the house with my biker wedding attire, I opened the fridge to grab a soda and exclaimed, "Oh my gosh, we need a gift!"

Pause.

"Don't we?!" I called this out around the corner of the kitchen and up to the sky.

What the heck do we bring to a wedding and offer to people we do not know, people who may not necessarily know we are crash- attending (crashing) their wedding? After a few moments of thought-searching, I said, "I got it." I marched to the den where my father used to sit and reached to the floor, just to the left of his chair and grabbed a giant unopened handle of Jim Beam bourbon whiskey. "We'll take this." I held up the bottle toward Angela who was walking past me to the kitchen.

I set the bottle on the kitchen counter and dug through the utility drawer. I managed to find a red ribbon leftover from a sweet package of bundt cakes a neighbor had dropped off after Dad died. I looped it around the neck of the bottle and made a bow. I felt a twinge as the thought came screaming to the forefront of my head: *Dad won't get to enjoy this.* It's funny, the things that feel nostalgic and those that don't. It did not seem wrong for me to gift these soon-to-be newlyweds the Jim Beam. It strangely felt like it fit. If we were not going to drink it, we might as well pay it forward as a gift for others to enjoy. Plus, my father would have wanted to hear about the wedding.

Angela typed the address Molly had sent us into her phone and we set out passing the street lights and onto the gravel roads to the west of town. As we neared the parking lot, Angela confirmed, "This is definitely it," eyeing the lines of parked motorcycles.

We parked.

For a brief moment before we entered, I stood there in the gravel lot. "Let me take your picture," Angela said, and she snapped a photo of me standing there in my new sundress, jean jacket, and sandals, the Jim Beam on my hip and taking it all in.

We walked into the reception, and it was a beautiful scene. I felt the wave of energy crash over me. It was full of life, music, and people mingling, drinking, eating, and dancing. Molly spotted us and came to corral us to her table. As she welcomed us and introduced us to her boyfriend and daughter, I stood there holding the whiskey as if it were my purse. I was busy chit-chatting when a young bartender came up to me. "Let me keep that behind the bar for you."

"It's for the bride and groom," I said without handing it over.

"Yes, of course. I'll need to keep this behind the bar."

"That makes sense." Angela added, while it did not yet click for me.

"Oh, I get it," I said, finally understanding and relinquishing the handle.

Of course. Of course. We all had a chuckle and then sat at the table together.

As we ate, the bride and groom made their rounds to each of the tables, greeting friends, family, and guests. As they neared us, I felt the nerves in my belly build. *What the heck are they going to think of us? Are they going to kick us out?*

They came up to us with huge smiles and a gleeful just-married glow and welcomed us. "We're so happy you're here!" they nearly shouted at us. Now, I am sure they probably had a drink or two (or a few) under their belts—it was their wedding after all—and, at the heart of it, they were kind, genuine, and made us feel welcome. As two people who were not even on the invitation list—a gay female couple—we were clearly not the typical guests for this wedding, yet they were all these incredibly generous things to us.

Molly, hospice, and medical equipment disposition—that's how Angela and I ended up at a biker wedding one week and two days following my father's death. And, carrying his last bottle of Jim Beam whiskey with me. It was surreal. Something I never would have imagined nor planned. I am comforted because I can feel in my bones that the experience showed up for a reason.

I did not get "white-girl-wasted" like Molly suggested, I did get overwhelmed by the human spirit of it all.

It strangely felt like it fit.
(Who isn't rough around the edges?)

Biohazard Bags and Bone Cement

"Do you want me to come over with some biohazard bags?" she asked openly.

"Umm…" I swayed.

"To help dispose of the tissue?" she continued.

"Ye- Yes. Yes, I do. Please. That would be great. Thank you," I managed to stammer.

"I will be there this afternoon after work, "she confirmed.

"Perfect."

A breath.

I hung up the phone amazed and relieved. Who was this kind woman?

It was a welcome offer. More than that: it was an offer without a request, without my having to ask, and it unexpectedly arrived providing much-needed support. And, it arrived in a unique situation: a need for biohazard bags. Her offer was specific, direct, and it provided immediate relief. It was the sort of relief that gave a glimpse into not being completely alone and made Angela and me feel like we were not utterly alone in a seemingly never-ending web of post-death problem-solving. It was one that this woman presented without hesitation—I could sense that in her voice. I was so eager to meet her.

It was my first phone conversation with my now friend, Marie. She worked at the organization for eye and tissue recovery and donation that my father originally started decades prior, and for which I now serve on the Board of Directors. I came to learn that she was Dad's mentee.

From my childhood bedroom window, I saw a red Cadillac SUV pull into the driveway. Just like when I was a child seeing my parents arrive home from work, I hurried down the driveway with an anticipatory gait. Who was this woman coming voluntarily with biohazard bags and to guide me on what to do?

There she was, actively gathering the bright orange, thick plastic bags labeled "BIOHAZARD" from the back of her vehicle as I walked up. We hugged. It was a hug full of kindness and knowing. She knew my father. She did not know me. Yet, her boundless care came through her hug that day.

I had so much more to learn.

I learned that she was a grandmother, although she looked far too young to be a grandmother with her long, curly hair; young, kind, wide eyes; and smooth skin. She told me the story of purchasing the wooden cradle from my parents for her "grand baby" —a cradle where my father had laid his head as an infant. He phrased it that way to her, and she relayed the story to me while we both stood in the driveway. Just a couple years prior, she had come to pick up the cradle from my parents and my father told her the story of that antique cradle. Marie told me about that day and the story instantaneously brought the strong, vivid presence of my parents back to life.

"Ya know, your mom was busy trying to sell things…" Marie began, peering to the side and leaning toward me as thought we were old friends. "Oh yes," I confirmed, "I do know," recalling the many times my mother mentioned wanting to sell things from the house. Marie continued, "Well, I came over to the house one afternoon to get the cradle from your parents. Your mom let me in, and I greeted your dad in the den right away." As she spoke, I could see her walking up the front steps and my mother trotting to the door to welcome her into the house. "Hi Marie!" Mom would have said with excitement. "Come on in!" Marie kept speaking as that vision sunk into me. I stood in stillness in the driveway clinging to her every word that described my parents together, not too long ago and while they were both alive. "When he told me it was the cradle he used as a baby, I couldn't believe it," she said. "Well, yeah," Dad had firmly stated to her, "it's where I laid my head." "Then I asked what I could offer for it," Marie continued. She told me how Mom had suggested fifty dollars while Dad simultaneously waved off the suggestion. I could picture the quick arm gesture he would have made in doing so. "Oh, just take it. You don't need to pay us." Dad had said. "Well, Tom, I would like to get *something* for it." Mom had replied while scurrying out the door to gather groceries from her car. "While your mom was outside, your dad opened his wallet and slid out a crisp fifty-dollar bill. He said, 'Here, give this to her,' and handed me the cash." Marie's laughter burst into the air and wrapped its arms around me. "Oh Doctor," she had said, "I'm happy to pay for the cradle." Then, my mother apparently appeared from the garage with Marie's husband, "Look, I found a handsome young gentleman to help me bring in the groceries!" Marie's infectious laugh grew into a chorus of smirks as she told me this last bit.

At that moment, I chuckled too, grasping for a lived memory I did not experience that Marie was generously sharing with me on the day I first met her. It was perfectly my parents: Dad conspicuously attempting to pull the wool over Mom's eyes, knowing she would not relent on her decision to sell the item versus gift it, regardless of who was interested in it.

I learned Marie had visited my dad at the house many times and fetched his books, medical tools, and trinkets that he would request. I learned that she would ask him for advice about her children and about work and that they had attended conferences together in earlier years. I learned so much about her—about them. And, I learned all of this after he died.

Dad never told me about Marie or the sweet connection they had formed through their shared passion for eye and tissue donation and helping people regain sight. He never mentioned her name as a topic or in passing. I would have loved to hear him talk about her.

She proceeded through the front door with a quiet confidence and knew exactly where to go. She was a true guide in a house I knew so well. She strode through the front hall toward the kitchen with purpose and moved immediately for the refrigerator. She opened it, scanning the shelving, then knelt and started gathering the samples of research tissue that were second nature to me and did not seem odd at all, even though I can recall Angela's facial expression the first time I told her what it was when we were visiting years ago and she opened the fridge to make a sandwich.

Research tissue resided in our kitchen fridge for as long as I can remember, just to the left of the produce and below the deli drawer. Marie looked closely at each one. “See, this one…Oh, your dad, he loved to investigate. He loved to research.” She had a comment for each one and methodically gathered every sample into an appropriate bag. After the fridge was empty of tissue, she turned to me, “Shall we check the basement?”

Marie had the wherewithal, the confidence, and the understanding of my father to know that we should check other spots. As we walked downstairs to the overpacked basement rooms, once again, Marie demonstrated her familiarity with the environment. She knew exactly where she was going. She marched toward the back basement room to check other medical grade cabinets to ensure there wasn’t anything more she needed to help with. It was incredible. I felt like a child, following a revered teacher while she provided guidance. She told me about her parents’ collectibles and how they have labeled each item for Marie and her siblings for when they pass away. *What would that be like?*

As Marie left that day, she reiterated, “Well, let me know if there is anything else I can do to help. Seriously, if I can help, please let me know.”

Another warm hug, full of kindness.

As she reversed out of the driveway to leave, I was turned to head back to the front door. But I felt myself whisper a pause: What just happened? Who is this woman? How amazingly helpful in all this craziness!

A few weeks later, I was standing just outside the garage, my shorts and tank top covered in dust and dirt. Angela and I had been sifting through cleansing bottles and jugs of chemicals, making sure to wear plastic nitrile gloves. It was a task we had been dreading yet were determined to ensure we properly disposed of old cleansers and chemicals we found in the basement and garage of the house. It was obvious that some of them had been transferred from my father’s medical lab over to the house following his retirement because they were associated with his medical research. I pressed my phone to my cheek waiting for

Maire to answer my call.

"Hey there, lady. What are you up to?" she asked.

"Hi Marie. Well, we're here at the house and have collected a bunch of chemicals that we found. I want to make sure we dispose of them appropriately, but a good portion of them we…Well, we just aren't sure what they are. Would you be able to swing by at some point and help us figure it out?"

"Sure thing! I could come by tomorrow after work. Is that okay?"

"Of course. That would be amazing. Thank you so much, Marie!"

She came by the next evening. Again, I was covered in dust and dirt from having gone through more things in the garage.

She walked up in scrubs, "Well, hello lady! Let's see."

She dug in and started looking at each of the bottles. "Yep, this one would be okay to go in the trash. And this one you need to take to hazardous waste. And this, hmmm…this one, I can take and dispose of for you. This one? No, you can't throw that away." She triaged all the bottles for us.

I came to a small cardboard box full of tiny brown glass bottles. "Marie, what about these?"

"Ah, well, let's see." She peered at each of the bottles, holding them up to the fading sunlight to make out the tattered labels. "Huh. That's bone cement. Yeah…geez, your dad. Well, keep that separate."

Bone cement? Bone? Cement? *What the hell was he using that for?!* "Is that something you can dispose of from your lab?"

"Uh, no. You're going to need to keep that separate and check with the hazardous waste facility." She noticed my gaunt face and questioning look, "Oh, your dad, he must have been using it in research or making molds or something" she guessed.

Following Marie's instruction, I had found the appropriate

hazardous waste location in town and had reached out to them to arrange for me to drop off a couple boxes. However, there was a handful of bottles leftover, including the bone cement, that the facility would not take. I ended up researching and finding a medical waste service in Minnesota, who would come to gather and dispose of the remaining chemicals. There was a decent amount of paperwork associated with this. It took another three months to officially close the door on the last bit of chemical disposal. I thought, *Of all things, what the hell?!*

More weeks later, we needed to go through my father's one remaining lab, which he had rented from the business owner who had purchased his office building when he retired. Dad, true to form, had negotiated a deal where he would be able to rent back one remaining lab space in the building, which was filled with ophthalmic machines, equipment, materials, files, and a stereo of mine from high school that he had taken once I went to college (Dad like to listen to opera while he worked in his lab). There were so many things in this lab room that were unfamiliar to me. That stereo was the one and only item I recognized.

I called Marie.

"Hi, Marie. Wondering if you'd be willing to join us at Dad's old lab to help us dispose of anything that needs specific handling?"

"Sure!" She barely let me finish my question. "When do you want to do it."

Wow.

"Marie, you are incredible. Well, it's a bit tricky. I realize there's a holiday weekend coming up, but the building owner said he'd leave me a key so we could get in the Sunday and Monday of Labor Day weekend next week. Would either of those days work for you?"

I was mortified that I was not only suggesting that she help us *again*, but that she do so on an upcoming holiday weekend. Ugh.

"Name the time and I'll be there."

I could barely respond. "Okay. How about ten o'clock on Sunday morning? We'll bring coffee."

"See you there!"

We spent nearly six hours with Marie clearing out that laboratory. Again, I learned so many things. Marie had better ideas of what some of the machinery was. "Oh that makes contact lenses." She found more things to fill orange, heavy plastic biohazard bags while Angela and I focused on the trash, files and paperwork. Once Marie had gathered everything that was medically related, she asked, "Okay, anything more you need me for?"

"No, Marie. You've been amazing. We can't thank you enough."

"Okay, well, I'll head out and you let me know if you need anything else." She said kindly, jovially, and gently all at the same time.

Godsend. In those moments (so many of them), Marie was the epitome of the word. I don't practice a religion, yet I do understand the meaning of that word—the magnitude of it. She was a godsend. If I open a Merriam-Webster Dictionary or look online at the definition of the word "Godsend," Marie's picture should be there.

At first, I was saddened and dismayed that Dad had not shared with me about Marie, about their conversations, visits, mentorship, and friendship. I was bummed that I did not know about her while he was living. And, I have come to learn that it was as he may have wanted, how he may have intended, or how he had no intention about it at all. I discovered it was an unexpected passing forward of a friendship to me. I learned that beautiful connections can blossom from crazy situations, from crazy shit. Each time I see a joyful text pop on my phone from Marie or hear her tell me about one of her new do-it-herself projects, or when I bake with her homemade vanilla extract, I am reminded of the relief I felt on that first day meeting her—the warmth of her kindness, the sparkle in imagining her sitting in conversation with my father, and the goodness in my soul for knowing her.

Godsend.

Can I Help You?

While Angela and I were at my childhood house for the additional weeks following Dad's passing, we were buried in organizing and figuring out the scope of what needed to be done to care for my parents' things and I was only a few inches into commencing the journey to close out the estate.

We opened the few windows that had mechanisms to open. We had Doug install a new screen door on the front door like the one he installed on the back door, so that we could allow as much fresh air into the house as possible—much needed fresh, clean air. Most moments, we would be inside the house working, sorting and cleaning.

One day, while I was juggling work meetings and shifting through the expanding and complicated list of "to dos," I heard a faint "hello" from an unknown voice. It was coming from the front hall, at the entrance to the living room. I rounded the corner of the kitchen from the dining room and found a stout middle-aged woman standing there. I had no idea who she was. I was startled and confused by the presence of this stranger in the house. *Why* was she here? *Who* was this woman? *Why* did she think it okay to let herself in?

"Can I help you?" I shakily asked.

"I'm Julie."

Okay, that does not begin to answer my question, but I guess it is a start. I was so taken aback and caught off guard, utterly confused by this woman standing before me, her bold behavior for entering the house uninvited and unsure what exactly to do about it.

She continued, "I'm Dean's daughter."

Oh, wow! Julie. She is the daughter of one of my mom's favorite cousins and someone I had not seen since I was eleven or twelve years old. Truly e-x-t-e-n-d-e-d family.

I stumbled, "Julie. Hi!"

My mom had a pretty large family. Well large compared to the rather smaller size of our immediate family and my dad's side. It was due to the thirteen siblings of my maternal grandmother, who was raised on a Minnesota farm and was twenty years younger than her eldest brother. Mom really tried to stay in touch with her side of the family, attending most annual family reunions; however, I grew up only having interacted with these cousins on rare occasions. So, while Julie technically *is* family, I felt no closer to her than the cashier at the Starbucks in Sarasota.

She told me she wanted to "check in" and find out "what plans" there were. *Plans?* Gulp. *Do I have to explain this on the spot? Yes. Yes, I do.* And, I did.

Over the next couple weeks, there were two more instances of people letting themselves into the house unannounced and unplanned. Neither were family but were "checking in," like Julie had stated. Was I missing something? Was this a norm of which I was unaware? It seemed completely normal—not at all awkward or odd—to these folks. To me, it was.

Am I in the Twilight Zone? Did I miss a memo? I continued to ponder these questions. Checking in on someone is typically a good thing, right? But what about when you do not know the person, and they do not introduce themselves *before* entering the house? Let alone—when you are in the midst of shock and grief?

I did not think locking the screen door while *in* the house was necessary. I learned it was. I realized that I am accustomed to people knocking on a door or saying "hello" through the screen, then waiting for an invitation to enter. I am okay with that. Of course, in certain situations and with close family and friends, "The door is unlocked, just come on in when you arrive" is an instruction I have used.

The funny thing is, I don't recall much of anything Julie said about my mom or my parents that day. She did talk to me about how to make sure to check for unclaimed property on a website. It was only as she turned to leave that I realized it was like watching a distant version of my mom walking away. She had the same build and gait as her. But it was not Mom at all. I did not know this woman. While we share distant blood, I do not know Julie.

After she left, I stood still in the front hall.

Angela walked up to me. "Who was that? Who does that?"

Julie does. Two other people do that. My mom would have done that. It was a moment that I cannot completely wrap my mind around. It could have been the start of something new, as so many things have been. Yet it was not. It was a moment in time—an awkward meeting. Whatever I shared with Julie that day, how I handled it was the best I could muster up—on that day.

To Julie, if you are reading this, while your entrance took me by surprise, and for as awkward and confusing as your checking in felt, I am glad you did.

Am I in the Twilight Zone?

Facebook Marketplace and Tap Dancing

"Who was your mom?"

There are so many thoughts, so many words for that answer.

"Nancy—"

She did not let me finish. "Oh my gosh! I thought you looked familiar! I am Nicole. Nicole Gade. My maiden name is Gade." Her voice accelerated as she spoke.

"Oh, wow. Hi. Hi!"

She turned to her friend, "We used to dance together. We tap danced at the same studio."

I introduced Angela, and she introduced her friend to us.

While Nicole had just purchased my parents' den couch, her friend had just purchased one of the needlepoint stools and a few of the needlepoint pillows depicting scenes from in and around the Twin Cities of Minnesota.

As we stood in Nicole's driveway, her friend had inquired about all the needlepoint we had shown her. I explained that my mom was the artist, that she and my dad grew up in Minneapolis, thus the tie to Minnesota. I mentioned offhandedly that Mom would needlepoint on road trips and at the dance studio while my sister and I took classes.

Nicole was technically in my sister's dance classes, a few years ahead of me in school, but every year there were routines (ballet, tap, and jazz) that combined our classes. My class, one level junior to Nicole's and my sister's which had half a dozen dancers, consisted of only three dancers, one of whom later became a neighbor of my parents, moving two doors down with her husband and daughter.

There we stood in her driveway, Angela, me, Nicole, and her friend talking about my parents and tap dancing. Nicole explained how she continued to dance and went on to teach tap dancing.

As Angela and I walked back to the truck that evening, she exclaimed, “How incredible is that? You danced with her, and she bought your parent’s couch! How cool is that?”

“I know, it’s unimaginable. It *is* cool, right?”

It was only a few days earlier that Angela had posted the couch on Facebook Marketplace and told me about a woman who responded almost immediately. When the woman inquired about wanting to come look at it, we had no idea it was a fellow dancer from my childhood.

“Is it okay if a lady comes to look at the couch this evening?” Angela had asked me.

“Sure.”

At five o’clock, a navy SUV pulled into the driveway. Angela and I had moved the couch out of the house to the driveway for ease.

The woman exited her vehicle, a friend in tow. She walked up the driveway and smiled. “This couch is in great condition!” Her friend convinced her that the couch would be perfect for her lake house, which she was working to furnish.

We mentioned a chair that Angela had also posted on Facebook.

“Oh, you have more pieces?” The woman asked.

“Yes, we do,” Angela confirmed.

We were trying to make space and told her there would be an estate sale later, though we had not even interviewed one of the estate sale businesses to whom we had reached out. We just were trying to get rid of a few things to create much-needed real estate inside.

Mention of needlepoint stools rolled off my tongue, and the lady’s friend perked up.

"Really?"

"Yeah, you're welcome to come in and see them, if you like," I said as Angela and I glanced at each other.

They were respectfully hesitant as we all stepped into the front entry of the home. I brought the two needlepoint stools from a bedroom while Angela showed them two bags of needlepoint pillows and ornaments.

Her friend immediately decided to take one of the stools and then zeroed in on four other needlepoint pieces. Then, she further convinced the woman to purchase the chair.

When we got all the things they chose to buy to the driveway, and they completed the purchases, we helped them load their vehicle. The couch was not going to fit so they were wondering if they could arrange to pick up the three-seater on a different day.

Angela looked over at our U-Haul rental Ford F-150, "We can just deliver it to you." We were so starved for space that getting any furniture out of the house and out of the garage would be a win.

"Are you sure? That would be great!" The woman said. "I just live over on Danper."

She stated the name of the street as though we were locals and knew where that was.

"We'll just follow you." I said.

The next morning, Angela and I took Charlie to one of our favorite parks in my hometown. As we walked among the plants and flowers, thoughts that came to me overnight paved a serpentine path in my mind.

"You know those needlepoint tap shoes we have hanging in Virginia?" I asked Angela.

"The ones your mom made you? Yeah, yeah, I do."

"When we get back to Virginia, I'm going to send them to Nicole. It feels right to give them to her."

"I think that is a great idea, love." Angela slid her hand in mine and we walked through the wet grass.

A couple months later, I walked out to our carport in Virginia and pulled the black and pink needlepoint dance shoes from the post where they were hanging. They had been so musty from years in my parents' home, that when my mom sent them to me, I had immediately placed them in our carport where they could get some fresh air and be protected from the elements by the carport's roof (similar to that Christmas stocking). I fondly remember Mom stitching these shoes, creating an ornament with sparkly silver ribbon connecting two one-twentieth the size of the shoes I used to slide on my feet to create rhythm on the floor. My very first tap dance was a "cane dance," a sing--and-dance routine. I practiced tapping on the laundry room floor in front of the washer and dryer in the basement and got used to looking straight forward while my feet shuffled, flapped, and tapped. "I'm setting a timer for fifteen minutes," Mom would say. "You need to practice until it goes off." Then, she would set another fifteen-minute timer, sneakily teaching me how to accomplish a thirty minute practice session. She made my pleated white skirt with a red and white vest for the dance, and we went to the hardware store together to get a dowel and red electrical tape so she could make my candy-striped cane accessory to go along with the routine. I can still belt out that tune and swing my hips side to side before flapping and shuffling. Practice pays off.

After carefully wrapping the needlepoint shoes in tissue paper, I slid them in an envelope with a notecard for Nicole. I knew her address from our having delivered that couch and chair. As I handed the package to the postal worker, a wave of calm, gratifying joy came across me.

Later, that wave of calm joy was countered, as I wondered, *What would Mom have thought of my giving away yet another something she had specifically made for me?* Adornment dance shoes that used to hang on the post of my bed while growing up, serving no purpose other than representing a gift from my mom, reflecting my love for dancing and her unconditional support of that activity over the years and her love. Then, I thought about that incredible and cool moment of unexpected reconnection with a former friend from the dance studio. Facebook Marketplace opened the door for reconnection and tap dancing formed the connection in the first place.

I thought about Nicole's kind words about Mom. I thought about her teaching other kids how to tap dance, how to get used to looking straight forward while shuffling, flapping, and tapping. And I knew, I just knew, tapping (this time) into my instinct and sending those ornament shoes was a good thing to do.

"Who was your mom?"

Creepy Clown

My dad's largest marionette—hung from its control mechanisms—was about three and a half feet tall. It had hefty yarn locks of hair, large round eyes, high painted eyebrows, massive ears (not to scale), a perfectly round and protruding red nose, a clown-white face, red-painted cheeks, felt eyelashes, purple eyelids, gingham pants, a pink bowtie, a yellow vest and a coat with tails. It hung just inside the full-scale puppet stage in my parents' basement.

Yes, we had a puppet stage in our basement.

The basement of my parents' home was deep and dark with multiple rooms. It could be really scary. Okay, it *was* really scary, just like any basement could be for a child coming up from a basement filled with things, including a large puppet stage, in the dark at night. Each time I would "make a run" for the stairs, I would look around me, scan my surroundings, make sure no monsters were about, click the light switch—which turned the entire basement into a black hole—and sprinted as fast as I could up the stairs and through the door, closing it abruptly behind me (but not too loudly so as to avoid Mom shouting, "Don't slam the door!"). In grade school I was the fastest runner of the 100 meter dash, and I am convinced to this day it was because of all those workouts every time I sprinted up from the basement.

So, a three and a half foot tall hanging clown behind a puppet stage in the pitch black of a dark basement was creepy. It was a creepy clown.

The puppet stage was a work of art, handmade by my dad. He built it as a teenager in order to put on puppet shows. It had alternating white and light blue vertical stripes and a wooden proscenium arch that was painted bright red and came to a center point that grazed the ceiling of the basement. The curtain was made of blue corduroy fabric and golden tassels of fringe from its bottom edge. A true curtain. How cool! There was a second puppet stage in the basement too. That one was made from wooden panels and painted white with hunter green accents (all the side doors and pop windows were green). That second stage I never saw put together; rather, it was folded up and leaning against the back room wedged between the water heater and door frame to Dad's study. These puppet stages were freestanding puppet theaters. They stood eight to ten feet tall and included perfect mechanisms for curtain openings and closures, each with three sides to provide a proper "backstage" for the puppeteers, and the puppets' stage floor was at least four feet from the top to allow the puppeteers to work their physical and vocal magic as the characters would come to life.

There were so many instances I remember playing with Dad's puppets and creating "shows" from that basement theater. My sister and I would try out any number of the props, even if they were mismatched with the characters' stories. For instance, I remember using the bridge from the *Three Billy Goats Gruff* for a story with the alligator and princess. There were times I would play with the puppets alone downstairs—lights on, of course! And times Dad would be down there showing us how to use a particular puppet or set item or show us how to transition scenes during a performance. It was a jolly form of make-believe.

In the world of puppetry, Dad gravitated more toward hand puppets. He was always gentle and coy when speaking about marionettes and ventriloquist dummies, recognizing the talent and skill required for them, but his pull toward hand puppets was one of a planetary force. He preferred it while fully recognizing the various qualities of the entire puppetry art form. Plus, he did his own share of puppetry with marionettes (hello, the clown!) and a ventriloquist dummy that he stored in a suitcase—also creepy.

Thus, my dad had a very large and diverse collection of hand puppets. It was a vast array of characters: animals, royals, witches, an opera singer, a princess, a mummy, a king, a lion, a pig, a magician, an alligator, a Scottish bagpiper, a dragon, an octopus, a snake, a turkey, a grandma, a marching band conductor, a train conductor, a wolf, a troll, goats, a ballerina… too many to name. Except of course the entire lot of *Punch and Judy* characters, arguably (without the argument) Dad's favorite, which included:

Punch (Pulcinella from roots of the storylines in 17th century Italian commedia dell'arte), Judy (Punch's wife), Toby the Dog, the Policeman, the Doctor, the Baby, the Lawyer, the Devil, the Ghost, the Hangman, the Crocodile (not to be confused with Dad's alligator puppet). Of all these puppets, some had hand-carved wooden heads (like all of the "Punch Puppets"), and some were made of cloth or fabric. Others were made of paper mâché. And all of them had vibrant clothing, accessories and costumes. Some had velvet bodies, others cotton, and others silk.

Dad found puppets wherever he traveled, mostly Europe and around the United States; he procured them in toy stores, small novelty shops, and directly from puppet makers. As much as Dad loved to play golf and to read books, he was the man who would venture into a children's toy store above all else. "They might have puppets!" He would say excitedly. "Let's go see."

The puppet collection resided not only in the basement of my parents' house, Dad had an entire collection of puppets at the condo in Florida, too. It was a combination of character puppets he had transported to Florida over the years, driving to and fro with my mom. Among them, there were safari animals, zoo animals, marine animals, a magician, a teacher, and an entire collection of carefully-handcrafted, super delicate puppets he had purchased in Prague. There was also a miniature wooden puppet stage at the condo, one he and Mom purchased in order to show the grandkids the art of puppetry.

Dad always spoke about his puppets with a certain reverence—a clear tone of love, memory, and play. It was a part of him as a young boy growing up, as a young man, as a physician caring for children, and as he raised his own daughters and played with his grandchildren. So when it came time for me to decide what to do with the boatload of puppets, their costumes, puppet show sets, and trinkets galore, it was a weight of heartache and supreme responsibility. I grew up getting to know these characters through my dad's imagination and his puppetry craft. I wanted to care for these characters in a way that would reflect the loving tone he used for them and that he shared with us and others.

When Angela and I were in Florida in 2020 clearing the condo, it was initially heartbreaking to think about Dad's beautiful characters there in a box being left at a random donation center or failing to cart them all back to South Dakota, which was not feasible. There simply was too much stuff to sort and prioritize.

"Don't forget my puppets!" Dad had expressed to me multiple times on the phone as I unzipped my soaked yellow rain jacket while Hurricane Eta (that was downgraded later to a Tropical Storm) blew into Sarasota, causing swells five to ten feet high on Lido Key.

"I'm not, Dad. I won't. I have a box here that I am putting together that I will bring to you."

I was triaging once again. This time, not bills and paperwork stuffed in reusable grocery bags, but wide-eyed characters in colorful clothing. While Dad's community of puppets at the condo was dramatically less than that at the house in South Dakota, there was a station wagon's trunk worth of faces staring back at me. Some were folded in half, some were dangling off the side of a box, some twisted together as if in an embrace. I carefully set aside an empty box and began to fill it with characters I would personally bring to Dad: a clown (yes, another one, but not a marionette), a raccoon, a 17th century Frenchman, three wisemen, a Spanish bullfighter, and a farmer's wife.

Then I came to a large box in which I found petite hand puppets—neatly stacked and carefully wrapped. Each had a hand-molded face with pristine clothing. This was the set Dad had purchased in Prague several years before.

"How was your trip?" I recall asking my parents at the time.

"Oh, it was absolutely delightful!" Mom exclaimed. "Prague is such a beautiful city…" she went on and on, then closed out "… don't get me started on the puppets your father insisted on purchasing!"

She loved Dad's artistry and recognized his talent for puppetry and for theater. Many times, she recounted stories about Dad's high school drama teacher, who was very strict but loved my dad. Mom savored talking about Dad in drama and later recounting his performances in local plays. He was active at the community theater and played leading roles in *Inherit the Wind*, *Sly Fox,* and *The Nerd* while I was growing up. From that red leather chair in the living room, I helped him rehearse lines for those plays. I would sit in my pajamas on the matching ottoman in the evenings and read every other characters' lines from the plays while Dad practiced his. I would have to correct him when he missed a line, or ad libbed, the latter of which he often liked to do. This always perturbed me. To me, the line should be spoken as written. To Dad, there was room to modify here and there. It was something he learned from working with puppets and crafting puppet shows for children. It was developing a storyline while leaving room to improvise with the freedom to respond to children's questions and reactions. There, Dad and I would sit, sometimes much too late in the evening on a school night, practicing. I loved the way it offered me my own practice of the scripts combined with helping Dad. When I attended his performances, I am almost certain the audience members sitting near me noticed my mouth moving along with each of the other characters' lines.

Later, when I was attending performing arts school in New York, I learned the acronym "DLP," which stood for Dead Letter Perfect. Wow, was that up my alley! When my professor in technique stressed the importance of DLP, I could not help but think about those nights helping Dad practice his lines. It was at that school that I also learned the sleeve of creativity that improvisation offers, and I found I was good at it. I must have gotten that from Dad. It led me to more fully understand his draw to ad libbing lines and improvisation. From classes on the fourth floor of a building in Manhattan, I would be transported to that red leather ottoman practicing lines and backstage of the puppet theater, soaking in Dad's rhythm of creativity.

When it came to puppets, Mom was strained about his need to continually add to the collection. "You have so many puppets. And we rarely see them!" She had a good point. For the most part, the puppets lived in boxes in the basement of the house (and later, some of them in boxes at the Florida condo).

Growing up, I always had imagined these puppets carrying on

activities and conversations with each other secretly in the basement, hopping out of the boxes on their own. I mused that they carried on with each other across storylines and themes, dancing, being mischievous, playing. The troll from the *Three Billy Goats Gruff* would be having tea with the grandmother from *Little Red Riding Hood*. Or the Ghost would be doing jumping jacks with the octopus. And one of the witches would be in cahoots with the alligator, spying on the Policeman.

To Mom's point, I had never seen these puppets hailing from Prague, and as I reached into the box and pulled each character out one by one, I was struck by the neatness of wrapping, each swaddled in bubble wrap, each secured with a single piece of paper-like tape. It was clear that the last time my dad looked at and played with these puppets was at the tiny store in Prague that resembled more of a woodworker's studio than a toy store, a store that I produced in my mind—the place I imagined he purchased them.

When I asked him where he procured them, he answered emphatically, "Prague!"

"I know that, Dad. They are really special. I mean, *where* in Prague?" I thought maybe if I found out, I could look up the store or the puppet maker and gather details that would help me locate a new potential owner, and of course, navigate that with Dad.

"Oh, some guy in Prague. You know, those are all handmade."

"I do, Dad. They sure look like it."

He was not able to tell me from whom he purchased that cast of characters.

I started to carefully unwrap each one. I stopped short, pausing after looking at the small face of a girl, the second puppet I unwrapped. *Should I keep them all wrapped?* Quickly, I answered my own question: *no.* My curiosity got the best of me coupled with the rationale that if I understood who each of these characters were, it would help me find them a new and proper home. For Dad. It took me at least an hour to delicately unwrap each member of this crew. I laid them out on the floor of the master bedroom in the condo. I took a photo, as I had already planned to do, and to follow Dad's clear instruction: "Take a photo of them!"

I was transfixed by these characters and found myself talking to each one of them as I straightened their clothing and lay them on the carpet.

"Hello, you."

"Who are you?"

"What a cool coat you have!"

I did not yet know how to take the deep breath that the situation required, but as I stepped back to look at them, I folded my right elbow over my left forearm, inserting my thumb nail in my teeth just like I used to do while trying to solve puzzles growing up. My heart twittered as I contemplated what would be a truly unacceptable outcome—simply dropping these off at a donation center. I needed a solution that would do right by them *and* do right by my dad. A solution that would offer the assurance that they would come to life as they were meant to. On that afternoon of unwrapping, I did not find the answer.

"Well, we have to figure out your next home," I explained to them as I gently re-wrapped each one, carefully placing them back in the box. Before I closed the lid, I hovered my mouth over the box and whispered, "Don't worry, you won't have to stay in here much longer."

I searched for all types of puppet organizations online. I reached out to several via phone and email and got a mix of responses, from "not doing anything because of COVID," to "no thanks," to no response. Ugh. One idea I had was to reach out to the puppet theater in San Diego, California that Dad and I had visited together in 2007. He was speaking at a conference, and my parents decided to stay an extra couple of days to visit me while I was living there. Plus, my parents got to meet Angela for the first time on that trip. The puppet theater is in Balboa Park, and it was one spot my dad mentioned off-the-cuff to me, so we ventured through the park together to find it. They did not specialize in hand puppetry, but I figured it was worth a try. They were not interested.

Ugh, again. A couple weeks went by, and I still did not have an answer. There in the corner of the master bedroom, the box of puppets sat.

Then, early in the morning on a Saturday, Angela and I drove into downtown Sarasota to get a cup of coffee after exploring a new neighborhood across town with Charlie. As we left the coffee shop and drove back to Lido Key, I noticed a small A-frame sign outside the Sarasota Opera. In colorful chalk it read, “Children’s Theater” with small blue letters below it: “Plus puppet shows.”

WHAT?!

I had already spoken to the Sarasota Opera costume department about some of my grandmother’s coats and hats that were at the condo. They welcomed the donation of pristine, vintage clothing for their costume department. My grandparents and parents had been members of the Sarasota Opera and loved supporting the opera and taking in the performances over the years. I had been so excited to find that their costume department was just as excited to receive these coats, hats, and accessories as my grandparents and parents were by supporting the Opera house.

“They surely will be worn and used for our productions!” the head of the costume department exclaimed to me over the phone.

I did not even realize they had a children’s theater, let alone theater activity with puppets! When we got back to the condo that morning, I immediately reached out to their children’s theater. Within days, I had an answer: indeed, they intermixed puppetry into their theater for children and would be overjoyed to receive the puppets. Hooray!

The day we drove back to the Sarasota Opera and pulled up to the children’s theater door, I carried the box full of Prague character puppets in with pride. This was a place they would come alive once again—and it was part of a place my parents loved and supported. Perfect.

“We are very grateful for these,” the gentleman meeting me said. He gently took the box from me.

"You are most welcome. They're from my father. He was an avid puppeteer and supporter of Sarasota Opera. Enjoy!"

I walked down the dark hallway to exit and whispered over my shoulder behind me, "Fare thee well, sweet puppets."

When Jim arrived in the driveway in South Dakota nine months later and offered to help with the puppets, I took him up on it right there on the spot. He walked up wearing a black t-shirt.

"Um, there is a man walking up the driveway right now?" Angela said as a question and statement.

I looked around our large rental SUV.

"Hi, um, I'm Jim. I heard the news about the doctor. I'm so, so sorry."

I looked at his caring eyes, trying desperately to place the familiar face.

"I used to do puppet shows with your dad," he clarified.

Aha! Yes, yes, I know this man! I silently shouted to Angela with a glance.

"Jim! Hi! Oh gosh, thank you. I know, I mean, I didn't recognize you, but…" I stammered.

It was crazy to see him after all these years and crazy to think I could have missed him that day had I not been there. Would he have left a note? I never asked him.

It was a welcome and generous offer from him to provide details he knew about Dad's puppets and help make connections to various puppetry groups and organizations. It was such a relief to connect with him. With Jim's support, I was able to get the notice about the estate sale directly to the regional puppetry guilds and make contact with the leader of a national puppetry organization. Jim had specific contact names and an account as a puppeteer himself and a member of the network, so there was so much more of a connection. Plus, by this time in 2021, it was later in the pandemic, and there seemed to be more of an "open door." Since the estate sale was advertised nationally, we knew that by specifically notifying these puppetry groups, we would reach puppeteers and puppet theater organizers, thereby increasing the chances of finding these small, colorful characters new adventurous homes. To do right by them. To do right by Dad. It was such a relief and such a help. It was comforting to know that I was getting to figure this out with the man who played alongside my dad as a puppeteer behind the stage, offering puppet shows to the children at the community library. Now, I realize that not all the puppets ended up with puppeteers or at puppet theaters, but I do know we set the stage (no pun intended) for the best new homes for them as possible.

I knew Dad had a lot of puppets. I did not know exactly how many puppets there were. And, I did not realize how well I had come to know them while growing up and then after Dad died. It was dreamlike to feel like I was getting to know my dad all over again, and getting to know these characters, some for the first time and some more deeply as familiar friends. A part of the puppetry, the stages, the sets, and these characters, was my dad. He and his various voices for each of their personalities were an embedded part of all of it. So, it felt bizarre to be with this world of puppets he curated without him.

Dad was an artist and a scientist. I think his greatest talent was his sense of play. He was a boy adventurer and loved to play so much that he continued to do so throughout his entire life, even as an elderly man. I admire that so much about him, and I know I was so fortunate to be raised by a father who could instantly jump in to play. Many people have told me, “Your dad was such a unique man.” He was—he played.

I kept two of Dad’s puppets. One is a Sesame Street Pirate Grover, whose arms wrap around your waist while you bring him to life. It was the puppet Dad kept at his medical office and would use with his child patients. It was stored on a tippy toes shelf above the drinking fountain in the hallway outside the patient rooms. “Who is that?” my seven year old self asked, standing on the boring dark brown carpet and pointing in the air while at his office after hours. “Oh, that’s for the kids,” Dad told me. On another occasion I was at his office on a weekday and about to leave through the back door with my mom when I witnessed Dad with the same bright blue furry Grover with a pirate cap and eye patch wrapped around his white doctor's cloak. He gave me a wink and a wave as he ducked into the patient's room. *That patient is a child,* I had thought.

I also kept a billy goat. It is one of the oldest of Dad's "self-made" puppets. Well, self-made in that he crafted the head, face, and horns. My uncle (Dad's brother) and aunt were also puppeteers and artists who helped make puppet characters with my dad when they all were in high school and college. Together the three of them worked for the Minneapolis park system during summers, providing puppet shows for children. My uncle and aunt went on to work at the Metropolitan Opera in New York later in life, and almost every year's holiday card depicted them in some costume from the opera, joined by hand puppets. It was my great-grand-mother who made the clothing for these characters. She was a seamstress, quilter, needle pointer, and cook. Basically, a woman of many talents. My sister knew her when she was a baby and toddler, but great grandma died a few months before I was born, so I never met her. I did know her sewing talents through Dad's puppets (and that puppet stage curtain), and the many quilts in our home. Not to mention, some of those needlepoint chairs. The billy goat has a gray face, black eyes, a cornflower blue waist coat with two white pearl-essence round buttons, and gold horns. "Watch the horns!" Dad would squeal. "You must be *ever-so-careful* of the horns. They are delicate."

I learned more about this billy goat after Dad died. Indeed, it was one of the early puppets that dated back to his puppeteering days of yore working the park system with my uncle and aunt. I found a newspaper article that my grandmother had kept that transported me back to those days of his puppet shows in the summers of the late 1950s and early 1960s. The photo in the article depicts my young dad bringing the billy goat to life in front of a small child, who is transfixed by the character. In the article, Dad talks about the importance of puppetry, explaining that it is an art form that offers children storytelling with characters who are more relatable because of the characters' child-like size. I had never heard him describe puppetry this way. Reading this gave me a deeper understanding of it from his perspective, one he offered when he was less than half the age I am now. It was about the art of play—the art of playing in a manner so that a child may participate.

So, when I say “creepy clown,” I say it with a loving smirk. I say it as the daughter of a profoundly artistic scientist who knew how to play, who showed me how to play, and who granted me the gift of play.

I miss all the puppets. It is hard to look at photos of them (and yes, I took photos!) and not have a sinking feeling in my heart, tears behind my eyes. *How could I let them all go?* It was like auctioning off Dad’s playmates, character friends and parts of his imagination. Then, I think of the smiles and laughter of the children watching Dad’s puppet shows; I think of his smiles and laughter as he greeted puppets in toy stores and showed them to children. I think of my smiles and laughter working backstage with him, watching him play; I think about the wink he gave me before greeting that patient. I glance at Pirate Grover and look over at the billy goat; I think about all those many characters coming out of boxes and playing together, and the sinking feeling dissipates.

“Fare thee well, sweet puppets.”
(Sense of play is immortal.)

Joy of Giving

A consistent theme for me that I discovered in the wake of Mom, Sharon, and Dad dying was the tremendous joy I derive from the act of giving. Just like my mom used to say about "giving something special" with her Candy, I found that I too crave the ability to find something special to give to another, to pass a positive meaning forward in thinking of someone else. Mom passed that trait along to me. Dad, too. And I saw it practiced further by Sharon. I knew this about myself before losing each of them and can recall birthdays and holidays when I would get butterflies of excitement in my tummy anticipating giving a gift. But it was only after losing them that I honed in with precision— an elevated exactness— on the joy that comes with giving.

"It's an act of love," Mom would say in reference to doing something for me, my sister, my dad, a neighbor, a fellow committee member at church, a friend. She was big on acts of love, like the playing of "Happy Birthday" on the piano, keeping up with correspondence, clipping out coupons and newspaper articles she would send to my sister and me once we moved to college, hosting dinners for friends, and of course, making and delivering her Candy during the holidays.

My mom loved to tell the story of receiving a set of china from my great-aunt, Hattie, and admired her giving nature. Hattie was the kindest, most loving soul I was exposed to as a young child. We would visit her in her apartment in Saint Paul, Minnesota, and she would make us root beer floats in colorful glasses. Each glass was a different hue from the rainbow, and I adored standing beside her at her small circular table as she scooped vanilla ice cream, poured the root beer, and explained how delicious a root beer float tastes during an afternoon visit with loved ones. She lived to be 106 years old, and I remember how impressive her 100th birthday party was at the nursing facility where she resided years after the root beer float days at her apartment. As a young woman, she had worked hard to earn enough money to purchase the Limoges plateware for her and her newlywed husband. Ultimately, she gifted the entire set to my mom and dad after they got married.

"How can you part with this?" my stunned mother had asked her. "Don't you want to keep it?"

"I've enjoyed it. Now it's time for someone else to enjoy it."

From that story, it was evident to me that Hattie was as clear about giving away the set of china as she was about how delicious a root beer float tastes during an afternoon visit with loved ones.

The day my parents rolled up in front of our home in (none other than) a minivan, my mother was determined to immediately unload the four boxes of carefully-packaged china she had insisted on bringing. Growing up, it was explained to me that the china set from Hattie was intended to be passed along to me. Angela and I barely had a chance to give hugs to her and my dad, welcome them inside, and gather their suitcases from the vehicle.

"We have to unpack the china!" Mom exclaimed.

"Now? Right now?" I asked.

"Yes!"

Angela and I carried the boxes from the van to our dining table, my mother hovering over us and lifeguarding the china the entire time.

"Be careful!" she shouted.

I sat at the dining table with my mom while my dad ventured into the guest room.

"Feel free to lie down, Dad," I called out. He looked tired from their three-day journey, and I was pleased to glance over and see him lay down on the bed for a rest.

I sat with my mom while she retold the story of Hattie purchasing the dishes, explaining how dear the set was to her, and how she generously passed it along to Mom and Dad. Each time Mom told the story, I knew Hattie's kindness and generosity had made a significant impact on her. It was an admiration of Hattie that Mom and I shared. For me, it was more so for the root beer floats, and for Mom more so for the giving of china.

"You must promise to *never* put them in the dishwasher!" Mom demanded for the umpteenth time. That was always the condition for ultimately receiving the fine dishes adorned with pink flowers and gold trim, a condition my sister and I would joke about. We wondered how anyone could put a condition on a gift. Mom's heart was in a good place; it just came across differently than I imagined the plateware hand-over by Hattie to her.

We carefully unwrapped every piece, and I showed Mom where Angela and I would store the dishes in our dining credenza.

When she said it was an act of love, she was right. There was a whole lot of love represented in these delicate dishes that I grew up with. My parents had served many Thanksgiving dinners on these precious plates and platters. A couple were already chipped, but that did not matter, except for the part where my mom got so animated when instructing us to be careful with them. I love the teacups and saucers and now enjoy using parts of the set at our own Thanksgiving dinner, serving special desserts like the post-turkey apple pie I love to bake.

With giving a gift, it is the act of love part that gets me. It is the act of kindness that adds onto that. It is the thinking of the other person and what they might like to have or what they might be surprised by that draws me in like a problem-solving challenge. And it is the exertion of immediate satisfaction, pleasure, and joy I feel by seeing or hearing of the other person's happiness, surprise (even joy) from receiving such a gift. It is partly selfish, because in the giving, I am satisfying a craving—a kind of "high"—which then turns into its own positive reinforcement. I suppose the thought behind each gift and the passing of positive meaning to another, the experience of the other, is the unselfish part.

The actual gift itself can take so many different forms. It can be intangible or tangible. It can be visible or invisible. A kind word, a card, an action, a thing, time—it can be anything in any form. I love the boundlessness of it. I also love the aspect of giving that I like to call "the cue to my imagination." What I mean by that is the capturing of an idea it promotes and excludes hesitation. Gifting

Dad's safari hat to Doug was like that, so were the needlepoint tap shoes for Nicole. I captured the idea of each and did not hesitate when the ideas arose. Then, I got to imagine (and in Doug's case, participate in) a joyful reaction.

Just like the honing in of this self-realization about the joy of giving, I honed in on my baking practice during this time period of loss. Since all of this happened during the throes of the COVID-19 pandemic, you might think, "how typical," since there were so many stories shared about people making bread and baking. But the origin of my own baking practice was not out of boredom or exploration of something new to try in solitude. The genesis for me came in the tangible actions of measuring ingredients and the practice of precision that baking requires, all providing a form of meditation, tapping into my soul. It was a meditation that gave me a sense of presence, pointed me in a direction toward getting better at something (baking), and granted me the joy to give the final product to another. For instance, I started making scones for the first time in my life and ventured into the land of new flavor combinations. Once baked, it was cheerful to offer a warm scone to Angela and see her enjoy eating it. And it was a delight to surprise a neighbor with a few warm scones to try on a random afternoon for no other reason other than they might enjoy it.

This is not revolutionary. Lots of people like to give and find joy in giving to others. I know that. The point is that in losing people I love, I discovered a new amplitude of giving that included hope. I found joy in giving under a magnifying glass, which allowed me to reflect on the root beer floats from Hattie and how she gave away her fine china before it needed to be given away. I get to ponder the thoughtful gifts my mom used to surprise us with (or absent surprise), the beautiful manner in which Sharon selected and wrote a greeting card, the unique items my dad would pick out and hold secret until revealing them as gifts. I had the joy of giving in me already, but now I had an even greater sense of it and expanded appreciation for it. Because of them, I uncovered the capability to precisely tune into the feeling from giving and from receiving gifts.

The crazy part wasn't my own joy of giving. What was absurd

was that I had to lose these three people I love in such rapid succession, and who were such prominent forces in my life, to gain the magnifying glass that would expand my perspective. It was grotesque to feel like losing them was the only way to grant me that magnification. Under my new magnifier also came my process of giving with newly incorporated characteristics that I can link to who Mom, Sharon, and Dad were in their lives. It is something in me *and* tied to the legacy of each of them, tied to the imprint they made on my life.

...I discovered a new amplitude of giving...

You, Me, Hector, Miguel, and Neso (… and Larry)

In the back and forth of errands—walking Charlie, triaging, organizing, shifting furniture and belongings, solidifying the plans with the estate sale team and more while in South Dakota the second time after Dad's passing in 2021—Angela and I determined that we needed to get a few temporary upgrades done at my parents' house.

Years prior, my parents were so excited to tell me that they had painted the living room and dining room walls a bright red. "It's bold!" they proudly explained.

"Red, Mom? Really? Red?" I asked over the phone. "That *is* bold."

Combined with the multi-colored paisley-textured wallpaper in the surrounding hallways, and top half of the dining room walls, along with the matching multi-colored paisley draperies in the same rooms, and a different patterned wallpaper in every other room, bright red paint created a dark, erratic, and loud sense of space. In my opinion, it was not welcoming nor relaxing. We decided a priority would be to transform those walls back to the original neutral cream that existed before those loud swaths of red paint.

The main bathroom in the hall was in desperate need of a tune-up and repair. The cream cupboards were scratched and in poor form. We decided a couple coats of paint would do the trick, and we chose a blue hue to play off the blue birds on the wallpaper in that room.

Painting interior rooms was something at which Angela and I had good practice, having painted walls in every residence we had lived in together to-date. However, we quickly determined that there was a limit to our "to do" lists. We already had too much on our plates. Taking on a painting job was not the wisest of endeavors for our energy expenditure. We needed to remain focused on the three-ring circus we were conducting and all the other balls we were juggling.

Angela found a local painter who was willing to come quickly (timing was key with the looming estate sale) and to paint for a very reasonable price. Enter Hector and Miguel. They showed up on time. They worked efficiently, and they transformed the rooms with brushes and rolls of paint within days. When the neutral color revealed itself in the living and dining rooms, we felt an immediate wave of relief. It was a swift sense of a calmer space. When blue came across the cabinets in the bathroom, the entire room felt recast.

In the meantime, a man named Neso, who had been hired by my father years earlier, was continuing to mow the large lawn (and plow the driveway in the winter). Ever since my mother died, and in managing my father's affairs, I had become versed in communicating with Neso and providing instructions for what to do and what not to do, like what weed spray to use and not to use.

Larry showed up mid-estate sale prep after I called one of the local plumbers because water had gushed into the basement during a huge rainstorm. It was Larry who stopped the leak, took the time to talk through the best fix with me, showed me how the house piping had been designed, and quickly fixed the issue in a way that would last.

Angela's and my energy output was grossly exceeding our energy input. In other words, we were continuing to operate on too little and low quality sleep; we were constantly in motion and treading water to keep things on track. Our batteries were constantly alerting us to "recharge," and that just was not possible. It was during this time that moments of creativity, brainstorming, and pure delirium set in. We were driving in my hometown, running errands one afternoon and expounding on our gratitude for Hecter, Miguel, Neso, and Larry. It was a rare moment when we gave ourselves pats on the back, recognizing all that we had accomplished to-date. We took a moment to acknowledge that we were managing a ton. We started imagining: *what if we just started managing upgrades and remodels?* All this stuff we were doing was educating us. The days of watching HGTV so very long ago popped into our heads. We would put a team together. Angela landed on what to call it, *You, Me, Hector, Miguel, and Neso.*

I chimed in, "… *and Larry.*"

We laughed. We smiled. It was delirium, we knew it. It was a playful fantasy and yet, that is what we were doing (to some extent) in those very days.

Those days of *You, Me, Hector, Miguel, Neso (... and Larry)* were an investment. We knew it was an investment. We knew the lawn needed to be cut. And, we knew bursting water pipes had to be fixed. We knew more calming walls and brightened bathroom cabinets would serve as a welcome ushering in for the estate sale. It would provide an environment more conducive for the passing along of so many things to others, and for passing the many, many things of my parents' collection forward to a new life. We knew such an investment upfront would have the potential to garner more for the estate—more for my parents' grandchildren, more for my sister and me. While it sounds like it was a focus on money, it was not. It was not a *sole* focus on money; rather, it was a focus on making the estate sale as successful as possible, making it as positive an experience as possible, to ensure a positive outcome. What would that be? It would be an experience with attention to the value of my parents' collection, a tribute to what they had curated and to them. We hoped for an outcome where each of the belongings would find new homes and be carried forward on new journeys. Each item, each belonging, would be taken care of with purpose.

"Each person will specifically select an item to carry forward," Debi's seasoned estate sale voice played in my mind.

Whenever Angela and I now take on a project at home, I cannot help but think, *You, Me, Hector, Miguel, and Neso (... and Larry)*. Ha!

It was delirium, we knew it.

Photos

Photos. Photographs. Film. Slides. Albums. There were thousands—maybe millions—of photographs in my family. My great-grandfather was an avid photographer hobbyist in the early- to mid-1900s, and my father, following in his beloved grandfather's footsteps, also loved taking photographs. He loved tinkering with cameras and film, capturing moments, documenting places, people, and experiences with each lens focus and click of a button.

"Stand there for a picture," Dad would say to my sister and me, while we stood outside a restaurant or on a ferry to Mackinac Island. He would raise a camera to his eyes, juggling at least three other cameras that hung over his shoulders, off his elbow, and around his neck.

"Smile!" Dad was not one to use the typical "Say cheese!"

He took a lot of home videos, too.

"Say the date. Tell us where you are *and say the date,*" my father would instruct us before hitting the bright red "record" button on the large machines of the 1970s, 80s, and 90s. He always wanted a record of a family outing, trip, or vacation—any shared experience, really.

"Daaaaaaaaaad…" I would heave, before he pressed his eye against the lens and the familiar beep of Rudolph's red nose "record" button hit my ear drums. Instantly, I would dive into a description of some monument, tourist site, or restaurant, swinging my arm like Vanna White from *Wheel of Fortune* revealing the letter "Z." When I forgot or failed to mention the date, Dad would ask me directly over the recording, "And what day is it?"

As a kid, it felt so embarrassing when groups of people and kids my age walked by. I never got completely used to it, but I did get better at embracing the practice of documenting family experiences this way. With time, I was much more fluid at producing the necessary location *and date*, waving arms, smiling, and squinting into the sun.

My father got film developed in prints of all sizes and forms. There were slide carriages and boxes filled with individual slides depicting pictures also found in 4x6, 4x4, 3x5 and 8x10 dimensions. Copies, too. *Lots* of copies. Multiple copies were always important to Dad. "Get a copy!" he would exclaim. When ordering photos from the local photo shop, he would get duplicates, triplicates, and twentyfold. He also did this for the older photos from my grandmother (his mom) and really old photos from his grandfather.

As an eye physician who was passionate about lenses, perspective and sight, my father also loved 3-D. I remember visiting Epcot Center and sitting next to him while we watched the 3-D movie. He would hand me the flimsy (but cool) glasses, and every time, I would slide them off my face to take in the comparison of the dandelion seeds blowing with and without them on. "Keep them on your face!" he would scold. The year Dad got a 3-D camera, he was a vivacious young boy sitting in his big red chair, so excited to try out this new camera. Like him, I was curious to see how those photos would turn out, but I was never as impressed with the resulting images as he was.

In September of 2021, I got full exposure (pun intended) to the bountiful universe of family photographs, films, and slideshows that existed in my parents' basement. Angela and I spent endless days and weeks scanning, peering, and flipping through photographs while the estate sale team was hard at work inside the house sifting through items and preparing for the sale that would occur a month later.

"There are many family photo albums and boxes of family photos that we'll need you to take," Debi had informed me. She had previously explained to me that things like family photographs were too personal and not appropriate for the estate sale. I completely understood and agreed, appreciating her instruction as to the rules-of-the-road in estate sale land.

There were cameras, too, many of which I had never seen

before whereas others were all-too familiar from our family adventures.

"Of course, the photographs!" I thought with a hand coming up to slap my forehead. I knew there were a lot from growing up with fields of framed photos in every room, staring at walls filled with photos at my grandmother's place, and watching my father reveal piles of photos on various occasions. "Tom, I love seeing these!" my mother would shriek. Yet, I had *no* concept what a lot, a LOT, A LOT equated to. I did not know that the collection from my parents' home would ultimately fill a five foot tall by three foot wide by five foot long section of the front porch once hauled out.

The dedicated and persistent photo-taking in my family dates back to the late 1800s (those photos are intensely cool) and the decades to follow in the 1900s, which was long before today's era of handheld take-it-with-you-everywhere phone cameras, where we now capture any moment with a swift touch of a screen and reveal an instant result. Now, instant feedback is provided for the next swift touch of the phone screen. When my great-grandfather and father were taking photos, it was a leap of faith for each click accompanied by an anticipation that would grow like an invasive plant while waiting for the film to get developed. When my sister and I were giving video play-by-plays of a family vacation, staring into the large lens of Dad's over-the-shoulder camcorder, we could only imagine how the resulting film would play out. The only way we got to relish a quasi-instant photo product was by way of the magical Polaroid camera, and that was not quite the standard of the time.

When Angela and I moved into our home in Virginia, the former owner said to us, "You cannot know how much we have put into this house." I feel that way about the universe of photography in my family: you cannot know how much there was. I am trying to describe it here with valiant aplomb, yet I know, to anyone other than Angela and those estate sale ladies, the description falls short of the actual quantity in reality. So, imagine. I ask you to imagine. As Angela summed it up, "My family has a lot of photos, and I never, ever, never in my wildest dreams have seen so many photographs."

Going through these special family heirlooms was an activity Angela and I were versed in from our work at the Florida condominium the previous fall, where there were other stacks of albums, framed photographs, and cardboard boxes full of free-floating photographs. I am certain, if stacked one upon the other, those albums and photographs (framed and unframed) would have filled the elevator shaft of that building up to the sixth floor where my parents' condo was located. It was not solely due to the many versions and copies of photographs, but also because there simply were so many photographs taken!

A fair share of the photos in Florida and at the house in South Dakota were ones I had never seen. It was a brand new discovery, another road on the curvy pathway of this post-loss adventure. Many were black and white, or "gray," as I would call them as a child. That always made my father chuckle. "Shall we look at some 'gray' photos?" he would taunt me. "Is it a 'gray' movie?" I would ask him when he or my mother would suggest a movie to watch. Some of the photos were "gray" photos that had been painted to appear in color, such as those from my grandmother's wedding.

The whole endeavor was overwhelming. No, it was severely overwhelming and emotionally demanding to go through generations-worth of family photographs. *How can I not look at each and every one? I must! I need to make a decision about each. And every. One.*

After our initial start with one or two boxes, standing in the basement amidst the estate sale team's activity of parsing items, it quickly became apparent that we had a problem.

"This is crazy!" Angela exclaimed.

My arms hung low, as if I were an Olympic swimmer with limbs for days. I pried my hands from my hips as I stared at the daunting piles before us. "This *is* crazy."

"We need a system." Angela was determined.

With that, we quickly set in motion the next game-plan. We craved fresh air, particularly with the cramped and stuffy air inside the house and the mixture of cobwebs, dust, and particles coming off the cardboard boxes, bags, and photos themselves that had resided in the basement for decades. Plus, we needed a large enough space to work. The boxes were heavy, too. I had to call Doug to come help us lug the giant paper weights up from the basement and out to the front porch. It was clear some of the boxes were from my father's parents, some from my mother's parents, shifted directly to my parents' basement following the passing of my grandparents. Others were taken by my parents before my sister and I were born, others from our childhood days growing up and more still from my parents' "empty nest" years. We purchased a folding table and set it up on the uncovered section of the porch to serve as our operating table.

There we were, triaging yet again. At least with the load in one spot under the covered part of the front porch, we would be able to gauge our progress as the pile inched smaller over the coming days and weeks.

We delved into boxes. We filtered. We studied. We examined. We investigated. We squinted. We peered. We decided.

I had a space sectioned off for photographs I would send to my sister, and a section for me.

"We found another box," Machelle from the estate sale team crept through the front door, gently hesitant to inform us there were yet more photos to go through.

Many were damaged. It was sad to find certain photos completely ruined because of the careless manner in which they were stored. Turns out, Heineken beer case boxes and old shipping boxes from who-knows-where are not the best for storing photographs. The manner of storage was not mal-intended, I know that. I think it was simply attention to the taking of the photos, the capturing of moments, and a lack of attention to the storage part combined with the overwhelming quantity. When there is so much stuff, what do you do? Answer: put it in a box—out of sight, out of mind.

I was ecstatic when I found the photo of my sister as a baby, reaching for a yellow flower. It was taken by my father (of course) and one my mother always raved about over the years. I had never seen the actual photograph before but recognized it as soon as I came across it in a stack. I found photos of my mother and her siblings from the 1940s; photos of my great- grandfather at a bowling alley with secretaries from his insurance company; photos of my parents with their friends on travel in Europe; photos of my great grandparents' dogs dressed up in costumes; photos of my grandmother with her two young sons; photos of my aunts and uncles at my sister's and my dance recitals from the 1980's, photos of my parents while they were in college—photos, more photos and more photos.

Angela and I stood. We sat. We knelt. We tried putting on music. For a while, we started setting timers to make sure we took breaks between bouts of combing through glossy and matte photos of all sizes. We worked to balance efficiency with due respect. We did our best. I did my best.

I developed extreme pain in my hip during this family photograph examination "Ironman" and only later learned that I was carrying excessive emotional pain in my hips. The emotions buried into my hips and dug in with sharp claws, refusing to let go. I became increasingly unable to walk. A former athlete, I found myself hobbling along in excruciating pain, taking breaks just to get around the block with Angela and Charlie. Only later, after a combination of physical therapy, emotional therapy, and energy therapy, did the pain start to release its anchored grip. Going through all those photos put into focus a picture I was not paying attention to at all: my grief was crippling me. The compounding layers of loss were stacking up, reacting to one another, and my entire being altered. The photos served as the thousands upon thousands (maybe millions) of pixels coming together to reveal that reality to me.

I know all these photographs are treasures. They are treasures beyond measure. Of course they are! How fortunate to have so many moments, over so many years, in so many locations, captured. To have a "record" (as my father would say) of these lives and their experiences. I know this is true. I feel it now as strongly as I felt the striking pain in my hips.

From all that sifting, and all the photograph discovery, including analysis, memory triggers, recollections, sighs for days of old, laughter at silly expressions, moments of re-lived experiences, tears of pain, aha's, and curiosity; from the young faces of my grandparents, great grandparents, great-great grandparents, their dogs, their homes, their celebrations and their lives; from the faces of my parents, my sister, and me; our celebrations, our lives; of all the thousands upon thousands (again, maybe millions) of photographs I peered at, there is one that grabs my heart with a string as mighty as the passion my parents had for life. The photo is candid—a profile of my mother wrapping a towel around me after bath time in the same hallway bathroom where we painted the cabinets blue. I am about a year old, sitting on the bathroom counter and my mother is kneeling, looking up at me while my arm stretches out to touch her loving face. The expressions on our faces captured in a click of a moment convince me that my father is there with us, on the other side of the lens. We are present and joyful. It is my favorite photo of us, and while my father is not in the frame, I carry it as the best photo of the three of us. It serves as a beautiful reminder of the lessons they taught me, the encouragement in life they offered me, and the love they gave me. And still do. Like others, I did not know this photo existed until after my parents died. I like to think the whole journey while they lived and after they died led me to it.

And then there is the photo of Sharon and me during our last ski trip together that appeared as a "photo memory" on my phone while Angela and I were doing all that sifting, flipping through and gazing upon family snapshots. The picture was taken two months before Sharon got sick, six months before she died, and a lifetime before I could imagine anything going wrong with her health. Sharon had no interest in skiing down the mountains, but she was the first to accept an invitation for a group trip to Utah. She was all in. In the photo, we are laughing— uproarious laughter really— about a silly, colorful map she had drawn for the trip, complete with sidebar notes of directions and places to visit. Perfectly Sharon. Angela swiped her phone screen at the time and took that photo, and just like the picture of my parents and me, though Angela is not in the frame of this one, I carry it as my favorite photo of the three of us.

These two photographs sit side by side in my heart, depicting two moments in life captured. They show that there is so much more behind a moment, so much leading in, and so much following. They remind me there are so many things in these flashes of time, in these stories. They serve as a reminder to be joyful and to capture a moment. And that beats in my heart.

We did our best. I did my best.
(There are so many ways to capture a moment.)

Playboy, Pipes, and How To Turn On a Lamp

My dad had a collection of *Playboy* magazines—a pretty large one. I cannot tell you how many issues, but I can tell you that it filled a few cardboard boxes in my parents' basement. I never saw my dad read, look at, or cram them into Heineken boxes. I do recall seeing the redacted, black-marked magazines arrive in the mailbox every so often, but I never actually saw him retrieve them from the mail. My dad could be sneaky. In any case, this was something I knew about but did not pay much attention to. I can probably count on two fingers the times I flipped through a *Playboy* growing up when I stumbled upon them in his study downstairs.

Dad revered women. He had a male ego like most men of his generation, and he admired women. He liked to be around and surrounded by them. He cherished my mom, savored bantering with the surgical nurses, and ultimately welcomed relying on the care of female caregivers at the end of his life. Perhaps the *Playboy* magazines were a mixture of Dad's love for women combined with his love for books and art. I imagine he would have considered *Playboy* magazines just another form of literature, photography, and artistic expression (can I call them that?) to go along with all the other mounds of books, magazines, newspapers, photos, and art he collected.

Plus, male ego.

Dad also had a beautiful collection of smoking pipes, the tobacco kind. Some were from his grandfather and some from his father and some he purchased during his various travels to Europe, South America, China, and Japan. Of course, he also had the tobacco smoking accessories—the fold-over envelopes that held various types of tobacco, stubbers (the tool to tamp down the tobacco in the pipe while filling it), and reamers (the cleaning tool to scrape out ash). As an adult, this made me think of the espresso tampers that baristas use at coffee shops. He had matches, lighters, and ashtrays of varying colors and sizes. A Sherlock Holmes porcelain head stared at us from a living room shelf, a tobacco cookie jar of sorts. When you lifted Holmes' hat, you would find a deep cavern for holding tobacco. And Holmes' pipe (of course he had a pipe) was a matchstick holder. That living room shelf was dedicated to Dad's pipe and cigar smoking arsenal. He also had other parts of his collection in his basement study. Special wooden racks to display the pipes facing forward and backward perched on his dresser, reflecting in his mirror. One of my favorites was smaller and looked like the bark of a tree.

Smoking cigars and pipes was a hobby, a thing my dad did every evening, a habit, and I dare say, an addiction. On some occasions, he would smoke a cigar in the afternoon, particularly when golfing. It was my dad who taught me that mosquitos don't like the smell of cigars. One afternoon when I was home from college, I was lamenting about the mosquitos coming after me on the fairway of hole number four. Dad reached into his tan golf bag and charged over to me with a cigar in hand, expertly lit it, and then shoved it in my hand. "You want me to smoke this?" I asked. "No!" He commanded. "Just hold it. The mosquitos hate it." Just like that, problem solved. I did not like holding that cigar—nor the smoke nor the smell—but I sure did like the mosquito repellant. Thanks, Dad.

Smoking was passed down to him from his grandfather, whom he adored and who "really felt more like a father to him than his own dad," my mom would tell my sister and me. Dad's dad also smoked but added cigarettes to his menu of smoking choices. Mom was always grateful that Dad did not smoke cigarettes, "At least your father does not smoke cigarettes," she would say, expressing both gratitude and disgust for cigarettes in one fell swoop. She would also vent her frustration with his smoking, "For how much grief you gave me for smoking cigarettes," tension in her throat, she would add, "and I cannot do the same about your smoking?!" Dad always claimed that cigar and pipe smoking were not as bad as cigarettes, not as addictive or harmful. "I don't inhale," he would state assuredly. Later in life, he would add a sly smile and chuckle after making that statement. Today, I am acutely aware of how ridiculous that argument was.

As a child, I always preferred the tobacco pipes to the cigars. Some of the cigars were really hard to take. My sister would scurry into the living room after having tried to go to bed and plead, "Can you please put that out? Or smoke a different one? It's giving me such a bad headache!" Dad would apologize. "Oh, I am sorry, honey," and though he may have put out the cigar for a different one, he usually kept puffing along. I think that is the nature of an addiction. He was genuinely sorry it caused her head to ache (and mine, too), but it didn't motivate him enough to stop. Some of the pipe tobacco smelled delicious. I would run into the living room in my nightgown and excitedly ask, "Which one is that, Dad?" I would add my own commentary. "I like that. Smoke that more, please." Not a strange request for a ten-year-old at all.

"Go put some lights on in the living room, will you?" Dad would ask me as night drew near and we settled in for dinner. I would go over and turn on the largest floor lamp in the house. It resided in the corner next to the piano and several feet behind Dad's trusty red chair. His evening routine post-dinner was to sit in that red leather wing-backed chair in the living room, surrounded by piles of medical journals, newspapers, history books, and a Mead notebook (for his notes and ideas, of course). These would sit, piled on that matching leather ottoman, on the floor surrounding him, and on the tiny, metal "cocktail" surface that attached to the wooden floor lamp residing just between his chair and the fireplace. Both lamps created a nice evening glow to the room. He needed the light for reading, certainly, and I think he liked that glow of light circling him. For all I know, in the wee hours of the night, while he read about the French Revolution, the Civil War, remedies for rare ophthalmic ailments, and artwork at the National Gallery of Art, he may have had a *Playboy* or two to flip through, too.

I do not exactly know when Dad's smoking ended. He quit pipes long before cigars, and I do not recall his ever picking up a cigar after he was diagnosed with pulmonary fibrosis. I have to guess that it was at some point leading into or after his diagnosis and when he started needing oxygen to aid his breathing when he called it quits. In his final years, as he struggled more and more to scoop in oxygen and breathe, I never asked him if he regretted smoking all those pipes and cigars over the years. I am not entirely sure what he would say. My instinct tells me he would give me that sly smile, add a wink, and say, "Nah, what for? I didn't inhale."

In October, 2021 in the final weeks leading up to the estate sale at the house, Angela and I had come back from that week working in Omaha, Nebraska because the estate sale team to finalize their preparations. (In a nutshell, they needed all the space to display and stage the heaps of my parents' things.) It was an afternoon when we walked back into the house. We found a team member, Machelle, working in the basement. She is the most talented staging artist I have ever encountered. She was incredible. We walked about the house and were amazed at the progress from the prior week. We could see it all coming together. "This is looking great, Machelle!" I exclaimed. "It looks like a home again." I was overwhelmed by what they had done thus far, and it was not hard for me to come up with a description for it: they had brought my parents' things back to life. While the three of us were in the basement, Machelle described how she was planning to showcase some of my dad's plush puppets. Then, she abruptly turned to me and softly stated, "I do have a question for you. It can be a sensitive topic."

Hmmm. What could this be about?

She escorted me to the back of the basement's main living area, toward my dad's study. She stopped at the round wooden table, which had been there for years, and which had also been hidden by the gross number of belongings stacked atop it. The table was now orderly and artistically decorated with books and newspapers, some of Dad's pipes, and that Sherlock Holmes porcelain head, including the matches sticking out of the pipe. Next to the table was my great-grandfather's plum leather chair. "I am designing this to be like a reading nook, like an old study with the pipes and books," she described gently, waving her hands over the space.

"I love that!" I nearly shouted.

She went on delicately, "And… I wanted to see what you thought about the *Playboy* magazines. Can we display them here?" She kept talking, "I mean, I thought it would be kind of cool to go along with the old-world study feel."

"Do it." Angela and I said emphatically in unison and without hesitation.

"Oh, okay, great," Machelle breathed. "You know, sometimes people are sensitive about them or want the magazines to be sold separately and quietly on the side."

"No. Your idea is perfect. Do it." I encouraged her.

In my heart of hearts, I knew without pause that my dad would have adored the nook Machelle was creating. And, sensitive? Ha! He would not have been sensitive about it at all.

The three of us walked back up to the main level of the home. I stopped by the kitchen for a glass of water while Angela and Machelle headed to the living room. We were interested to see how they decided to display things in the large central room of the house. "We need some light," Angela said, as she walked over to the large floor lamp in the corner by the piano. She looked under the lamp shade and at the cord, searching for a switch. Machelle called out from across the room, walking toward her, "It's on the pole. Pull on the rod." Angela continued to look up, down, sideways at the lamp, trying to problem-solve for a switch. I rounded the corner from the kitchen, ready to help. Having turned on that lamp so many times before while preparing the living room lighting for Dad's post-dinner routine, it was more than second nature to me. Before I could squeak out an instruction, I saw Machelle lean over, "It's kind of like an inappropriate sexual gesture." She pulled down and up on the lamp's rod and a glow of light immediately filled the space around us.

I burst into laughter. It was such a *good* moment—such a great series of moments. It was crazy good: my dad's *Playboy* magazines, pipes, and how to turn on a lamp, an "inappropriate sexual gesture," indeed. I am smiling as I write this, and I bet my dad is, too.

"It looks like a home again."

Piano

Some things in life are fixtures. Growing up, the piano was a fixture in our home. While I write those words, it is hard to call it a fixture because it felt so embedded in our lives, as though it moved with us, like the sound produced from its keys—the music—moving through rooms, memories, and hearts.

It was a Steinway & Sons grand piano. Black and shiny. My father used to tinkle the ivories, and I loved to dance when he would spontaneously play *The Wild Horseman*, Robert Schumann's Opus 68 Number 8. What immediate joy I would feel upon his playing that tune! I recall twirling with my sister and marching around the living room, careful to avoid knocking into the many breakables my parents kept around.

I remember when my legs would dangle off the black wooden bench and how smooth the keys felt on my fingertips.

My sister began lessons in the third grade. She and I would sit alongside one another while she taught me *Peter, Peter, Pumpkin Eater* and *Mary Had a Little Lamb* on the black keys. We would play *Heart and Soul* together before I even began piano lessons, which was also in the third grade.

My parents were adamant that we both learn starting in the third grade and continue to play until we were at least eighteen, "And then you can decide for yourself." It was my mother who drove that train, though. The commitment until age eighteen was clear—no flexing on that.

I had fun with the piano and learning to play over the years. My draw to the instrument had ups and downs. I had waves of interest and cheer for playing, and my love for it ultimately came from the joy it offered us all.

My sister is a talented piano player. She embraced the instrument with an admirable ardor and reverence. Over the years, she grew closer to music and her talent. She outgrew teachers and had long lessons at the university's music school, and at one point, an instructor drove the sixty mile route from the state university to teach her from our living room on Wednesday afternoons. I think it was that teacher who encouraged a new framework for my sister's practice schedule: she started practicing nearly four hours per day. One to two of those hours in the morning starting at five o'clock, never mind that three other people in the house were trying to sleep. I still remember putting a pillow over my head every morning. To this day, when I hear one particular piece, which was an emotive pounding (not a gentle lilt), I am taken back to my twin bed during those wee hours of the morning. I was intrigued by how there wasn't alternate timing for her practice. She needed to practice, wanted to practice, and that took priority. I guess our morning discomfort was our way of supporting her.

When she graduated high school, my parents and sister orchestrated an individual senior recital that she performed at the local college music auditorium, printed program and all. She had practiced so hard, demonstrated so much dedication, and was on her way to study piano performance at a music institute. So cool. She fully embraced the instrument and a path forward with music.

Every birthday, Mom would insist on pulling out the "Happy Birthday" sheet music from the wooden bench and wrestling out the familiar tune. This was something for which she nearly never practiced and that she viewed as a demonstration of her commitment to the celebratory nature of birthdays and one of those "acts of love" she would reference. It was something she felt was special to do for each of us on our "special day."

My father kept up with the piano tuning schedule. Many times the tuner would arrive on a Tuesday afternoon. I recall being there to greet him and listening to him check the strings. I found it fascinating. Hard presses of the keys, soft presses, banging as he would check the exactness of the sound.

As a member of the local Lions Club, my father became the gent to pound out the "Don't You Hear Those Lions Roar?" mascot song each week at the local chapter meeting.

At rare times, I wondered what it would be like if we

rearranged the living room and reoriented the placement of the piano. I even brought it up a couple of times, to which even the slightest consideration was quickly abandoned. There the piano would stay, situated opposite our dining room, alongside the large living room window. It was a steady, stable fixture that would remain in its place.

We used to put Christmas decorations atop it each holiday season, and over time, we opened the top more often to reveal the beautiful strings and allow the sound to more fully spread throughout the house. In later years, my parents began displaying framed photographs of our family on top of the instrument.

When my sister was married and her family had a home of their own, my parents offered her the piano. She was not ever able to accept it, citing the difficulty and expense of moving it and the lack of space in her own home.

So, there it remained, in the living room of my childhood home.

Not nearly enough years later, after Dad died, and with Mom already passed, and the time had come to go through the house, once again, the piano was a key topic. *The piano.*

My father's final wishes were that my sister had the first right of refusal. It was to be offered to her, but if she did not accept it, the piano was then for me to keep or decide what to do with it.

My sister ultimately decided it was too difficult for her to take, which was a very emotionally taxing decision for her. Rightfully so.

I considered keeping the piano, but could not imagine it as the living musical battery of my home today. I could barely imagine my childhood living room without the piano. Remove everything else, but do not take the piano.

I learned through copious amounts of research and talking to dealers and musicians that large instruments such as pianos are "tricky" to sell, "tough" to find buyers, and "difficult" to get good offers. The art auctioneers for the paintings and other items of my parents' belongings did not agree to auctioning the piano. They recommended including it in the estate sale. "That's really the best way," they advised. So that was my answer. It would serve as a "welcoming piece to draw in estate-sale goers," according to Debi from the estate sale team.

As the team leader and owner of the estate sales business, she was enthusiastic about the presence of the piano and arranged to have someone play it during the sale. She was giddy with excitement about how it would create a certain mood and ambiance. Once again, the home would be filled with music. I liked to imagine the sale as a party, a social event of another era, like those hosted by my parents and grandparents. The piano would play its role for my family in that home one last time.

The evening of day one of the estate sale, a text flashed onto my phone screen. "We have an offer for the piano. Do you want to accept it?" It was Debi notifying me of the offer. I immediately stopped in my tracks, my breath suspended. The pressure of tears behind my eyes swelled. *Here it is*, I thought, *an offer*. A precipice of letting go of something my parents loved, something my sister loves, something I love—something we all loved together as a family.

I knew from all that prior research that the offer was a good one—smack dab in the middle of the expected range (one where "You would be lucky to get the high-end of the range," the auctioneers had said.). But, this was our family's piano. *The piano.*

I was balancing on the tip of a pointy fulcrum: which way to lean?

I could not respond.

Pick up the phone. Set down the phone.

Pick up. Set down. Turn it over.

Walk away. Come back.

Read the text again.

Make a phone call.

Make a call. Make a decision.

Again, decide.

Then, my phone rang—a phone call from Debi. "I have the woman who wants to buy the piano here," she said. She explained that it was an offer from a mother with two young daughters who was really excited to buy the piano and who would arrange for the pick up and transport of the instrument. Debi asked the question again, "Do you want to accept the offer?"

"Can I please have a few moments, and I'll text you back?" I committed to making a decision. I would text her back. I needed another breath. I needed a moment.

I hung up the phone.

Angela asked, "What did she say?"

I retold the conversation. As I did, clarity inched forward. The call helped. The context helped. The challenge remained: the tug of reality and logic with emotion.

"What should I do? Do you think I should accept it?" Angela knew the weight of this decision, the feelings tied to it. She wrapped her arms around me and gently asked, "What do *you* think?"

With sadness and acceptance, "I think so."

A few moments later, with Angela's arms around my shoulders, I texted Debi, "Thanks for calling Debi. Yea."

I eked out a "Yea" with my fingers typing. I could not manage a "yes," not a "yeah," but my intention and meaning were there with that "yea."

It makes me sad to write this, and I struggle. It is hard. I sit with the feelings of loss and hear the music played by my father, my mother, my sister, and me. The truth is, we all really *loved* that piano. We loved its comforting presence, the hope of music and harmony it promised, and the sound it filled the house with morning, noon, night, holidays, birthdays, and every days.

A few days following the estate sale, I asked Debi if she could share the name of the woman who purchased the piano.

She wrote back with two words: Sara Mark.

Another stop in my tracks.

Sara Mark?!?! I knew that name! I *know* that name! Sara is the youngest daughter of my parents' friends from the medical community, who I held when she was a baby, whose father was our orthopedist, and whose grandfather repaired my finger when I was two years old.

Debi went on to tell me that Sara's two young daughters were excited to learn piano and were taking up lessons.

My breath suspended yet again. The pressure of tears behind my eyes swelling, again - this time with comfort and resolution.

As sad as it was to let the piano go, the connection to its new owners and the bridge to a new life of music for a family, for *that* family with two young daughters, just like my parents with two daughters eager to play music, is the universe's way of comforting me and reminding me that the piano has been paid forward to play its role for another family, with all the promises such a fixture can hold.

I was balancing on the tip of a pointy fulcrum: which way to lean?

Skull

"By the power of gray skull!"

He-man would reveal himself in order to defend against Skeletor, the evil villain of the He-man cartoon. *He-man* was a television cartoon from the 1980s and a popular entertainment for my sister and me for a couple years in the early part of that decade. We would watch while sitting on the lime green carpet of the basement. We did not grow up watching many cartoons since we mostly had extracurricular activities, like dance and ice skating on Saturday mornings, so finding moments to watch a *He-man* rerun, or even *Scooby Doo*, was a real treat to us.

When the owner of the auction house in Minnesota who advised about the piano, and worked with us to auction a number of my parents' collectibles, including those Old Masters paintings, reached out to me about the skull just before the final of three auctions, "by the power of gray skull" ran through my mind. He informed me that they would need to return the skull to me.

What?! I had to squeeze my eyes closed and reset myself for his message. I had completely forgotten that they had found a medical model human skull in my dad's study.

At this point, it was months after Dad had died, the estate sale had ended, and two auctions were complete. Angela and I were back at our home in Virginia, and I was in regular contact with my dad's estate attorney, in the throes of working to close out his estate, preparing tax documents for the accountant, and continuing to ignore my extreme exhaustion and pain in my hips.

I called him back.

"Do you know when your dad purchased the skull?"

"Uh, no."

"Do you know where he purchased it?"

Again, "No."

"We cannot confirm the provenance of the skull, but we believe it comes from a small company in Michigan."

He went on to explain to me that they do not handle items believed to be from that company because that it has a reputation for bad practices in the acquisition for the selling of medical models.

I did not have the energy to speak what my mind said: *Well, that's great—just dandy.*

"I just need to confirm the address where to send it to you."

"Okay. Well, um… here. You can send it to me here." I gave him my address after a hurried analysis in my brain.

Two days later, a perfect cube of a cardboard box arrived at our front stoop. I carried it around to our back patio to open it. After all the cardboard Angela and I had been surrounded by and amongst the past twenty-four months, I did not want to bring more cardboard into our home. And I did not want to open a medical model of a human skull in our front yard. I knelt on the patio and opened the box to find loads of packaging material spewing out. I cleared the packaging popcorn pieces, wishing I had had the forethought to put a trash bag next to me. Inside, I found another cube: a hard black case. I slid it out of the cardboard box. It had a handle and old-fashioned clips securing its closure. I gently landed it on the patio table, lifted up on the two clips, and opened the lid. There it was: a to-scale human skull.

It was only after I lifted the skull up and out of the black case that I saw a flimsy paper, tarnished by years of storage. It had the name and address for that small company. I stared at the skull's no-face.

Wow. What remains, I thought, not intending a pun; rather, feeling the pang of desire to call up my dad and ask him all about it. "Where did you get it, Dad? When? How did you reference it?

Was it in your office? I think it was on your shelf next to your desk in your office. Am I right?"

Angela came out to the patio.

"The skull arrived," I said flatly.

"Oh geez," she peered over my shoulder. "What are we going to do with it?"

With a shrug of my shoulders, I delicately slid that skull back into the case and closed the lid.

"I don't know. I'll have to figure it out. For now, I guess it goes back in the box."

When I think about what remains, somehow a skull with its delicate pieces, tiny hinges, and medical labels is part of it. Hell, at this point, why not? Why shouldn't it be? Why *wouldn't* it be? After all that remains, a skull too. Crazy! The unknown story where and when Dad got it, the journey of it before those auctioneers found it, the story I imagine, and the journey I have taken is what remains.

Among He-man's superpowers are increased stamina, endurance, and strength. Part of my journey, including the skull, is that it all has pushed me, rocked me to my core, requiring increased stamina, endurance, and strength (among other "powers"). I did not transform into a he-man, and I do not think I have superpowers. I have taken a human journey.

…the journey I have taken is what remains.

It's Not About the Skates

Mid-afternoon on a sunny, breezy Friday of October 2021, Angela and I were packed up with Charlie, ready to drive the large, black Ford Expedition rental back to our home in Virginia. After showering and checking out of our rental a few neighborhoods away, we made one last stop at the house to check with the estate sale team before heading out on the 1,269-mile journey from South Dakota to Virginia. I did not consciously think about it as we entered the house; I only realized as I walked from room to room that this would be the last time I saw my parents' home, my childhood home, as just that.

The estate sale was scheduled to kick off the following Thursday, and it was going to run for two weekends. Angela and I would be back at our home in Virginia, awaiting word from Debi and her team about how it all was going. When we first met Debi, months prior she had shared her strong recommendation for us not to be present at the sale. It was never our plan nor intent to be there, but I distinctly recall her describing that it is much better for family members to spend time elsewhere while a sale takes place. "It's too hard to watch other people look through, comment on, and purchase your parents' things," she had said. It made sense. She also informed us that for this particular estate sale, multiple weekends were in order. "Typically our sales run for one weekend, Thursday morning to Sunday evening, but we will need to run the sale here for two weekends," she had told us. "And, we'll need to advertise it nationally." This was due to the "size and scale of the sale," as she had phrased it. In other words, due to the sheer volume of items and unique items that my parents owned and that were to be sold.

My final visit to each room was masked by the checking in and farewell to the wonder-women estate sale team: Debi, Machelle, and Megan. As if my own secret in the wide open, I visited each room of the main level first. I wandered into my childhood room, which they had transformed into a delightful kids room, displaying everything for a child: the doll house, dolls, books, toys, blankets, the lace-covered pillow I knew so well from nap time. My sister's room had transformed into the holiday room. Everything holiday and Christmas-related was neatly displayed. I picked up a needlepoint mouse ornament and brushed my fingers along the Santa placemats. My parents' room was a fashion department store with frocks and purses, hats, scarves, and shoes from the various decades of my parents' marriage. I put on one of Dad's European hats and felt the warmth and weight of it. I picked up one of Mom's purses and felt the chain strap that used to make an annoying clink on the entry-way slate floor when she set it on the front hall chair. I stopped at the doorway of the hall bathroom, which had transformed into a cosmetics counter. A variety of perfumes, colognes, unopened bath salts, hand towels, and beautifully-organized bathing sets rested on the counter, across from the bathtub, and on the back of the toilet. I walked through the living room to the dining room and scanned the colors and textures surrounding me. Books, figurines, needlepoint pillows, more books, sheets of music displayed near the piano, a case filled with higher priced items of crystal and silver.

I found myself breathing it in, breathing it out. I gazed at how well each family treasure was displayed, taking snapshots with my eyes. *Click, click,* the button of my memory camera clicking with each eyelid closing and opening—letting go and holding on all at once.

"Your childhood must have been magical." Debi startled me from my trance while I scanned the bookshelves, the fireplace and the piano. "Your parents had so many wonderful things; it must have been magical."

"It was. It really was." I sighed, the flip book of my childhood flashing before me. *Magical. What a perfect word for it,* I thought. I believe that to this day. All the joy, chaos, stress, the love, the challenges, all the music, all the adventure—it *was* magical. It was wild to me that Debi could name it, could describe it, without knowing me very well and without ever having met my parents. I am certain it was a testament to the lives my parents curated that were represented by all these beautiful things.

I strolled through the kitchen and noted the vertical shelves of teapots my father had mostly picked out over the years: the hexagon pot with four accompanying mugs, which depicted scenes and various characters from Shakespearean plays; the blue, yellow, and red engine train car pot that was so tricky to pour; and the hand-painted red geranium on the squatty, white teapot from Mackinac Island. The penguin pitcher resting in the corner of the countertop stole my gaze. Oh, how Mom liked penguins!

I rounded the corner and made my way down to the basement, feeling the creak of the third step, just as I would hear as a child when I would carry caffeine-free diet Pepsi up from the basement for my mom (it would stay cool in the back basement room). I walked through the utility and laundry rooms, stopping for a few seconds in front of the skeleton to honor it in some way. "Oh, there you are," I said under my breath, "nice to see you again." That same skeleton that enjoyed time in the living room (and the garage) was now a focal point among cards and decorations highlighting Halloween. To the left on my mom's old sewing table, I noticed the inventory of painted needlepoint canvases not-yet-stitched. I floated past stacks of five hundred and thousand piece puzzles depicting old villages and landscapes in Germany. I strolled back to the main basement living area. I rested my hand on more than a few of the plush puppets that snuggled among each other on a large table: the turkey, the octopus, the elephant—each a separate character and personality. I grabbed the paw of the wolf from the *Little Red Riding Hood* set as I walked past the puppet stage. I strode past that 'reading nook' Machelle designed, into my dad's study, noting the box of old newspapers from Minnesota, and around to my dad's old tool bench. I zigzagged my way past the cupboards displaying Kodak film and the Polaroid cameras. I criss-crossed to the shelving units near the heating and air conditioning systems. Rows of Dad's cameras earnestly gazing at me. I was struck by the quantity of lenses staring back at me. In one small area, I peered back at one of the old 1970s film machines. Suddenly I was six-years-old again and my mom, my dad, my sister, and I were in the living room watching stacks of family movies together. I could hear the tick-ticking of the film reel while the videos scrolled across the large projector screen my dad had hauled up from the basement. The sound of the film overlaid by my mom exclaiming, "These are wonderful, Tom! It would be nice to see these more often!" Mom was always dismayed that so many of her favorite family photos and videos were tucked away in cardboard boxes "somewhere in the basement" and "never to be seen" as she worded it.

I breathed in. I breathed out. I passed the area with Dad's old medical cabinets. The table-top model of the human eye was featured on the second shelf of one cabinet, resting squarely between a variety of ophthalmic posters and medical journals. The door to the back basement room creaked as I opened it and the oh-so-familiar hard snap of the light switch pierced my eardrums as light burst into that back room. The room was no longer a zone of trip hazards I had come to know so well over the years gathering that caffeine-free diet Pepsi. It was now a clear pathway featuring newly organized shelves lined with you-name-it: trinkets, outdoor equipment, and more needlepoint decorations.

As I turned to leave that cold, back room in the basement, I stopped short and suddenly, an immediate locking of my feet to the chilly concrete floor, as if my legs were posts nailed into the ground. Amidst all the things, my eye caught a pair of black speed skates poking out of a giant, dusty and bent cardboard box on the floor. My breath halted, pure ache. "Oh, Dad," I whispered. The rush of memory and emotion flooded to me and prevented any bodily movement on my part. My mind racing, another flip-book of memories scrolling rapidly through my mind: Dad in his Scottish cap, red plaid pants and tan sport coat, striding in speed-skating style around the local ice rink while his cheeks deepened in pink color from the cold air; my sister and me practicing our figure skating: frontwards, backwards, spins, T-stops, hockey stops, snow plows, spirals, jumps; the sound of the rink's wooden door swinging open, creaking, then slamming hard, abruptly shutting each time a skater entered the warming room. The smell of the fifty cent hot cocoa Dad bought from the concession stand for me and my sister. This was an ice rink he had conceived of with a handful of other people in the community and then successfully negotiated a land lease from the city; a rink for which the original Zamboni ice machine was named after him due to his generous donation. "The generous gift of…" it read in italicized black paint across the front, my dad's name written in bold cursive. He was passionate about that rink because he wanted people in the community to have a way to stay active in the bitter cold of winter because skating is an activity you can do "When you are young and also in your older years," he would say. Dad was driven to make it accessible because he enjoyed skating, and he wanted to see children from the community learn just as he had done growing up in Minnesota learning from his beloved grandfather. And, he wanted a place where his two daughters could skate. My dad put me in skates when I was two years old. Skating across a sheet of ice is like walking for me, thanks to my dad.

It was then, just then, that it hit me: this would be the last time I see these things. I knew it. I felt it with all of my being. It would be the last time I would see the house as it was. With these things—with all the things representing my dear parents and my childhood with them and my sister.

"What?" Angela asked. "What is it?"

"Dad. My dad's skates," I squeaked. "What do I do?" I stood frozen, as if I were a sheet of ice.

"It's not about the skates, honey." Angela grabbed my hand, gave it a squeeze, and we walked steadily out of the room, up the stairs, and out the front door of the house.

I kept moving. I just kept moving. One foot in front of the other. Breathe in. Breathe out. Moving. Doing. It was one of those times in life when you have every reason to stand still, yet you must keep moving because if you don't, you may never move again.

As I walked across the front door's threshold to the outside, the sun warming my face, I heard Angela call out to Debi, Machelle, and Megan, "We're headed out. Thanks for everything."

Debi's voice breezed through the air, "Have a safe trip! We will be in touch and let you know how things go."

I yanked my sunglasses over my face and loaded my person into the SUV. Breath in, breath out.

"Are you okay?" Angela touched my arm.

"Yep. Let's go."

We pulled out of the driveway and drove down the hill. 1,268.8 miles to go.

Angela was right. It was not about the skates. It is not about the skates.

I was right, too. It *was* about the skates. It *is* about the skates. It is about what the skates represent: the joy, the memories, the loss, the pain, the mourning. It is about it all. E-v-e-r-y-t-h-i-n-g. Every tear, every laugh, every smile, every cry. It is about the glisten in Dad's eyes, his joy in telling a long-winded story, his will to live. It's about Sharon's *joie de vivre*, frankness, and purple nails. It's about Mom's passion to learn, to give gifts, and her love of family. It is about the craziness when they were living, the crazy shit that happened when they died, and all the crazy shit that is yet to be. All of it. Because that is life. This is life. And I would be crazy not to soak it all in. Breathe it in. Breathe it out, and breathe it in again. That is what I do. That is what I will do.

And that is what I will offer to others: soak it in. Soak it all in. It is about none of it, and it is about all of it. Death, tragedy, loss, mourning, fear, illness, grief… they magnify life. The magnifying glass that you held as a child over the summer sidewalk creates a sizzle in the sunshine and now—new perspective. New feeling is born. The amplitude of life increases and the underlying feeling establishes a grounding you had not yet known.

...letting go and holding on, all at once.

Most Exceptional Emotion

One of the most exceptional emotionally present experiences in life is that of laughter through tears. My recollection of the first time I experienced this sensation for myself was when I saw the movie *Steel Magnolias*. What writing! What a cast! The most delicate and strong moment of the film is when Sally Field's character, M'Lynn, is beside herself with grief and Clairee offers their ornery friend, Ouiser, as a punching bag. I remember I was wearing a purple Benetton sweatshirt to the movies that afternoon, and it was soaked—soaked from the tears streaming down my face. And suddenly, I was laughing a deep belly laugh. It was a beautiful moment of exceptional emotion. The combination of sadness and humor, evidenced by way of laughter through tears.

We see and feel meaning through what we experience. A meaning far greater than any one circumstance or situation and far greater than us. At most unexpected moments and in most unexpected ways, we get the rare glimpse into these meanings. We get distinctive and atypical opportunities to see the intersection of these experiences and the broader universal pull that is happening to connect them. It is unique and rare moments of "aha" that serve as both wonder and confirmation of something grander out there. Something bigger in the universe connecting all of these tiny moments, these large moments, all of the in-between—connecting us to each other.

Some of it I learned the hard way. Some of it made me older for having learned it. Some of it made me believe in the goodness of the world, and some of it made me question that there ever was goodness. Some of it made me question everything. And all of it was crazy shit because it felt crazy. It felt wild. It felt odd and unique. And, it also felt precisely as it was meant to be. At times in foresight, at times in the present, and at times in retrospect. I felt it all. I feel it all. Still. I think I always will. Recently, Angela and I reconnected with a former athlete we had coached years ago. She put her hand on her chest as I told her about my writing this book. She said, "We are carrying these things with us. They are personal.

They are ours." Her words were consoling, and I was grateful. She was right. These things—all this crazy shit—I carry with me. It is personal. It is mine. I believe it, too, is universal, and so it is ours. And it all has been absolutely as it was meant to be.

Maybe not all of this was crazy shit that happened. Maybe some of it was just shit that happened. Maybe it would have happened anyway, and it felt absurd because of the heightened emotion on this very human journey. Maybe some of it, a slice of it, was crazy shit that happened as a result of the effort I put in, the thought I put into it, the follow-through I did. And maybe I did not have anything to do with it.

Maybe.

And it doesn't matter. Any which way I think about it, it all happened. At the time, I could not emotionally process these things other than feeling them as the crazy shit they were. I was not the human I am today because of these things. I had not yet developed into the person I am today because of the life hijacking, the grief, and the mourning. I could only press forward and warrior through the new life before me. I had to get to know this new life and release the hijacked one. I had to get to know me. I did not grasp the unwelcome (and now welcome) wisdom I newly gained. I felt all of these things as purely, roughly, and rawly as possible. Processing it all came later. Much later.

What I have come to learn is that, all of the loss and the crazy shit is part of the beautiful, vibrant, shocking part of life and of living. It goes along with all the pure ache and pure joy we experience, and it enhances that joy. All the crazy shit served as the universe compelling me to laugh through tears—to cry, to laugh, to hope, and to dream. The universe compelling me to tell a story and to share it. The universe reminding me to trust in it. That it works out in uncanny, unimaginable, and unforeseen ways. When your heart is breaking, broken; when your heart is healing, and recovered. When *you* are breaking, broken. When *you* are healing.

Recovered, alive.

I had to get to know this new life and release the hijacked one.

Music

Below is a playlist —a music therapy —that helped bring Crazy Sh*! to the page:

"Bad Thoughts"

Vocals by Rachel Platten | Composition and Lyrics by Rachel Platten, Nick Lee, Kyan Palmer

"I Still Haven't Found What I Am Looking For"

U2 | Composition and Lyrics by Bono, The Edge, Adam Clayton, Larry Mullen Jr.

"Only You (And You Alone)"

The Platters | Composition and Lyrics by Buck Ram, rand

"Easy on Me"

Lead vocals by Adele | Composition and Lyrics by Greg Kurstin, Adele, David Campbell

"Where I Stood"

Performed by Missy Higgins | Composition and Lyrics by Missy Higgins

"When I Get There"

Lead vocals by P!nk | Composition and Lyrics by David Hodges, Amy Wadge

"We Can Do Hard Things"

Lead vocals by Tish Melton | Composition and Lyrics by Patricia Melton

"LA Song"

Vocals by Beth Hart | Composition and Lyrics by Beth Hart

"Pawn Shop"

Brothers Osborne | Composition and Lyrics by John Osborne, Sean McConnell, John Thomas Osborne

"Meet Virginia"

Train | Composition and Lyrics by Charlie Colin, Jimmy Stafford, Patrick Monahan, Rob Hotchkiss, Scott Underwood

"A Step You Can't Take Back"

Vocals by Kiera Knightley | Composition and Lyrics by Gregg Alexander, John Carney, Danielle Brisebois, Sandra Park

"Crying"

Vocals by Roy Orbison | Composition and Lyrics by Roy Orbison, Joe Melson

"Red Red Wine"

UB40 | Composition and Lyrics by Neil Diamon, UB40

"Crazy"

Lead vocals by Patsy Cline | Composition and Lyrics by Willie Nelson

"Don't Give Up on Me"

Lead vocals by Andy Grammer | Composition and Lyrics by Andy Grammer, Bram Inscore, Jake Torrey

"Don't Get Around Much Anymore"

Vocals by Etta James | Composition and Lyrics by Duke Ellington, Bob Russell, Riley Hampton

"Out Of The Woods"

Lead vocals by Taylor Swift | Composition and Lyrics by Taylor Swift, Jack Antonoff

"Sail Away"

Vocals by Noël Coward | Composition and Lyrics by Noël Coward, Peter Matz

"Middle Ground"

Maroon 5 | Composition and Lyrics by Andrew Watt, Jon Bellion, Pete Nappi, Adam Levine, Marvin Hemmings, Gregory "Aldae" Hein, Rodney Jerkins

"The Way You Can"

Vocals by Joshua Hyslop | Composition and Lyrics by Joshua Hyslop

"Lullaby"

Lead vocals by Shawn Mullins | Composition and Lyrics by Shawn Mullins

"Eyes Closed"

Lead vocals by Ed Sheeran | Composition and Lyrics by Ed Sheeran, Max Martin, Shellback, Fred Gibson, Rob Moose

Act II Curtain

Intermission

When I was growing up, I had the good fortune of attending many theatrical and musical performances. It is safe for me to say that I come from a long line of theatergoers. Not to mention, I also went to performing arts school. Being present for a performance on stage is in my blood (either in the audience or on the stage) so intermissions are something I am well-accustomed to, and I understand their value.

Every year in December, I watch *The Sound of Music*, and each time the screen displays the word "Intermission" in large yellow cursive writing, I appreciate the time to listen to the music and "step away" from the performances for a few moments. I know this classic film by heart. However, I do not anticipate the intermission. It shows up and each time I think, *Ah yes, it is time for the intermission.* The intermission provides a space to soak in the story thus far, get curious about what may happen next (even though I know exactly what is next in this movie), and it gives me a break. It offers an obvious moment to "push pause" on the story if I so choose, which I sometimes do.

Up to this point, you have read my story through my written voice. You have taken in words that have shown up in the form of memoir and source narrative. As you turn the next pages and the curtain goes up on Act III, you will quickly see that it takes on an entirely different style and varies in voice and format from the prior two acts. While I wrote this entire book in the depths of my grief and mourning, I wrote Act III once I reached the fulcrum point of an acknowledgement: the magnitude of my sorrow. Recovering and healing were born from my acknowledging the shock and sadness in my bones. It was only after this awareness that I was able to find Act III. It is dynamic. It is lyrical and it has no steady format. It is how Act III showed up for me. It is how I live it and feel it. It is how I want to offer it to you. It follows no mold, because grief and mourning know no sculpted form. There is no manual nor protocol, no runtime or timeline. Grief is unyielding and shows up as it is. Act III is an interpretation— my interpretation— of forging ahead, of healing, finding steps forward, recovering.

This is your intermission. It is a time to stretch your legs, use the restroom, get a glass of water (or wine). It is time to step aside and take in what you have read and (hopefully) grow your curiosity for what is next.

Wait until the lights of the playhouse flicker to alert you that Act III is about to begin. (Hint: only you will know when that is.)

Then, turn the page.

Act III: A New Mo[u]rning

Gifts

For You.

Scenes

Overture: Nothing Now

The first time I was exposed to WH Auden's poem, "Funeral Blues" was while watching the film *Four Weddings and a Funeral.* During one particular scene, Matthew, played by the actor John Hannah, recites Auden's words at a funeral in front of dear friends. He is shaken and poised, holding back tears.

The film was released in 1994. I was seventeen years old.

I recall the scene having a profound impact on me. I specifically recall hearing the last line of the poem– an acknowledgement of bleakness that nothing will ever come to any good– and thinking, *How awful. How tragic. How real.*

I asked myself, "Can someone really feel that way? That nothing will ever come to any good?" Then I thought, *It is so very sad. And I believe it.*

I believed it from a distance.

What I did not know then and have come to learn is: yes, of course someone can feel that way. Now, I *know* what that feels like. Believing it from a distance transformed into an intimate knowing.

That is the brilliance of Auden's words: they touch on something universal.

My belief about that sentiment has expanded further: it is a certain feeling. *I can feel* that way. *I have felt* that way. *I will feel* that way. And if I can, if I have and if I will; anyone can feel, has felt, and will feel that way.

What also is certain (and arguably critical to know) is that the feeling of *nothing now* will metamorphose; it will become layered with new goodness in life to be had.

John Hannah's recitation and character portrayal in the film is perfect. In my mind's eye, I will hear his voice saying those words each time I feel them.

The following included in this book are tips for grief. As my partner, Angela, offered, they are gifts.

They are gifts *of* grief, *from* grief, and *for* grieving.

While mourning, I *so wanted* a list of suggestions, a checklist, a manual or suggestion-box-output to help me.

You can think of these as that.

I put this to the world and offer it to you.

Please understand, I am not a psychologist, psychiatrist, or a therapist. I do not have a medical degree or PhD.
I have an undergraduate degree in psychology and philosophy, a professional degree in the arts, I love to problem-solve and spend time in nature, and I have (what feels like) a life's worth of experience.
I offer ~~my tips~~ my gifts from that perspective.

To You.

For You.

From me.

If you combine these things, you will find your way.

I did.

B. R. E. A. T. H. E.

Breathe.

Square your shoulders. Inhale with purpose. Count to five (if you have to). Exhale. Exhale until you cannot exit any more air. Then, keep exhaling. Start again.

Breathe.

Square your shoulders. Inhale with purpose. Count to ten (if you have to). Exhale. Exhale until you cannot exit any more air. Then, keep exhaling. Start again.

Breathe.

Square your shoulders. Inhale with purpose. Count to five (if you have to). Exhale. Exhale until you cannot exit any. more. air. Then, keep exhaling.

Start again.

And know that sometimes you won't be able to...

Breathe again.

Indulge.

I discovered that Costco sells massive bottles of Woodford Reserve and Grey Goose. Along with bottles of rosé.

Indulging in a delicious, strong cocktail felt numbing and felt freeing. They helped me focus; focus on the potent potion in front of me.

And yet, a bourbon *does not* make the sadness go away.
"Rosé all day" is not an option.
I indulged in wine and cocktails, yoga, baking and baths.

I indulged in these and they helped.

With time, the yoga, baking, and baths outnumbered the cocktails and wine. (Mind you, I still raise a glass like the best of them.)

Yoga offered daily routine, stability, and balance. Literally and figuratively.

Baking became a necessary indulgence. I activated the kitchen like sugar and warmed water activated the foam of dry yeast. With the activity of baking precision, I found new ways to bring smiles to others. I indulged in the energy I discovered by offering the warm goods from our kitchen to unsuspecting neighbors and friends.
Baths offered time to reflect. To feel warmth. And to cleanse.

My mom used to speak of indulgences, and Sharon lived a life crafted to indulge in the present, modeling it for those around her. I had to lean on the memory of each of them to take care and indulge.

Indulge in what feels good; and make sure it is for good. If it is indulging in an entire bottle of wine, that is not good. If it is indulging in a warm bath with aromatic bath salts, that is good. If it is eating cupcakes instead of doing yoga, that can be good.

Receive Hugs.

Receive hugs. Receive each. And every one.

Every

time.

And let the person offering the hug be the last to let go.

Full stop.

CRY.

Cry.
It can be the most present thing you do.
Cry.
Let the tears flow.

Sniffle,
scream,
gulp.

Let your tear ducts flush, exercise.

Know this is your body's and mind's
way of connecting to your soul,
and listening.

Release.
Welcome this form.
It will show up in so many varying ways
And in so
many

moments.
Cry.

My partner and I used to live in a condo that had a magnificent bathroom. There was a spacious standing shower next to an oval-shaped soaker tub, a long counter with two sinks, and a linen closet that had just the right amount of shelving. We used to comment how fortunate we were to live in such a place with a perfectly designed bathroom.

One day, I walked in and found her, wrapped in a white towel, sitting on the edge of the tub. I asked, "What are you doing?"

She said, "I'm sitting here. Sometimes it's nice to sit and do nothing."

Years later, I recall this moment and define it as a perfect frame on taking a pause.

In music, the pause symbol was one of my favorites. To me, it looked like an eye. It is a dot, with a parenthesis facing down. In Italian, it is called *fermata*. I remember my music teachers instructing: "And now, pause." It signifies capturing a moment. Capturing that which comes before and that which will come after.

Until that morning while seeing my partner on the tub's edge, my association to pause was *fermata*. An instruction to capture a moment.

Pauses are strategic, simple, telling. And so hard to do.

My partner is good at it. My pause has improved.

Take it as an instruction. Or take it as a suggestion.

Either way, capture a moment by pausing to consider everything, nothing, and all in between.

When you have really tough times and really dark days—pause. When you have really good times and bright days—pause.

Stare at what your eyes see (like the *fermata* symbol "eye"). Look for exactly what you see. Notice something new, notice nothing at all.

And consider the moment. Capture it.

Savor Memories.

I have been blessed with a great memory. I have always had a great memory. For me, my first memory scales way back to my first year in this world. It sounds hard to believe, I know, but I can distinctly recall my hands pasted to the cold glass window of the front storm door at my childhood home, watching my father come up the front stairs with our white poodle.
My memory (both quality and quantity) is a blessing almost all the time and sometimes a curse. It is a blessing, in that I can recall the most vivid details and faint memories. It is a curse, in that I recall even the less-than-desirable moments.

In the house where I grew up, we had a playroom that transformed into a den once my sister and I grew "out of" childhood toys. It was a small room off the front entryway and had lime green carpet covered with a large square, hunter green shag rug. The shag rug had large tassels on the four edges. I used to try and braid the yarn of them before I even knew how to braid, so I really was just twisting the yarn strands between wooden puzzle-playing and cooking at the miniature kitchen. There was a lot of imagination happening in that small room. Funny to me that it was this small room that served (I believe) as the foundational scenery for the growth of my imagination and cultivation of my memory.

It was in this very room that my mother would periodically sit on the floor and play "Memory" with me. I was great at that game.

As an adult, and now, through everything, I can consider my memory ability as a near one-hundred-percent blessing. My gratitude expands to include this ability as does the desire to practice it and to savor it, along with each and every detail that comes to mind.

Of my mother. Of Sharon. Of my father.

In the quietness and stillness, in the rigor and chaos—savor memories and let them flow.

One Thing.

I am a creature of routine. I thrive on routine. I think most people do, to a degree.
My theory is that operating on some sort of routine is not only healthy, that as a need, it varies from person to person.

> *Pick one thing to be your joy-thing of routine.*
>
> *And do it every day.*
>
> *Be specific.*
>
> *Brush your teeth every morning precisely before washing your face because clean teeth and fresh breath bring you joy? Perfect.*
>
> *Hot washcloth draped on your face just before bed? Perfect.*

One thing leads to two things, leads to more.

For now, pick one.

Pick one.

And do it every day.

Garden (as the verb).

"You certainly got your green thumb from your father.
It was *not* from me!"

My mom had uttered this many times to me, but she said it with an increased fervor one Saturday morning on our back patio in 2014. The four of us were enjoying breakfast outside and it was a beautiful, breezy morning, the leaves on the trees creating a familiar hushing sound. I poured coffee into their mugs while my dad asked me about the irises in our front garden. I had just walked him around the yard, showing him all the plants, pointing at the rose bushes and the water lilies in front the pond, then the milkweed and daisies in the perennial garden. When we made it to the backyard, my mom had come out to join us just as we stopped at one of the large colorful hydrangea plants. It wasn't typical for Mom to browse in a yard, but her urge to participate overrode that. On the walking tour of our yard, I felt pride in our garden and the hard work Angela and I had committed to in maintaining the gorgeous plants the previous owners had planted. I felt the brilliant joy of sharing it with my dad. And my mom.

We were hosting my parents for a few days, and this was the morning after their arrival the previous afternoon. They were on their way to Florida and made the round-about path toward Virginia for a visit.

"We would love to see you, Mom. Are you sure, though?
It isn't really on your way..."

"Of course it is!"

She cut me off while we spoke on the phone a few weeks prior, stating the myth that Virginia is on the way to Florida from South Dakota. She went on assuring me that it did not matter the distance, they wanted to come see us.

My dad loved to tinker in the yard and the garden when I was growing up. Every early spring, he would venture to the local ACE Hardware and find marigolds, geranium, petunias, and pansies to plant in gigantic pots for our front stoop. I would sit on the retaining wall, my legs dangling off the edge, while he instructed me on the planting of them.

"You see, they are delicate. You have to push them out of the plastic containers ever-so-carefully. Don't pull them."

My eyes wide, he would patiently watch me as I placed the orange, red, and white flowers into the pots.

"Yes, just like that," he would encourage me.

In our backyard, Dad kept a large tomato garden plot each summer and would proudly bring in the large fruits so we could enjoy them in a salad or as thick slices on our burgers. "Maters!" he would excitedly shout as he paced through the back porch.

That morning in 2014 on our patio, we weren't caring for the garden other than admiring it. We were talking, laughing, smiling, and enjoying each other's company. It was one of the more calm, stress-free, and present scenes with my parents. Dad was sporting one of his most colorful shirts, and Mom complimented him with her own bright turquoise top.

They asked about Sharon, and we told the stories about how she loved to visit our yard and garden or watch the dogwood trees blooming from our dining room.

"They are so gorgeous!" she would cry out. "I am going to sit here." She pounced on one of the chairs facing the back window. "I want the view of the dogwoods blooming!"

Angela and I both love to plant, to garden, and to work in the yard. Sharon always encouraged us to get help, claiming we worked too hard. After Mom, Sharon and Dad died, I discovered a new form of gardening: the verb. I recognized that I certainly got my green thumb from my dad, noticing an act of love from my mom and relishing in the beauty around me from Sharon. I discovered that caring for plants and flowers and baking and cooking a meal for others is all a form of gardening. Moments pruning the herbs started from seeds, or checking on the flowers in the side yard, or slicing apples for a pie became meditative for me. They became quiet, restorative moments of calm, stress-free presence. They became moments to feel the warm sunshine, hear the quiet wind, smell the tart fruit and bask in the hues before me, my surroundings in entirety.

I want to pass that discovery forward the way Mom made a path that was (most certainly) out of the way— on the way; the way Dad patiently taught planting and carefully attended to flowers and tomatoes; the way Sharon appreciated the beauty surrounding us and called it out.

Garden (as the verb).

Whether it is in an actual garden with plants, in a kitchen with dishes and food, or out on a walk—garden. It can be anything of your choosing that sets in motion your senses.

Garden.

Sleep Well.

"You fall asleep as soon as your head hits the pillow."

That is what my mom and dad used to say about me. And it was true. Nighttime stories occurred sitting in two red chairs in the living room after bath time. I posit now, that was due to the fact that I would be asleep for the stories if I were in bed.

I have come to find as an adult that I cherish sleep. And sleeping well.

After losing Mom then Sharon then Dad, there was an extended period of time (way too long) when I was not sleeping. Nor was I sleeping *well.*

So many nights were spent awake. Awake. AWAKE. Yearning for sleep and unable to do it. Or to do it well.

I went back to the basics:
Eat well. Avoid inflammatory foods. Avoid alcohol before bed.
Exercise and move. Move well.
My therapist had to talk me through sleep-training.

Therapy coupled with eating well and moving well, consistently, helped me to fall asleep as soon as my head hit the pillow again after months of zero sleep and bad sleep.

I cherish each and every night of good sleep.

Eat *well.* Move *well.* Care for your emotions *well.*

So that you may sleep *well.*

Feel.

Feel every emotion that comes to you.

Be Stunned.

Thump!

It was a crisp, sunny morning in early spring, and there was an amazing glow of colors from our stained-glass window reflecting on the walls of our kitchen. Angela and I were enjoying our post work-out coffees.

Suddenly, we heard a clear *thump* against the large kitchen window above our sink. We rushed to look outside. As suspected, there was a bird, a cardinal to be exact, standing on the ground, clearly stunned.

No movement. Simply standing there. Exposed.

We knew from prior bird watching with our dear friend Sharon that birds are very nearly always (or appear to be) moving: head tilt, feather fluff… something.

This cardinal was standing m-o-t-i-o-n-l-e-s-s.

As a counter to that, we sprung into motion. My partner, Angela, rushed to the mud room and found a small cardboard box while I found a soft towel to nestle inside the box. She put on medical gloves and proceeded outside. She quietly approached the vibrant red bird, who let her gently pick it up and place it into the cushioned box.

We briefly spoke about where to place the box. Where would be most safe? We settled on the top step to our patio, in the sunshine, yet protected from the openness of the patio itself.

Our aim was to create a safe space to let the delicate creature be alone—to give it a moment, allow it permission to be stunned and regain itself.

On its own.

The placement of the cushioned respite was designed also to allow us the opportunity to keep a distant and watchful eye on the cardinal.

Over the course of the next hour, we first noticed a few small fluttering motions (hooray!) and then more episodic twitters. Then, a few hops. Each motion we witnessed increased our hopeful state and our silent cheering for the creature.

Before we knew it, the fluttering became more frequent, until ultimately, I experienced the immediate joy upon observing the cardinal lift off and fly away.

It took time, yet it ultimately flew away *so fast*.

Sometimes we need to recover. We need to take a moment from time.

Allow yourself to be stunned. Allow yourself to recover. Give permission to yourself. Be comforted by the silent cheering that is happening all around you.

Say, "I need a minute." Sometimes you just need a minute.

Or two.

Or 1,051,200.

Then fly.

Learn.

Grief is a raw learning.

It is definite. It is definite that you will experience it.

Grieving, as with other things in life, offers a potent experience from which to learn; to get better at it: life. And grief.

I believe you can get better at both.

While grief is not necessarily something at which we strive to become an expert, we can gain an expertise in grieving such that it serves as a map for recovery and in lending a heart to others who are experiencing it.

And a gateway to an enhanced way of living.

The intimate knowing of it hastens a knowledge and capacity to withstand and thrive.

GROW.

"Growing pains." I remember my father's answer when, at six, I would complain that my legs were sore. They were. It felt like a dull ache resonating in my legs at night.

"You're growing. And it hurts," he would say. "Drink your milk."

I am not sure the milk helped. Maybe?

Just like my legs when I was a child, my heart is growing. And it hurts.

I have the same complaint: My heart is sore. And I have to remind myself of my father's words, "You're growing. And it hurts."

In this case, drinking milk certainly will not apply. Yet, the final unspoken part does: there is hope in that growth. There is goodness. It will be okay, and it may even end up great.

Feeling deepens and expands from pain. Grief is "muddling through" that expansion of feeling.

It's new, raw, and impossibly real.

Hearts Flutter. Hearts Break. Hearts Mend. And Hearts Grow.

Person to Account.

Sharon was my person to account.

And she died.

I had to tap into her spirit: *What would Sharon do? What would she say?*

Sharon believed in taking care of yourself in entirety. From facials, to massages, to exercise, sex, doctors, therapists, and everything in between. She firmly believed in taking care of our whole selves and being unapologetically upfront about it.

She also had a fervor in encouraging others to "get on board" with this notion. She would exclaim, "Seriously! You have to take care of your body, your mind *and* your emotions!"

It was laudable.

Not only that, it was something I so admired as a part of who she was and what she brought to the world. I so admire it *in* her.

Through Sharon, and with encouragement from my other person to account (Angela), I found and started working with a therapist.

And it has been amazing. It feels healthy and good.

What started out as healthy has proven to be healthy *and rewarding*.

Yet again, I have found that Sharon was right.

This is important: Find yourself a person to account. Pick someone who exudes confidence in your healing and bravery in sticking with you. Here or not. Take care of your whole self.

Find Your Nowhere.

Find your nowhere.

Where sad comes untrue and truth from sadness grows.

Just like a tree. Steady and strong. Grounded and expanding.

Stable and reaching.

Old and new.

Rough

and smooth.

Scarred.

And recovered,
alive. Alive. Alive.

Coda: Gifts

B. R. E. A. T. H. E. And know that sometimes you won't be able to…Breathe again.

Indulge. Indulge in what feels good; and make sure it is for good.

Receive Hugs. And let the person offering the hug be the last to let go.

CRY.

𝄐 When you have really tough times and really dark days—pause. When you have really good times and bright days—pause. Look for exactly what you see. Notice something new, notice nothing at all.

Savor Memories. In the quietness and stillness, savor memories and let them flow.

One Thing. Pick one thing to be your joy-thing of routine and do it every day. Be specific.

Garden (as the verb). It can be anything of your choosing that sets in motion your senses.

Sleep Well. Eat well. Move well and care for your emotions well. So that you may sleep *well.*

Feel. Feel every emotion that comes to you.

Be Stunned. Allow yourself to be stunned. Allow yourself to recover. Be comforted by the silent cheering that is happening all around you.

Learn. Grieving, as with other things in life, offers a potent experience from which to learn, to get better at it.

G R O W. Feeling deepens and expands from pain. Grief is "muddling through" that expansion of feeling.

Person to Account. Pick someone who exudes confidence in your healing and bravery in sticking with you. Here or not.

Find Your Nowhere. Discover the place where sad comes untrue and truth from sadness grows.

Finale: Music

As you now know, music plays an integral role in my life. It has played an integral role in my mourning, my healing, my recovery.

And so, with Act III, I offer the following list of tunes in concert with ***Gifts:***

"Visiting Hours"

Lead vocals by Ed Sheeran | Composition and Lyrics by Ed Sheeran, Amy Wadge, Johnny McDaid, Kim Lang Smith, Michael Pollack, Scott Carter, Ant Clemons

"Sleeping at the Wheel"

Matchbox Twenty | Composition and Lyrics by Rob Thomas

"Some of It"

Vocals by Eric Church | Composition and Lyrics by Eric Church, Jeff Hyde, Bobby Pinson, Clint Daniels

"Sanctuary"

From Nashville TV-series, featuring Charles Esten, Lennon Stella and Maisy Stella | Composition and Lyrics by Jill Andrews, Gary Nicholson, Sarah Siskind

"Lay Down"

Lead vocals by Ella Henderson | Composition and Lyrics by Ella Henderson, Ben Kohn, Pete Kelleher, Tom Barnes

"In Between"

Performed by J.J. Pfeifer | Composition and Lyrics by J.J. Pfeifer

"Have You Ever Seen the Rain"

Vocals by Willie Nelson featuring Paula Nelson | Composition and Lyrics by John Fogerty

"Better Place"

Vocals by Rachel Platten | Composition and Lyrics by Rachel Platten, Sally Seltmann

"Fix You"

Coldplay | Composition and Lyrics by Guy Berryman, Will Champion, Jonny Buckland, Chris Martin, Audrey Riley

"If This Is Love"

Vocals by Ruth B. | Composition and Lyrics by Ruth B.

"Castle on The Hill"

Lead vocals by Ed Sheeran | Composition and Lyrics by Ed Sheeran, Benjamin Levin

"Song Sung Blue"

Vocals by Neil Diamond| Composition and Lyrics by Neil Diamond, Lee Holdridge

"Memories"

Maroon 5 | Composition and Lyrics by Jon Bellion, Michael Pollack, Stefan Johnson, Vincent Ford, Jacob Kasher Hindlin, Adam Levine, Jordan Johnson

"Hold Me Closer"

Vocals by Cornelia Jakobs | Composition and Lyrics by Cornelia Jakobs, David Zandén, Isa Molin

"All I Know So Far"

Vocals by P!nk | Composition and Lyrics by Alecia Moore, Benj Pasek, Justin Noble Paul

"Lease On Life"

Lead vocals by Andy Grammer | Composition and Lyrics by Andy Grammer, Bram Inscore, Jake Torrey, Nolan Sipe

"Let Somebody Go"

Coldplay with Selena Gomez | Composition and Lyrics by Apple Martin, Bill Rahko, Chris Martin, Guy Berryman, Jonny Buckland, Leland Wayne, Max Martin, Olivia Waithe, Oscar Holter, Will Champion

"I've Been This Way Before"

Vocals by Neil Diamond | Composition and Lyrics by Neil Diamond, Jimmie Haskell

"Landslide"

Fleetwood Mac | Composition and Lyrics by Stevie Nicks

"Sweet Creature"

Lead vocals by Harry Styles | Composition and Lyrics by Harry Styles, Thomas Edward Percy Hull

"The Promise"

Lead vocals by Tracy Chapman | Composition and Lyrics by Tracy Chapman

"Rainbow"

Lead vocals by Kacey Musgraves | Composition and Lyrics by Kacey Musgraves, Natalie Hemby, Shane McAnally

"Afterglow"

Lead vocals by Ed Sheeran | Composition and Lyrics by Ed Sheeran, David Hodges, Fred Gibson

Act III Curtain

Epilogue: New Realm

The thing about losing loved ones and those most dear to you is that they enter a new realm that transcends the living life you knew them in. And somehow, you get to know them all over again. They show up in unexpected places, expected places; they speak to you with words so familiar and new words for conversations you did not yet have, and ones you had so many times before. Their memory shows up in skeletons in the living room (because it's as good a place as any), fallen trees, handwritten recipes, cardinals at the window, purple ribbon, delicious cocktails, and Cheez-Its. You enter a new realm of life, grief serving as the entry point. It is a new part of the galaxy you did not know existed and the universe reveals to you: "Kindly enter here, no turning back now."

Loss, grief, mourning—they are the universal, perfect example in life of gaining deeper understanding and individual wisdom from personal experience.

Today is the anniversary of my mother's passing and I cannot believe it has been four years.

1

2

3

4

How fast it has gone and how slowly, too. Tears well in my eyes, and I feel their wetness while aching for one more hug, one more sound of her laugh. I can hear it even now. And, I can see my father trembling in laughter with a wide smile as they both recall a comedic story of a dear friend they lost all too young. Just like I quiver in laughter, recalling Sharon's giant personality and fervor for life. I am venturing in this new part of the galaxy, and while I cannot turn back, "forward," I say. "Forward," with a deep, full breath, as yoga has taught me. I move forward with them and with it all.

These losses and the associated experiences are incorporated into my being, folded into how I now move through the world, the way chilled butter is folded into pastry dough. They are incorporated into my alive-ness. My way of being is transformed. It is metamorphosed into a new way of moving in the world. Layered and connected.

When all is said and done, this has been a journey. It *is* a journey. We are all on a journey full of twists and turns, heartache and anguish, laughter and turbulence; a journey full of growth, pain, renewal, and discovery. It is a journey full of joy, hurt and recovery; full of loss, crazy shit, and gifts.

The soul would have no rainbow,
if the eyes had no tears.

-Native American proverb

Acknowledgments

Part of this journey is the gratitude I carry from it all, along with the desire and responsibility to feel it, recognize it, speak it, write it, and show it.

There is so very much to be thankful for and to celebrate in life. I am grateful for every moment: the unexpected moments of laughter, tears, fear, profound joy, and grief. Yes, the grief too. The prominent force of my gratitude can be defined by the amazing individuals who showed grace, patience, courage, urgency, encouragement; love and care; demonstrated exceptional empathy; and who, in each of their unique ways, taught me more about humanity than I could ever imagine.

Thank you to:

Amy, for reiki and breaking Mom's fever.
Marge, for saying goodbye to Mom.
Jessica, for profound care and respect in Mom's final hours. And for pronouncing her.
Sara, for your deep eyes.
The Saint Armand's Circle Starbucks cashier, who asked, "What are you up to today?"
The couple from Boston, for the lobster rolls that Dad so enjoyed.
Di, for coordinating Mom's service announcement to the condominium community and orchestrating treats.
The woman who bought the never sat-in needlepoint chair.
The gal who drove from Alabama to purchase the needlepoint to stock her *Alice in Wonderland* bed and breakfast.
Connie "MS. KITTY," for perfectly "poached" eggs, earning Dad's trust and describing the truth of a moment.
Staci, for holding Dad's hand and asking about family vacations.
JegBeh, for laughter and getting Dad "excited" to see you.
The Judy-s (all three), for watchfulness.

Kim, for winning the clinical conversations with Dad about medications.
Jessie, for a gentle nature with Dad.
Molly, for the candid and caring discussions, winks and the white-girl-wasted biker wedding.
Slava, for demonstrating care and confidence in having Dad's back.
Nora, for jumping in with both feet.
Lesly, for digging up every ounce of courage to knock on our door.
Bruce, for patience and second- try grace.
Allison, for immediate kindness.
Wendy, for repositioning Dad on your own, earning his trust and asking to sit at the table.
Stacy, for compassion and patience. And for pronouncing Dad.
Doug, for prompt responses, screen doors, trailer haul away, box lugging, chats and that wide smile wearing Dad's safari hat.
Sara, for the cookies.
Angela, for the bundt cakes.
Jody, for taking my calls every time, for navigating the basement, gathering the mail and stopping by with a sweet smile every time.
Marie, for biohazard removal, chives, a picnic, Dad's doctor wing and new friendship.
Jake, for beer, ribs and neighborly kindness.
Dick, for mail delivery and help with magazines.
Chuck, for patience and flexibility.
Nicole, for buying the couch, chair and reconnecting about dance.
Jim, for walking up the driveway and helping with puppets.
Robert and Sean, for making the full day trek to assess and load (including that giant marble bust).
Debi, for letting me know that each person "will specifically select an item to carry forward."
Machelle, for transforming each room and showing Angela how to turn on the lamp.
Megan, for airing things out on the ladder.

Sara for buying the piano.
Boris, for showing me energy healing.
Nancy, for teaching me how to breathe from my core.
Marya, for tracking context, listening, reading and support.
Nan, for cookies.
Julia for the star.
John, for draft reading.
Erica, for offering to drive Charlie.
Brian, for walks, talks and sharing grief.
Mitsie, for using the word "exfoliation" with reference to my writing.
Adena, for connecting me with Dave.
Sean and Andrew, for cocktails, listening and advice.
Natalie, for introducing me to Dan, and teaching me the power of a hug.
Kristina, for treats, excitement about my writing and encouraging me to say the thing that is hard to say.
Brie, for coffee talks, so much laughter, steadfast love; and *The Boy, the Mole, the Fox and the Horse*.
Gretchen, for surprises at the side door and the garden ornament that moves in the wind.
Ashley and Marco, for your clear and confident support.
Todd and Terri, for the tremendously warm welcome back.
Ann, for evening patio time and stories with Mom and Dad.

To my creative writing cadre, your insights and creative spirits have helped fuel me.

> Alisa, for sharing the joy of writing and offering your artistic talents for the cover.
> Richard, for providing input that pointed me in a direction to shape this as one book.
> Dave, for being open to a conversation and feedback that led me to new words.
> Katie, for your editing expertise and mushy love of words.
> Joe, for reconnecting me to the voice for my words and (unknowingly) helping me decide the book's title.
> Dan, for endless encouragement, sound advice and stating my courage.

Each of the artists of the aforementioned playlists for releasing music to the world. I hold each note and lyric close.

To the beautiful tribe I have the pleasure of calling family and friends, for exercising so much enthusiasm and support. I feel you cheering for me. You are all so dear to me.

To the many strangers, who offered kind glances, showed grace and humanity. You made a difference.

Charlie, for your wiggles, "pointer-stink," nuzzles, and yoga-disruption.

Louie, for introducing me to perfectly present joy after loss, and staying there with me.

Thank you to the love of my life, Angela. Words cannot sufficiently express how thankful I am *for you* and *to you* for being with me every step, driving (literally and figuratively) alongside me, filing my edges, embracing my heartache, and bringing me joy. I found my strength only because of your boundless love. My world is so beautiful because you are here with me.

My mother instilled in me the importance and power of saying a proper thank you:

To each of you,

Thank you from the tips of my toes to the top of my mind; and from the depth of my heart to the expanse of my soul.

Recovered, Alive

Amelia Chiarenza

About the Author

Amelia Chiarenza is a writer, speaker, and storyteller.

From a renaissance career spanning radio, NCAA Division I coaching, technology development and aerospace, she made an intentional pivot and now spends her time as a podcast host, death doula, kinesiologist, and cottage baker.

She believes in the power of humanity and the ability of stories to strengthen bonds. Her writing offers engaging and sage advice through the lens of her experiences. She aims to share personal stories so her readers can find tangible connections to their own.

Her best days are those spent in nature with her partner and German-wirehaired pointer.